SECURITY OPERATIONS PRACTICE

BCS, THE CHARTERED INSTITUTE FOR IT

BCS, The Chartered Institute for IT, is committed to making IT good for society. We use the power of our network to bring about positive, tangible change. We champion the global IT profession and the interests of individuals, engaged in that profession, for the benefit of all.

Exchanging IT expertise and knowledge
The Institute fosters links between experts from industry, academia and business to promote new thinking, education and knowledge sharing.

Supporting practitioners
Through continuing professional development and a series of respected IT qualifications, the Institute seeks to promote professional practice tuned to the demands of business. It provides practical support and information services to its members and volunteer communities around the world.

Setting standards and frameworks
The Institute collaborates with government, industry and relevant bodies to establish good working practices, codes of conduct, skills frameworks and common standards. It also offers a range of consultancy services to employers to help them adopt best practice.

Become a member
Over 70,000 people including students, teachers, professionals and practitioners enjoy the benefits of BCS membership. These include access to an international community, invitations to a roster of local and national events, career development tools and a quarterly thought-leadership magazine. Visit www.bcs.org/membership to find out more.

Further information
BCS, The Chartered Institute for IT,
First Floor, Block D,
North Star House, North Star Avenue,
Swindon, SN2 1FA, United Kingdom.
T +44 (0) 1793 417 417
(Monday to Friday, 09:00 to 17:00 UK time)
www.bcs.org/contact
http://shop.bcs.org/

SECURITY OPERATIONS IN PRACTICE

Mike Sheward

Published by BCS Learning and Development Ltd, a wholly owned subsidiary of BCS, The Chartered Institute for IT, First Floor, Block D, North Star House, North Star Avenue, Swindon, SN2 1FA, UK.
www.bcs.org

Paperback ISBN 978-1-78017-5065
PDF ISBN 978-1-78017-5072
ePUB ISBN 978-1-78017-5089
Kindle ISBN 978-1-78017-5096

British Cataloguing in Publication Data.
A CIP catalogue record for this book is available at the British Library.

Publisher's acknowledgements
Reviewers: Wendy Goucher and David King
Publisher: Ian Borthwick
Commissioning editor: Rebecca Youé
Production manager: Florence Leroy
Project manager: Sunrise Setting Ltd
Copy-editor: Gillian Bourn
Proofreader: Marion Moffatt
Indexer: Matthew Gale
Cover design: Alex Wright
Cover image: iStock/mthaler
Typeset by Lapiz Digital Services, Chennai, India

CONTENTS

FIGURES AND TABLES

ABOUT THE AUTHOR

Mike Sheward, CISSP, CISM, CCFP-US, CISA, HCISPP, CEH, OSCP, CHFI is a Seattle-based information security professional with 15 years of experience in the field. Mike has worked primarily in security operations, incident response and digital forensics roles, in both the UK and USA, and across both the public and private sectors.

Mike worked with BCS in 2018 to publish his book *Hands-on Incident Response and Digital Forensics*, and has previously published tales of his work in the field in his 2017 book, *Digital Forensic Diaries*.

FOREWORD

The world of information security is ever changing. I hadn't even heard of the industry when I began working in it over a decade ago. Back then, the attitude in the workplace was more along the lines of 'let's avoid security, and keep them out of the loop as they slow us down', rather than the 'let's proactively approach them so we can develop more securely and ensure compliance', that it's heading towards today. With the introduction of the General Data Protection Regulation (GDPR), and the dissolution of Safe Harbour (to have the Privacy Shield implemented), we can clearly see that over the last 5 years alone we have come a long way in understanding that the security of not only our financial data, but also our personal data, should be a priority. In Europe, we have already seen a 50 per cent increase in Subject Access Requests, and we're also seeing security-related commercials between TV shows, which I personally have never seen before, proving that our appetite to understand our own online footprint is more security based.

As we are aware, social media has been hit quite hard from a privacy standpoint over the last few years. A slightly newer and increasingly concerning information security trend is the rise in 'internet of things' (IoT) devices and just how willing we are to give our data and privacy away for free to save a few minutes of the day. There has been growing debate around just who is listening to us, what they are listening to and what they can do with that information. The dangers that surround the potential 'spying on us' aspect of these devices is something to which many are turning a blind eye. In this interesting time we live in it is ever more apparent that we need to head into the future with the best protection we can; following best practice and guidelines as outlined in Mike's books will certainly help in easing some of the concerns this threat brings.

I met Mike after I had been in the industry about 5 years. I found him somewhat intimidating in the beginning, as my first impression was 'this guy knows what he's talking about'. The intimidation faded away after a few socials and we became not only colleagues but friends. Mike is a family man who is dedicated to doing a great job. It is clear through knowing him (as well as through his writing) that he is keen on making security clear and understandable in a way that is relatable and enjoyable to read, rather than the never-ending stream of 'must' and 'must nots' we are used to. Even though we no longer work together and live in different countries, we have remained friends and follow each other's career paths keenly. I am always excited to hear about a new plan he has hatched, or a new book he is writing. Now that I have my own software-as-a-service (SaaS) information security compliance company, I use principles that I learned with Mike to help build our company. We focus on making InfoSec compliance accessible and easy to understand, rather than the minefield some larger companies can make it seem. At RiscPro, we believe that having good security practices should not equate to having a large security budget, just a willingness to create them.

I firmly believe that with the increase and sharing of knowledge through our various mediums, we will only improve the ever-evolving security and privacy industry.

Tamlynn Deacon,
Founder and Managing Director, RiscPro

ACKNOWLEDGEMENTS

First and foremost, I wouldn't be able to do any of the things I get to do without the love and support of my family, Jessica and Oliver.

Second, perhaps a more unusual acknowledgement. In November 2018, the local transit authority in my county, directly across the waters of Puget Sound, opposite Seattle, began a fast ferry service from my home town to the city. The twice daily 40-minute crossing that I and a number of other commuters undertake to get to and from our day jobs is probably one of the most beautiful commutes in the entire world. It's also probably one of the most productive, as I glance around and see most people working at their laptops and tablets every day. Indeed, the majority of the book you're about to read was written during those trips between North Kitsap and Seattle. With that in mind, I'd like to thank the folks at Kitsap Transit for establishing and operating the service safely so I could type away for all those hours, and to the M/V *Finest* for being a pretty awesome vessel and mode of transit. I'm not sure how many information security books have been written primarily on water, but I'd like to think this is one of the few.

Thanks to my family 'back home', including my parents Geoff and Angela, and Paul (sorry I broke the shower), Lisa, Toby and Rosie.

Thanks to everyone in my work family whom I enjoy working with so much, including Mike McGee, Darcey Axon, Courtney Rust, Eli Sohl, Chris Guarino and Dan Yeager.

Finally, I'd like to thank BCS and Rebecca Youé for allowing me to write on their behalf once again.

ABBREVIATIONS

ACL	access control list
AES	Advanced Encryption Standard
API	application programming interface
APN	access point name
APT	advanced persistent threat
ARP	Address Resolution Protocol
AS	autonomous system
AV	antivirus
AWS	Amazon Web Services
B2B	business-to-business
B2C	business-to-consumer
BCP/DR	business continuity planning and disaster recovery
BGP	Border Gateway Protocol
BYOD	bring your own device
CASB	cloud access security brokers
CCTV	closed-circuit television
CEO	chief executive officer
CI/CD	continuous integration and continuous deployment
CIS	Center for Internet Security
CISO	chief information security officer
CPTED	crime prevention through environmental design
CPU	central processing unit
CTO	chief technology officer
CVSS	Common Vulnerability Scoring System
DBA	database administrator
DDoS	distributed denial of service
DLP	data loss prevention
DNS	Domain Name System
DR	disaster recovery
GDPR	General Data Protection Regulation

GPO	Group Policy Object
GRC	governance, regulatory and compliance
GUI	graphical user interface
HR	human resources
HRIS	Human Resources Information System
HTTP	Hypertext Transfer Protocol
HVAC	heating, ventilation and air conditioning
IaaS	infrastructure-as-a-service
IAM	identity and access management
ICANN	Internet Corporation for Assigned Names and Numbers
IdP	identity provider
IDS	intrusion detection system
IoT	internet of things
IPS	intrusion prevention system
ISECOM	Institute for Security and Open Methodologies
ISP	internet service provider
KPI	key performance indicator
LAN	local area network
LDAP	Lightweight Directory Access Protocol
MAC	media access control
MDM	mobile device management
MEL	minimum equipment list
MFA	multifactor authentication
NAC	network access control
NAS	network attached storage
NAT	network address translation
NIC	network interface controller
NIST	National Institute of Standards and Technology
NPM	network performance monitoring
NTP	network time protocol
OSI	open systems interconnection
OSINT	open-source intelligence
OSTMM	Open-Source Security Testing Methodology Manual
OU	Organisational Unit
OUI	organisational unique identifier
PaaS	platform-as-a-service
PCI-DSS	Payment Card Industry Data Security Standard
PFS	perfect forward secrecy
PGP	Pretty Good Privacy

PIN	personal identification number
PIR	passive infrared
PoC	proof of concept
PR	public relations
PTES	Penetration Testing Execution Standard
QA	quality assurance
RADIUS	Remote Authentication Dial-In User Service
RAID	redundant array of independent disks
RAM	random access memory
RBAC	role-based access control
RDMS	relational database management software
RDP	Remote Desktop Protocol
RFID	radio-frequency identification
RSoP	resultant set of policy
SaaS	software-as-a-service
SAML	Security Assertion Markup Language
SCM	source code management
SDLC	software development life cycle
SFTP	Secure File Transfer Protocol
SHA	secure hashing algorithm
SIEM	security incident and event management
SNMP	Simple Network Management Protocol
SOC	security operations centre
SP	service provider
SQL	Structured Query Language
SS7	Signalling System 7
SSH	secure shell
SSO	single sign-on
STAR	Security Test Audit Report
SYN	synchronise
TCP	Transmission Control Protocol
TCP/IP	Transmission Control Protocol/Internet Protocol
TLS	transport layer security
TTP	tactics, techniques and procedures
U2F	universal second factor
UDP	User Datagram Protocol
UI	user interface
UPS	uninterruptable power supplies
USB	universal serial bus

UTC	Coordinated Universal Time
VLAN	virtual local area network
VPN	virtual private network
WAF	web application firewall
WAN	wide area network
WLAN	wireless local area network
WPA	Wi-Fi Protected Access
XSS	cross site scripting

GLOSSARY

Active Directory: A Microsoft directory services product in widespread use for identity management and policy enforcement in Microsoft Windows environments.

Chief information security officer (CISO): A position within an organisation that typically bears overall responsibility for an organisation's information security programme.

Compliance: The state of complying with any applicable regulatory or legal requirement. Also used to describe the team responsible for ensuring compliance.

Confidentiality: The state of secrecy or privacy of a given piece of information.

Debug: The process of using a software tool to deconstruct running applications for the purposes of detecting, understanding and fixing errors.

Denial of service: A condition caused when a system is unable to service legitimate requests because it's overwhelmed by malicious traffic, or otherwise taken offline.

DevOps: A software development model in which the same group of people build the software (develop) and operate it post deployment in production (operations).

Encryption: The process of taking a piece of information and encoding it in such a way that only authorised parties are allowed to view it.

Endpoint: A term originally used to describe the device on the end of a networked conversation, which is now widely leveraged to describe various device types in use by users in an enterprise network, for example desktop, laptop or tablet computers.

Ephemeral: Something that lasts for a very short time. Commonly used when describing container images.

Exception: In information security, used to describe when something is done in violation of a specific policy, with approval.

Exfiltration: The act of surreptitiously removing data from a computer, or network.

Exploit: A piece of software written to take advantage of a vulnerability in a computer system.

False positive: An incorrect indication that a condition is occurring. Commonly associated with intrusion detection systems, or vulnerability scanners.

Hashing: A mathematical process performed on data of any size, which results in the generation of data that is a fixed size, otherwise known as a hash digest. Frequently used to ensure data integrity.

HTTP: HyperText Transfer Protocol, the primary protocol used by web browsers and servers to communicate. A set of standards for transferring text and other media across the internet.

Hypervisor: Computer software that is responsible for running and managing virtual machines.

Jailbreaking: The process of bypassing restrictions imposed by the manufacturer of an electronic device (such as a smartphone), usually for the purposes of installing software, outside of that approved by the manufacturer.

Lateral: Used to describe the path an attacker takes from one host to another, once they are inside a compromised environment.

Microservices: An application architecture model that leverages multiple small components, or services, to implement a function, as opposed to building a single large application.

Open systems interconnection (OSI) model: A conceptual model that describes seven layers of communication functions to be implemented by an operating system and a telecommunications system, for the purposes of inter-system communication. The OSI model covers everything from data input at the application level, to physical transmission of data as an electrical signal.

Packet: A formatted unit of data carried across a packet-switched network. A packet includes addressing information, to help it get to where it needs to go, as well as the data it is transmitting.

Penetration test: An authorised test that is designed to simulate actions taken by a malicious attacker attempting to gain access to an organisation, application or network.

Phishing: An attack that involves sending phony emails purporting to be from a legitimate source, such as a financial institution. The intent of the attack is for the victim to respond with sensitive information, such as a set of credentials. A spear phishing attack is a phishing attack that is specifically targeted at a victim.

Process: In a computing context, used to describe an instance of a running program.

Responsible disclosure: A manner in which details on a newly discovered software vulnerability are provided to the software vendor in such a way as to minimise the risk that vulnerability could be misused by a malicious party.

Security operations: A sub-discipline of information security focused on the day-to-day management and monitoring of an organisation's security controls and procedures. A security operations centre (SOC) may be responsible for trigging an incident response upon discovery of a specific condition.

Systems admin: A position within an organisation that is generally responsible for the day-to-day management and maintenance of computer systems.

Timestamp: A representation of the time an event occurred, of particular importance in information security when reviewing the times files were created or modified.

Universal serial bus (USB): An industry standard specification for cables that provide connectivity between computers and peripheral devices. This standard also details the communications protocols and power supply standards leveraged by these cables.

Vulnerability: A weakness, typically within a piece of software, that can be exploited by an attacker to create an unwanted condition. For instance a vulnerability in a web application could allow an attacker the ability to bypass authentication and access sensitive information.

USEFUL WEBSITES

https://aws.amazon.com/blogs/security/
AWS Security Blog focused on Amazon Web Services security, run by AWS themselves.

https://www.cisecurity.org/
Homepage of the Center for Internet Security (CIS), the non-profit organisation behind the CIS benchmarks and hardened images leveraged by multiple security organisations across the world.

http://www.digitalforensicdiaries.com
Homepage of Digital Forensic Diaries, one of this author's other works, a series of short stories based on real life forensic investigations.

https://blog.erratasec.com/
ErrataSec blog run by Robert Graham and David Maynor, two highly respected security researchers.

https://www.hacker101.com/
Hacker101 online tutorials and a Capture the Flag (CTF) run by HackerOne, which specialises in running bug bounty programs.

https://www.healthcareinfosecurity.com/
Healthcare Info Security information security news site specific to the healthcare industry.

https://www.kali.org/
Official site of the Kali Linux penetration testing distribution, a widely used operating system image pre-loaded with many penetration testing tools.

https://krebsonsecurity.com/
Krebs on Security blog run by investigative journalist Brian Krebs. If you're a blue teamer, your job is to keep your company off this site.

https://www.offensive-security.com/metasploit-unleashed/
Metasploit Unleashed: a free (small donation to Hackers for Charity suggested) Metasploit training course created by Offensive Security.

https://nvd.nist.gov/
NIST National Vulnerability Database: the US Government's database of software vulnerabilities, hosted by the National Institute for Standards in Technology.

https://software-security.sans.org/blog
SANS AppSec: application security blog maintained by the SANS Institute.

https://sectools.org/
Sectools catalogue of the top 125 security tools, including a mixture of open-source and commercial products. Maintained by the team behind the Nmap port scanner.

https://www.threatminer.org/
ThreatMiner: a free (donation suggested) resource for searching across an aggregated collection of threat intelligence data.

https://threatpost.com/
Threatpost: an independent information security news site.

https://docs.microsoft.com/en-us/sysinternals/
Windows Sysinternals: a collection of tools for Windows systems that are of particular value to blue teams.

PREFACE

It's Friday, and I'm heading home for the week. The week started off with a pretty big celebration; after a couple of months of configuration and development work, my team and I wrapped up a major identity and access management (IAM) project. The final out-of-hours changes that needed to be made were made successfully on Sunday, and importantly, nothing was broken on Monday morning.

The celebration was short-lived, however. Out of the blue, in the middle of the morning, an intrusion detection system (IDS) alert was triggered by a strange outbound connection being made from a non-production host running a corporate application. Having jumped on the host, about 30 seconds after the alert hit, it was obvious that there was a malicious process running that had spawned a reverse connecting shell. A few calls to get the right people on the incident phone bridge, and after about 3 minutes the host was isolated, forensically relevant data was offloaded and the malicious processes were killed. Next, the machine was restored from a backup taken the previous Friday.

The log files that had been offloaded revealed a malicious request, designed to exploit a newly discovered vulnerability in a component of a Java-based web application, which had been leveraged to get the shell on the machine. It had been 5 minutes from incident detection to the completion of the response process. That's how it should be done. I was pretty happy with how the response process ran.

The vulnerability was patched, the post-mortem held to discuss what could've been done better (such as being a little bit quicker in applying the patch in the first place). The post-mortem took the most time out of any part of this response.

On Tuesday, the team and I were back to evaluating a couple of products from competing vendors for a new container image hardening project. Wednesday, I worked with a development team to ensure their application was logging events as per our published guidance. On Thursday, I helped an executive confirm that their machine was clean, after they opened a malicious attachment by accident. Earlier today, I was distracted by helping an engineer investigate something, and missed a call with one of the vendors we were evaluating earlier in the week. Whoops! That something turned out to be nothing, but the investigation was more interesting than any phone call would've been.

That's security operations folks. The pace is quick, the scope of responsibility is immense, and just when you think you've got time to switch off for a minute, the next thing pops up. It's exhausting. I wouldn't change it for the world.

With this book, my aim has been to explore the most effective ways to perform the various functions of the security operations team, and provide real-world examples that should supplement the theory. Nothing is worse than a textbook that teaches the theoretical best way to achieve something, when there is absolutely no practical way for that to work in reality.

I've always strived to be brutally honest in my assessment of any security topic, and share times when I've made mistakes, and what I learned as a result of those mistakes. Mistakes are inevitable by the way, when you move as fast, and are expected to provide so much coverage as you are in the world of information security. I really hope this honesty is apparent throughout the book, and you turn the last page not only having learned a great deal, but also having appreciated my candour and most importantly having enjoyed the read.

WHO SHOULD READ THIS BOOK?

This book has been written for anyone who needs to understand the various responsibilities of a modern-day security operations team, and what it takes to operate them effectively.

If you've been charged with creating and developing a security operations programme, and are sitting back, looking at a mountain of tasks ahead of you, and wondering where to get started, then this book is for you.

If you're an active member of a security operations department looking to expand its suite of offerings and move the team into new areas of focus and take on new roles, then this book should provide inspiration.

If you're new to the field of information security, or planning on getting into information security, this book will hopefully give you more than enough ideas around areas you'd like to concentrate or specialise in.

Whoever you are, I'm extremely glad you've chosen to read the book. There are so many voices in the field of information security, that for the quiet, anxiety-ridden ones such as myself it can be heard to break through the noise. The written word provides perhaps the best medium to share our thoughts and experiences, and that's what this book is all about. I'll always be in awe of the privilege it has been to write it for you.

1 INTRODUCTION

Much of what we read and hear about the relationship between information security professionals and the end users of the systems that we're working to protect is often overly adversarial. We're not at war with our users. Far from it. We're there to serve them. We're there to make it so difficult to violate a security policy, by providing the right tools and techniques, that no one can be bothered to do it another, less secure way. That's what security operations in practice is all about. Throughout this book we'll be discussing how to build an effective security operations team that can serve, protect and enable end users and the organisations they're a part of.

The idea of service and building a service-focused culture within a security operations team will be core themes within this book. This is deliberate, because I believe a security operations team that serves will be a successful security operations team. At this point in my career I've overseen the build out of security operations teams at a couple of different software-as-a-service (SaaS) organisations, and I hope to lean on the various experiences and lessons learned along the way to better prepare the reader who may be about to embark upon the same journey. It's not always a smooth journey, but it's one that is worth taking.

Perhaps one of my earliest memories in the security operations space was a meeting to introduce a project my team and I wanted to run to tidy up user accounts and permission levels that had been assigned within a finance application, in a somewhat haphazard fashion, over the course of several years. We wanted to align the application with our new organisation-wide identity and access management (IAM) programme.

I went into the meeting expecting little resistance. After all, the application contained sensitive information that could do the company significant harm if it was exposed. It was a complex application 'managed' by a couple of long tenured folks from the corporate IT organisation, who had knowledge of its innards. I needed support from the senior IT executive for the project, as I needed to borrow a chunk of her people's time to get the project done. I felt confident this wouldn't be an issue, since it would make the application more secure, easier to manage and in the long term, reduce the overall burden on those two specific people.

The response I got was surprisingly negative, and I was told the needed resources wouldn't be forthcoming. When I defaulted, as so many of us in this industry do, to 'but...but...security!' the response came as follows: 'Security is great, but we're not in business to be secure.'

This took me back and although it was a frustrating response it was 100 per cent correct. To this day, it has defined my thinking on the role of the corporate security team. Businesses aren't in business to be secure, but it sure helps them if they are. Understanding that security may not always play the leading part but has a role to play in the overall production is tremendously important. If you understand and appreciate this, often you can define and gradually increase the scope of that role. If you get offended, upset or confrontational by this notion, then emotion can take over and security can be seen as sulking off into the background.

WHAT IS SECURITY OPERATIONS?

If Hollywood movies or even just TV adverts produced by the major public cloud providers are to believed, security operations involves a group of people sitting in a room surrounded by monitors, making split second defensive decisions based on what those monitors are telling them, billions of times a day. Of course, real-life security operations, while it may involve such a room, frequently known as a security operations centre (SOC), is markedly less movie-worthy. In the movies, they always show you the SOC, but they never show you the meetings or processes you had to go through to get all the purchase orders, tickets and other documentation in order, to actually build and maintain the SOC.

Security operations is where the words and aspirations committed to information security policies are put into practice and a person, or people, begin the information security equivalent of painting the Forth Bridge – the never ending, always evolving tasks of detecting, responding, patching, analysing and understanding.

The understanding portion is key. Understanding and differentiating between the cause and effect of an event helps a security operations team determine severity, which in turn drives how the team decides to respond, and the response is ultimately where value is realised.

Processors of events and incidents

The majority of the time, security operations teams are dealing with security events rather than incidents. There is a crucial difference between these two terms, which is worth clarifying before we go any further. Various information security standards and publications have slightly different takes on the two terms, but many have followed the lead from the National Institute of Standards and Technology (NIST) Special Publication 800-61, *Computer Security Incident Handling Guide* (Cichonski et al., 2012).

The NIST definition of an event is 'any observable occurrence in a system or network', which covers a broad range of activities, both legitimate and otherwise. A user logging into an application that they are entitled to with valid credentials is an observable event. Likewise, a file being copied between two machines on the network is an observable event.

An incident, however, is something altogether more severe. According to the NIST definition, a security incident is 'the act of violating an explicit or implied security policy'. A person attempting to gain access to a system they are not authorised to use would be an example of an incident. Attempting to steal data from a web application would be another.

Now, this is all pretty foundational stuff, but it's important to get this distinction right. Security operations teams typically receive data pertaining to events, and they set about figuring out which of those events constitute an incident. This is typically done by correlating a group of events to figure out which ones might be related to something that warrants further investigation and response. The challenge here is that there are often quite a lot of events received by the operations team. We're talking thousands, tens of thousands or even millions of events per day in some cases. So how on earth are the security operations team supposed to deal with that level of 'noise' and figure out where to concentrate their efforts? Well, we've just arrived at a core challenge faced by security operations teams and one that, depending on how they choose to respond, can have a real impact on their effectiveness within an organisation.

There is no simple answer as to how you deal with this problem. There is no one size fits all approach. There are plenty of vendors who claim they will solve it for you with their software, but the truth is, while they might get you some of the way there, no single vendor makes software that can reliably detect every incident in your specific environment. We'll be walking through the various strategies for effectively extracting the signal of an incident from the noise of routine events throughout this book. For now, I'll mention one strategy that is doomed to fail: attempting to offload the event noise onto other teams within an organisation, or to put it another way, your customers.

It's tempting for a security operations team that is drowning in events to attempt to offload some of them directly to other teams in the hopes that they'll be able to stem the tide. Security operations teams should be service-focused, and most service organisations aren't there to increase the workload for their customers, they're supposed to lessen it. When it comes to 'noise', security operations should be a filter, not an amplifier. A great way to lose credibility and trust with your customers is to bombard them with useless, irrelevant or unactionable data. In the early days of a security operations team, this situation is more likely to occur, as a combination of new eyes, new tools and new insight into how various systems are running leads to an increased amount of paranoia and greater number of false positives.

I've been in a situation where a new security operations team had a rough start to life for the exact reason I've just described. The team was created in the shadow of a well-established incident response team, who were also doing a lot of event triage work. The aim of the security operations team was to reduce the workload on the incident responders, therefore allowing them to concentrate on more in-depth investigative work. At the same time the team was being created, a security incident and event management (SIEM) suite was being deployed and other security tools were starting to come online. The result was a lot of new people and a lot of new tools.

This was a big organisation and the event count ran extremely high. The security operations team, determined to prove their value early, set about alerting various contacts and teams to every event they were able to get their hands on. It soon became unmanageable and the security operations team ran the risk of losing credibility, as the defined escalation paths outside the security department started to refuse to respond to every escalation.

To fix this, I made a change to the way the new team would escalate. Rather than escalating directly, we leaned on the incident response team, who temporarily acted as a second tier. Using their prior knowledge of the environment, they proved to be an effective filter before escalations made their way outside the security team. Over time, both sides learned from each other how to recognise what was worthy of escalation and what was not. The temporary second tier was removed and the company started to realise the benefit of their investment in security operations.

When building a security operations team, always remember to take raw, unfiltered events as an input and produce actionable, detailed reporting and instruction as an output. This will result in a more secure organisation, which is ultimately what we're working towards.

Built to fit

Security operations teams should understand the business they are supporting, and build security to fit that business. Teams that attempt to operate things the other way around will always run into problems that limit their effectiveness, cause frustration and ultimately lead to the development of a less secure environment. This was true 10 years ago, is true today and, despite the explosion in awareness of cybersecurity issues, will probably still be true in another 10 years. It can be disheartening at first, but I promise you the reward comes later, when the security operations team is seen as a trusted entity that enables the business. You will be invited into more projects to get ahead of what is coming. You will receive more reports from end users and customers about potential incidents and problems if they trust you. Developers will be more willing to work with you to address important security problems if they know you don't pull the alarm cord continuously.

When an enterprise purchases a large, complex piece of software, the vendor often provides professional services to get the thing set up and rolled out properly. The same thinking should be applied to a security operations team, except, obviously, it's a group of people rather than a piece of software. To get the most out of the team there has to be some time set aside for orientation and to fit them into the day-to-day operating rhythm of the business. Considering the question 'what do we want from security operations?'

will go a long way towards defining what exactly security operations does for your organisation.

If your organisation is a SaaS provider, chances are you'll want security operations monitoring the software you provide to your users via the internet, keeping their accounts and data secure as they do so. If your organisation is running a power plant, you'll probably want security operations focused mainly on keeping the internal networks and computers that keep it ticking over free of malware.

Security operations is a form of risk treatment in this regard. You've identified a risk to your business, and one of the ways to lessen that risk is to employ a team to be on the lookout for signs that it may be about to materialise. Therefore, it's important to remember that the scope of a security operations team not only differs between organisations, but can change depending on the direction the business takes. For this reason, you always hope that a member of the security leadership team is present when those business decisions are made, which (thankfully) is increasingly the case. The best security operations teams are those who are seen not only as a force for good inside an organisation, but also as an enabler of the business, and perhaps even a differentiator in the sales cycle.

As general awareness around information security has increased in recent years, so too has the role that the security team plays in the sales cycle. This is especially true when considering business-to-business (B2B) deals, involving the handling or hosting of sensitive information. Once relegated to a darkened room and kept out of public gaze, these days it's not uncommon to find a security professional called up to join a sales call. This is fantastic news, for all parties, as exemplified by this next story.

I was asked to join a meeting with a particularly cloud-averse prospect (while working for a cloud-based software company). At this meeting the customer's IT compliance officer started to list their concerns with our product. An incredibly specific risk case was cited; one that, to this day, I believe was invented because the officer wanted to kill the deal and not have to do any more paperwork.

While the heads of the product, sales and development teams started to talk about how they could solve the particular issue raised by the compliance officer, I opened my laptop and went to the SIEM. I was able to create a new event condition, based on correlating values from two different logs that came from different parts of our application, in about 3 minutes. Meanwhile, back in the conversation, new features were being proposed that would take weeks to implement.

'Hey, so I just created a new event type to detect this occurring – obviously I'd like to test it, but I'm fairly sure this'll alert my team if that ever pops up', I said, somewhat smugly. Well, extremely smugly, actually.

And with that, the number of prospect meetings I was invited to increased dramatically. More importantly, the number of alerts for events that pertained to things our customers actually worried about increased, which is of course what it's all about.

In, or on?

While talking about what security operations is, we'd be remiss if we didn't discuss what security operations shouldn't be. Although security operations teams vary from organisation to organisation, one common factor that binds them together is that they rarely have extra people floating around looking for things to do. There's usually more than enough work to keep everyone busy. There's never really a quiet period either. Teams are either going 24-7 in shifts or have at least one person on call 24-7. It's operational, it's all hands on deck and it's a critical business function.

No surprise then, that most security operations team members are 'thrilled to bits' when they are invited to all day meetings to discuss more long-term security strategy, or write a policy to ensure compliance with a particular standard, taking precious time away from being on the front line. Security operations shouldn't be continually leaned on as security theorists or architects. These are the people who like to roll up their sleeves and deal with the issues that are actually occurring in real time.

There is a balance to be had here and it's related to a classic resource management problem: do you spend time 'in the business' or 'on the business'? 'In the business' refers to time spent doing the actual job, in this case, triaging events and being on the lookout for potential security problems. 'On the business' means time spent improving the way you do those things day to day, so that you can become more effective when you are doing them. The answer of course is that you need to spend time doing a bit of both. The size of your team and therefore the resources you have available have a dramatic impact on how you choose to divvy things up.

If you have a team of many people, the chances are you can hire specifically to fulfil both types of duty. The deployers and maintainers of tools on one hand and then the people who use them on the other. If you have a team of, say, you, then things might look a little different. Chances are you'll feel conflicted. You'll want to be part of the big decisions early on, since you know you'll be expected to respond to whatever comes your way, and any influence you can have on that is clearly going to be a bonus for your future self. At the same time, the pressure is on not to miss things that are going on in the now, as anything that you do miss could lead to an incident and create problems when it comes to proving your value and the value of security operations in general.

The key to solving this problem, especially if working in a smaller team, is to set ground rules and guidelines for those wishing to leverage your precious time. Make it very clear that operational work comes first. When you respond to meeting invitations, make meeting organisers aware that you might need to run if a serious situation warrants your response. Ensure that all meetings have agendas and desired outcomes. Prepare yourself by reading and digesting any pre-read material prior to the discussion. It can be hard to do this without feeling that you're throwing away, or putting a dent in that service-focused mentality that we're discussing throughout this book, but it is possible. As long as you're professional and polite, it is entirely reasonable to ask why you're expected to be at a meeting and what value the organiser is seeking from you.

The same rules apply to meeting with vendors and potential vendors. As someone who works in information security, you'll have no shortage of suitors vying for your affection, in terms of selling their product to you. There are some folks that accept every invitation for a pitch and there are others who decline or ignore automatically. Again, the right answer lies somewhere in the middle. If it's a product that fits with your needs or strategy, by all means have a meeting; if not, don't bother. The trick I've found that works with balancing vendor pitches is to have a 2-hour blocked out window on a Friday morning, and if I'm approached by a vendor that interests me, I know I always have that slot open to talk.

As security operations continues to grow, those who are in leadership roles will of course tend to take on more of the meetings, and cascade down the decisions that are driven from those meetings. This frees up the hands-on technical folks to stay focused on the job, while their leaders are busy filtering and deflecting. Of course, one of the great challenges about leadership roles, especially in information security or technology in general, is losing touch with the hands-on and technical work that you used to love so much. Good leaders will always consult with the people that report to them before agreeing to something that will directly affect their day-to-day lives and, ultimately, their happiness.

A security operations team can consist of anything from a fraction of a person (that is to say, one person spending a fraction of their time working on security operations, rather than focusing on it full-time) to thousands of people working full-time. I will always refer to a 'team', because any good security operations process, even one that is designed, deployed and managed by an individual, should scale to be workable by many.

Being a founding member of a security operations team is often a good way to set yourself up as an information security rock star within your organisation, but even rock stars need to take time off occasionally. Real rock stars, of course, tend to go through their various ups and downs in a very visible fashion. It's the price they pay for being constantly in the public eye. The very same can happen within an organisation to the information security rock star, although to a smaller audience. For this reason, I always think it's better to be an information security librarian. Librarians are reliable, know where to find anything, are well respected and, although you might not always notice them, you become very aware when they are not there.

Service, security and scale – three important and conveniently alliterative core tenets for a successful security operations team to embrace. All three will be a common theme throughout this book.

BLUE AND RED

Blue teams and red teams are an oft-used classification scheme to draw the line of demarcation between the defensive security and offensive security roles within security operations. Blue teamers are the valiant defenders of the realm, seeking to frustrate the ever-crafty red teamers who seek to find new and creative ways to sneak in to the organisation.

While these two opposing functions may be designed to directly compete with each other, they share a common goal, to keep an organisation secure. If you're lucky enough to be a part of a team that is large enough to have defined blue and red team roles, then you likely have tremendous resources available to build an effective security operations programme. If not, do not fret, it is entirely possible to do the same in teams with mixed responsibilities, which is still a common configuration (see Figure 1.1).

Figure 1.1 An overview of blue and red teams

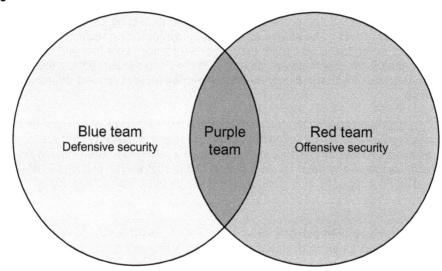

The evolution of security operations

Generally speaking, when establishing a security operations team, building defensive or blue team operations is the first priority for an organisation. Over time as the team grows, value is realised and roles focused on red team tasks such as penetration testing are added to the job boards. The reasoning behind this approach is fairly easy to explain, why concentrate on attacking yourself if you have no one in place to build and operate the appropriate defences? That said, there are exceptions to this. In some cases, the desire for opening security-focused job roles can come from the software or technology development departments, rather than the corporate IT side of the house. In such situations it's not uncommon for that first hire to be more of a traditional 'red teamer', such as a penetration tester or application security specialist. More often than not, if this situation occurs the newly hired individual finds a number of issues and coincidentally (of course) a blue team role is hastily approved.

However a security operations team is organised, the blue and red categorisation is a great way to prioritise and divide responsibilities among team members. It can also help with building career paths, by allowing people to focus on either offensive or defensive security work, and attracting people with different skillsets to your team. Some folks are die-hard blue teamers, who love the thrill of detecting, responding, containing and shutting down potential security incidents following a meticulous methodology. On the other side of the coin, many red teamers shudder at the thought of being so structured in their work, and instead enjoy the creative freedom afforded by being given a broad assignment to break into an organisation. Both perspectives have their place in building a well-rounded team, and being able to draw from a diverse range of candidates is always a positive.

It's for this reason that this book is broken into two parts with a focus on roles and responsibilities afforded to both blue and red teams. While in practice they might be conducted by the same people, at least initially, understanding how the typical functions of a security operations team are divided up between these two sub-teams can help down the line as the team grows.

THE BLUE TEAM

If you think of a team sport, football (soccer, for US readers) for example, and then think of the most famous professional players from that sport, there is a good chance you're going to think of Messi, Rooney, Ronaldo or Zidane. Those names have one thing in common: they're all attacking players who, as a part of the offence, have been given greater opportunity to score goals and make the headlines when their teams win. Of course, football is a team sport and we know that while those individual players are more likely to score goals, it takes a strong defence to win games and championships. This analogy is extremely relevant to information security, where as a member of the defensive side of the house, it can often feel like your daily efforts go unrewarded, while the superstar red teamers who find interesting vulnerabilities are lauded. So why would anyone want to be on the blue team?

It's a fair question, but thankfully an easy one to answer. Blue team work is incredibly interesting and extremely rewarding, even if you don't get all the accolades all of the time. In fact, perhaps the best indicator that you're doing a really good job on a blue team is when you go unnoticed, in some cases for several years in succession! It's a truth that many who work in this industry will attest, that people only tend to notice the work you've been doing when things go wrong. Now, while that might sit nicely for some folks, it's of course always worth making sure that people do know you exist for various reasons: proactive outreach, understanding the capabilities your team can provide, being aware of changes to your monitoring responsibilities, to name but a handful.

When you think of a blue team, you'll likely think of tasks like firewall management, monitoring of intrusion detection and prevention systems (IDS/IPS), responding to antivirus (AV) software alerts and using tools such as data loss prevention (DLP) software to keep sensitive information contained. While these are all good examples of the daily work that a blue team will be involved in, in the modern enterprise it's important to think beyond these traditional responsibilities. Blue teams, and their leaders, are finding tremendous value in being seen not just as a technical function, but as a self-promoting business unit with internal customers. A well-connected blue team adds value, not just to the security team, but to the entire organisation. It's not uncommon for a blue team that has done their homework to know more about the way a custom-built application works than the team of folks who originally built it, not least because of organisational changes and staff turnover. Throughout this book, we'll look at a number of traditional and not-so-traditional blue team functions.

Monitoring

Blue teams spend a lot of time monitoring using various tools, such as SIEM suites and log aggregation tools, to look for signs of intrusion or incident, and responding accordingly. Monitoring typically refers to studying network traffic, application logs, or endpoint and user behaviours. In the modern enterprise, monitoring will transcend the confines of an enterprise network and extend to public cloud and SaaS offerings.

Endpoint protection

The endpoint (desktop, laptop, tablet, phone or watch) and the organic mass that is operating the endpoint are frequently critical players, for better or worse, in the event of a security incident. Therefore, protecting that endpoint, which is often seen as a balancing act between allowing a level of trust and flexibility needed to get the job done and enforcing a stricter set of conditions that will reduce the likelihood of a security incident happening, is usually a big part of the blue team's daily responsibilities.

Data protection

Every company is a data company. If you're working on protecting a dataset, you're working on protecting an entire company and, in many cases, a whole slew of people who have entrusted that company to handle personally sensitive data. We've all seen, multiple times, how devastating it can be when data ends up in the wrong hands. Through various technologies including encryption, specialist monitoring, permission assignments and endpoint protection agents, a blue team is on the front line when it comes to keeping data safe. As a security professional you cannot, and should not, bear the sole responsibility of being the conscience of the entire company when it comes to data protection. However, you can work to build that conscience across all areas of the company by being an advocate for the safety and security of your end users.

Identity and access

Identity and access management (IAM) is an area of blue team responsibility that has seen tremendous growth in recent years, not least because of the increase in SaaS products that leverage single sign-on (SSO) and federated login. IAM has two equally important facets. The first, and the one most people tend to think of when they think of a security team's involvement in access management, is taking access away. Ensuring that access is removed from a system in a timely fashion when an individual leaves the company or updating it to reflect a change in role are routine but highly necessary actions to ensure the prolonged integrity of a system. The second facet is ensuring that a person gets the appropriate level of access required to do their job and that this is done in a timely fashion. Nothing is worse than waiting 2 weeks to be able to access an application; in such a case you might even be tempted to ask a colleague if you can borrow their account. In organisations that leverage role-based access control (RBAC), security operations teams can be responsible for building the job role to access mappings, ensuring this situation never occurs, since all access is directly aligned with an individual's position within the organisation, rather than being assigned on a case-by-case basis.

The increasing popularity of Zero Trust access models, which do away with the familiar concepts of trusted networks, such as an internal company network, and untrusted networks, such as the internet, and treat everything as equally untrusted and in need of strong authentication, is another factor in the increased importance of IAM. Security operations teams can find themselves deploying products and tools that support enterprises in implementing a Zero Trust model, without causing their business to grind to a halt. Technologies such as password-less and continuous authentication ensure users don't have to manually reauthenticate every time they access a new resource.

Incident response

Incident response is a topic so worthy of its own book that I wrote one (Sheward, 2018). Incident response is a critical information security function, and one that, when done correctly, can prevent a bad situation from developing into something much worse. The blue team will likely find themselves the lead incident responders for their organisation. Incident response requires cool heads, solid relationships with other members of the organisation and most importantly – trust. In many cases, you develop that trust during your routine daily work prior to an incident occurring.

Vulnerability management

Few defensive information security activities are as underappreciated as vulnerability management. It's a critical foundational activity for any security programme, yet more often than not, a task that is quickly assigned to the newest or most junior member of the security team, and subsequently passed around like a hot potato. I get it; it's not the most exciting task. It takes a lot of work to keep track of all the various systems in an organisation, the software components they are running and the remediation states of pages and pages of various vulnerabilities.

Vulnerability management platforms help with the tracking significantly, but they cannot always talk to the appropriate ticketing systems to ensure tickets are opened in the correct queues or formats, and they definitely cannot navigate the human political or emotional factors at play when it comes to actually getting patches applied in a timely fashion. It's for these reasons that a good vulnerability management programme is about more than just running scans and collecting results – it's also about cross-functional collaboration with systems owners and working to ensure that expectations about which patches are to be applied and the time frame in which they are to be applied are clearly communicated.

Work beyond the enterprise

Having a trusted and approachable blue team can feel like a perk of the job for many employees, and that's something that, if attained, should be celebrated. Not just because it's great that people like and want to interact with them, but because it actually serves to improve security for the organisation and beyond.

Many people have the option to work from home, connecting from their own networks, and in some cases their own devices and equipment, to systems under the purview of the enterprise blue team. Therefore, if that same team can help with queries about the most secure way to set up a personally owned device, they should. If they have the bandwidth to support an employee when a personal email account gets compromised, why not? It helps keep them, their networks and ultimately your systems secure.

THE RED TEAM

One of the most frequent statements that you'll hear from an external penetration testing consultant is a variation on 'if only I had more time', referring of course to the limited window of opportunity they're afforded to conduct a penetration testing engagement for a client. Well, guess what, join an enterprise red team and suddenly you'll have a lot more time to probe, understand, break, fix and repeat.

There are clear advantages to having external eyes on an enterprise for the purposes of testing security posture, but if you have resources available internally to bolster and more directly focus your consultant hours, you're almost certainly going to get more out of the engagement and come away with a more secure environment. That's the beauty of red teaming, a group within your four walls that is set up to attack you like an adversary would, but with the ability to file tickets to drive remediation of issues, rather than compromise, disrupt and damage your business operations.

Red teams, and offensive security functions in general, might seem like a no-brainer if you can afford them; however, outside the information security profession they're not always so well received. In some cases an organisation might steer clear of greenlighting offensive security work, not because they question the value it can provide, but because it might not sit well within the political landscape of the corporate environment. Folks have a tendency to become somewhat perturbed if a team within their organisation shows up on a regular basis to challenge and question the work they're doing. There is often a feeling that the red team is 'out to get me', or on a mission to deliberately embarrass, for example, if an employee fails a phishing simulation carried out by the red team.

To counter this resistance, it's critical that the red team be set up in such a manner as to accurately communicate and reassure their targets about the purpose of their work. Yes, we test aggressively and intrusively, but we do it together, for the purposes of making everyone more secure. No one is going to be singled out; security is an organisation-wide function; and everyone has a role to play; we're just reminding everyone of that role. Remember, as mentioned earlier, security operations is a service-focused function, and that notion still applies to the red team. The red team is there to serve, and educate end users.

Legislation such as the General Data Protection Regulation (GDPR) can help make the case for red teams. Nothing says 'secure by design', one of the accountability requirements of GDPR, like an entire team dedicated to the role of security testing at all stages of product design and development.

As we move into the second part of the book, we'll focus on red team and offensive functions.

Penetration testing

The bread and butter work of the red team, performing penetration testing is often the first thing you'll think of when you consider offensive security. A penetration test involves simulating the actions of a malicious attacker, seeking to gain entry to a network, a server, an application and, ultimately, an organisation.

The scope of penetration testing can be limited to a specific target or be limited only by the tester's imagination. Most typically within an enterprise red team, highly targeted tests on new application features or following significant code changes are the name of the game.

Threat hunting

Why sit passively and wait for something to pop up in an IDS/IPS alert or a SIEM tool when you can go looking for it proactively? That's the idea behind threat hunting, a red team function that is gaining popularity and momentum within many security operations teams around the world.

It's often said that if someone has had the time to write a signature to detect a piece of malware or a network intrusion, it's already too late. That same threat could already have been in your environment, doing its malicious deed for some time. Honestly, that way of thinking is probably a little alarmist for most organisational threat models, but it's not without credence. AV software developers have to first capture and observe a piece of malware in a lab so they can write an appropriate signature for their product to detect it. Even AV software vendors aren't privy to every variant of malware, especially in industries running highly specialised equipment or systems (think industrial control systems, for example). This is an example of where a threat hunting programme can be very effective.

Building bespoke tools

Every organisational computing environment is unique. There are endless combinations of hardware and software components that can create equally unique attack surfaces. It's for this reason that we often say, 'security isn't for sale'. You can't go out and purchase security for an organisation. Sure, you can buy individual tools to help you secure an environment, but it takes a combination of people, process and technology to really get the job done.

Some of the best security tools aren't purchased at all. They're custom-built in house and designed to fit the system being protected, like a suit of armour. It's increasingly common to find the task of building such tools to be a red team responsibility. Many red teamers (but not all) are coders by nature, so revel in the opportunity to create a tool that will fulfil a specific organisational need, while at the same time making it possible to increase the scale and repeatability of their testing.

Physical security

One of the most devastating ways technical security measures can be bypassed is via a breach of physical security. It's surprising then, that physical security often plays second fiddle when an organisation is building out its security programme. Many times, this is because there is a divide in responsibility between the corporate security team and the facilities team. It's not always clear what falls on each side of the divide. Ultimately, physical security is an area that impacts everyone, and there should be a unified approach driven from the top down.

One aspect of physical security that the red team can excel in is putting it to the test. Ensuring that door alarms are active, testing badging systems and making sure physical security controls are applied at all branch office locations. For this reason, red teamers frequently find themselves including physical security assessments in their scope of responsibilities.

PURPLE TEAMS

So-called purple teams (a mix of blue and red) are found with increasing frequency nestled within the organisational charts of businesses around the world. The truth is, many organisations, especially those that are smaller in size, leverage purple teams simply because they don't have enough staff to warrant separating out their offensive and defensive security work into distinct groups. Opinion is split on whether or not the purple team is a good or bad thing.

Proponents of the purple team model argue that, by defending a specific system with an attacker's mindset, the defensive work is more effective than it would be if you were simply building defences, even if you were doing so in accordance with best practice. Every target is different, after all. Controls can be adjusted and updated while the attack is ongoing, which feels like a more 'agile' approach to deploying enterprise security.

Opponents suggest that if you have enough people to separate out your teams, you should do so. A purple team shouldn't be necessary if both blue and red teams are run properly and working together well. Red and blue teams should be sharing information at all times, in any case. They work for the same organisation after all.

A good compromise is for the purple team to be a cross-functional meeting, or even a virtual team, made up of various members of the red and blue teams. In the case of a meeting, the cadence may be multiple times per week, and involve note sharing or actively working on defending and attacking a target. In the case of a virtual team, rotating members of the team is a great way to expose red teamers to blue team methods and vice versa, while still allowing those individuals the reassurance of having a speciality, be it offensive or defensive security.

Whichever approach is leveraged, red, blue or purple, the security operations team will perform the same core functions as those covered in this book.

HOW THIS BOOK FITS IN

Over the course of the next 12 chapters, we'll delve deep into the areas we've just introduced. We'll look at the goals of each of the tasks, as well as ways to effectively introduce them into your security operations programme.

Blue, red, purple or a one-person show – however your security operations team is set up, we'll use a combination of theory and real-world tested methods for building and practising effective, modern security operations.

REFERENCES

Cichonski, P., Millar, T., Grance, T. and Scarfone, K. (2012) *Computer Security Incident Handling Guide* (rev 2). National Institute of Standards and Technology, Gaithersburg, MD. Available at: https://nvlpubs.nist.gov/nistpubs/SpecialPublications/NIST.SP.800-61r2.pdf

Sheward, M. (2018) *Hands-on Incident Response and Digital Forensics*. BCS Learning & Development, Swindon, UK.

2   ESTABLISHING A SECURITY OPERATIONS TEAM

If I were to provide a generalised summary of the typical life cycle of a corporate security team, it would probably look something like this: The genesis is a customer requirement to meet or prove compliance with a particular information security standard. The company responds by selecting or hiring a person to lead the effort of understanding and applying the standard to the business via a series of written policies. That person is more often than not less technical, and typically from a financial, legal or IT leadership background. They might be the sole person with 'information security' responsibility for some time, and during that period they rely heavily on partners in other teams to actually enforce, and adhere to, what is listed in those policies.

Now to be clear, just because that person isn't necessarily someone from a technical background, it doesn't mean they have less of a right to be there, nor does it mean they won't be successful. A lot of the time the success of the founding information security professional within an organisation comes down to how well they can influence and work with others, versus their ability to be hands-on in applying security controls. The effectiveness of that person and their early stage, compliance-driven security programme can make or break the perception of the security team at an organisation for years to come. Therefore, it's important that they build their programme to support and enable the business from day one, rather than declaring security to be an 'all or nothing' arrangement. In fact, it's for this reason that having someone other than a purely technical resource running the show can be beneficial, as we techies tend to be more binary in our thinking, which can lead to flat out frustration and burnout.

I can say with complete certainty that I wouldn't have written the preceding paragraph at the beginning of my career in information security. However, over time, having experienced working for different types of leader, and in information security functions at different stages in their development, my thinking has definitely evolved on this particular topic. There are positives and negatives to having both non-technical and technical leadership.

Back to the life cycle, once the compliance-driven programme is in place, has had a couple of victories with customers, and the person running that programme is starting to build momentum, they are typically given their first staff. That can go one of two ways. The hiring manager can either seek to hire someone with a similar background and skills to their own to provide backup and scale the function horizontally, or elect to make a technical hire to provide more direct control over the implementation and management of security controls, therefore making the enforcement of policies somewhat easier. A lot of the time, the technical hire is the path taken, and with that you have the early stages of a security operations function.

Aside from getting stuck into firewalls, monitoring tools and all that other fun stuff, that first technical hire has another critical responsibility. They often find themselves owning the perception shift from security as a legal or financial enforcement and policy function, to security as a technical function, which is a big deal in most organisations. If the security leader has done a good job in managing cross-functional relationships to this point, then this shift is made considerably easier.

In this chapter, we'll explore this cycle in more detail. We'll discuss how to hire for those critical roles, how to prioritise those first security operations tasks and what it takes to put it all into practice effectively.

HIRING FOR SECURITY OPERATIONS

One of the common themes to develop in the information security industry over the past few years is typically referred to as the 'cybersecurity skills shortage'. It's the notion that while the demand for information security professionals has grown (thanks to greater awareness of the information security risks and stricter data protection laws, to name but a couple of factors), the number of qualified people available to fill those roles has not. With this in mind, you might be concerned that even if you get the opportunity to hire people for your security operations team, you won't be able to find high quality candidates. Fear not. The candidates are indeed out there. They're great candidates too.

While I agree that there is a skills shortage impacting the information security industry today, I don't think it's for the reasons that everyone has been led to believe. I believe, and it has been my experience hiring people over the last decade, that the shortage is not of suitable candidates willing to do whatever it takes to succeed in the industry, but is instead in the vision and creativity of those charged with hiring them. We cannot build up a supply of experienced information security professionals if no one is willing to give them the chance to gain relevant experience.

Information security is a field that lends itself to people who come from a diverse range of backgrounds. After all, one of the most commonly used messages in security awareness training is 'everyone is a member of the security team', meaning, of course, that everyone has a role to play in keeping an organisation secure. So, why should that message be forgotten when folks actually want to join the security team? Part of the challenge is that people like to set entry-level criteria for an information security professional based solely on the certifications they have attained. Yet, most of those certifications require an experience level measured in multiple years before they can be issued. It's a vicious cycle. Certifications are a great way to demonstrate your experience and solidify your knowledge in a particular area. However, they should not be the be all and end all when it comes to hiring, and organisations that use them as a filtering or gating mechanism for candidates will ultimately lose out.

Traits and skills

There are some personality traits and core skills that do not require certifications or experience to obtain. And these should be considered before everything else when hiring for an information security position.

Being honest and trustworthy

Being honest and trustworthy is number one on the list. Anyone who works in any information security role must have high levels of integrity, must never seek to distort the truth and must be prepared to be trusted with some incredibly sensitive responsibilities. In the modern organisation everything travels across the network. Emails, instant messaging conversations, internet traffic, secrets and data. All things that the information security professional might be expected to monitor to look for signs of a security problem. This level of unfiltered exposure to so much information means a great deal of trust is placed in the security professional. Break that trust for any reason, and the ability of a person to continue to function in a security role is gone in an instant.

Passion for the work

This industry is a tremendously rewarding place to work. It can also be bone-crushingly infuriating at times. Having a passion that means you'll keep coming back for more is critically important, even after the phone goes off at 3 a.m. every morning for a week when you're the on-call incident responder. You can't afford to hire someone who'll bail the second something aggravating happens. Security is about persistence and creating positive change through trust and influence, as well as technology. That doesn't always come easy.

Conversely, an important point is that it's entirely possible to be very passionate about your work in information security and still have a life outside the industry when you're not at work. There is this undercurrent of pressure in our industry to always be finding the next vulnerability, posting the next research paper, blogging and tinkering at all hours of the day. Be passionate, and do those things if you enjoy them, but take time for a break too.

Always learning

No one can ever truly know everything about information security. The rate at which things evolve and the ever-changing threat landscape make that an impossibility. You need people that recognise and apply this. Thankfully, that is most people in the field, but there are some out there who paint themselves as all-knowing oracles. Be cautious of this kind of personality.

Flexibility

In an information security team, especially a smaller one, priorities can shift quickly. Having someone on board who is okay with stepping outside their comfort zone and away from their primary responsibilities on occasion is a huge plus when change happens. We can't hire people to do one thing and then set them up for something else altogether, of course, but it shouldn't be too much of an upheaval to ask that person to temporarily back up another function if the business or team requires it.

Understanding and respecting the team
As already discussed, information security lends itself to a diverse array of candidates with different skills and experience. If you have a team of multiple people, they'll all bring something different to the table. It's important that when you hire for your team you hire a person that also respects and understands this. Not everyone who works in a security team can break into machines and pop command shells on them with custom built exploits at will, and nor should they be able to. Those who can, should still have respect for those with a different skillset.

Being a builder
A tool, a program, a policy, an application programming interface (API); whatever can be built; hire someone who wants to build it. In information security there is frequently opportunity to build something that will live on for years. Therefore, people who embrace the builder mentality tend to do very well in the field.

Personas

When building out a team, hiring people from diverse backgrounds provides you with a broader range of skills to draw from. This in turn leads to a more effective group and, because we're focusing on building out a security operations team, a more secure organisation. Let's take a look at examples of the types of backgrounds and perspectives that are key in building out a security team with depth.

The businessperson
Having someone on your security operations team who understands how your organisation makes money is vital. Typically, the people you're defending against want to either disrupt or exploit the way that you make money, so that they can stop you from doing so or use that method to line their own pockets. The businessperson will also understand the goals and objectives of the organisation, and can help the team align seamlessly with those goals. Finally, they should be able to fully analyse business processes, to identify potential weak spots. There are always vulnerabilities at the business logic layer that might escape even the sharpest security technician.

The systems admin
Having someone on the team who knows every single configuration setting on an operating system, what every error message means, where the important logs are and where to look when performance is not as it should be has countless advantages.

The network engineer
When you strip down almost every significant breach that has ever happened, it happened because 'host X' communicated sensitive information to 'host Y' over a network connection. Network engineers are prolific packet capture analysts; they know network equipment command lines like a first language and are well-versed in firewall administration: vital skills for a security operations professional.

The law enforcement professional
If you get the chance to have someone on your team who has investigated 'real-life' crime, particularly fraud, I highly recommend you take that chance. Never forget, bad things don't just happen on the internet autonomously. At the root of all malicious

activity, even if abstracted behind a bot or automated scanner, is a human being. Having someone who understands the motivation, techniques and psychology of a criminal adds a new dimension to your team's abilities.

The developer

Developers make great penetration testers because they know exactly how developers think. This gives them a highly valuable perspective when it comes to disassembling an application. They can also create tools that empower the rest of the team through automation. Some of the most effective security tools are those created in-house, built like a well-fitting suit of armour specific to the organisation, rather than purchasing an off-the-shelf tool.

The communicator

Sometimes the more technical folks on your team will need a little help from someone who can 'translate'. They'll need to take a technical concept, such as the justification for a control, and explain it to someone who maybe isn't quite as comfortable with the language in use. Having someone on point who can break through communication barriers for your team will help them make new and useful connections.

The accountant

Because of the meticulous nature of their work with numbers, accountants make great information security professionals. They rarely miss a critical detail.

ROLES

Of course, a very significant consideration when deciding who you are going to hire is what exactly you are hiring them to do. A security operations team, like any other organisation, will have different wants and needs from its people, and that'll be driven by a number of factors, including:

- budget;
- size of the organisation;
- maturity of the team;
- responsibilities relative to other departments within security.

Every security operations team will be built differently to cater for the unique needs of the business it serves. Two people with the same title at two different organisations might have entirely different responsibilities. That said, some common types of role have emerged, and it is possible to give a general overview of their typical activities.

Analysts

The information security analyst position is typically an entry-level position in an organisation's security operations team; although, there might be different levels of seniority attached to the role. A person in this role is usually seen as a generalist who may be assigned to work on a series of routine technical security or compliance tasks, or work on specific projects or initiatives.

In a security operations setting, the folks who triage and respond to events are commonly categorised as analysts.

The position typically provides people with their first hands-on experience with enterprise security tools and allows them to start thinking about areas in which they'd like to specialise (for instance, penetration testing, incident response, security architecture).

The entry-level nature of the position doesn't make it less important than any other information security role. In fact, in many organisations, information security programmes are still being shaped, and there is tremendous scope for an information security analyst to help provide direction for that programme.

Engineers

The tools that the analysts use to detect events and incidents don't just magically appear in an environment; someone has to put them in place and then feed and water them to ensure they stay operational. This is usually the role of a security engineer in a security operations team.

Thinking back to the description used in Chapter 1, if you have both analysts and engineers, you can clearly identify who is spending time on the business (engineers) and in the business (analysts). It's a luxury to have both.

You might also see the title 'network security engineer' within a security operations team, or as part of a networking focused team. Here, there is generally an assumption that a person with this title will be working mainly on firewalls and other network-based security tools.

Specialists

In a larger security operations team it's not uncommon to have specialised roles for various tasks. A red team is a prime example of this. A common job title for someone working in a red team might be 'Application Security Specialist', which is typically used to describe someone who primarily works on application level penetration testing.

Other common specialisms within security operations include:

- Physical security technology – the management of security technologies in support of a physical security programme, such as a cameras and badging system.
- IAM – responsibility for the systems and workflows used to approve and provision access to applications.
- Compliance operations – performing tasks to ensure ongoing compliance with regulatory, industry-specific or contractual requirements.
- Vulnerability management – performing scanning to identify vulnerable systems, and working to ensure timely remediation of identified vulnerabilities.
- Incident response – leading an organisation's response to a security incident in accordance with defined procedures.
- Digital forensics – the scientific process of collecting evidence and investigating a computer crime, with the aim of identifying a perpetrator.

Leadership

To enable those who work hands-on to get the most out of their time, a security operations team benefits from having both technical and people leaders in the fold. The technical leaders can often take titles in the form of 'principal'; 'Principal Security Engineer' for example. They remain individual contributors, but are often the first to be sent to other areas of the business to make sure the security operations team is engaged in what is going on.

People leaders, on the other hand, are responsible for hiring and assigning responsibilities to the security operations team members. A good people leader also clears roadblocks that may be holding a person back from achieving their full potential, and helps them develop throughout their career. Titles like supervisor and manager tend to be used to identify these types of leader.

Sometimes you'll find people who act as both technical and people leaders. Balancing both can be tricky, and if you find such a being, and they're good at what they do, I'd advise you to keep them close by at all times. Never let them out of your sight, because they'll be very hard to replace.

PRIORITIES AND PROCEDURES

Once you've made your hire, they've completed the mandatory orientation tasks at your company, and they are eager to start, what exactly should you task them with first? There's probably a mountain of tasks and ideas that you could have them tackle. Simply unleashing your new hire to pick and choose from that mountain can have mixed results. Some people, mainly those with some experience, could be in heaven. There are plenty of people who can walk in, provide a quick assessment of a company's needs and start to build accordingly. If you're hiring a more experienced person and are early in the life cycle of your team, this might be exactly what you want, and precisely why you hired them. For others, perhaps people with less experience in information security, the mountain of tasks could prove overwhelming, and the experience both damaging and off-putting.

In either case, it's extremely important, and a trait of a good leader, to be able to accurately convey what your priorities are and how they relate to the priorities of the organisation, and to set an expectation for what success looks like when tackling those priorities. Yes, give people the freedom they need to be creative and build good security into your organisation, but make sure that it's directed creativity and not a complete free for all. That can be a recipe for disaster, as someone might be spending hours working on something that doesn't fit the needs of the business, and therefore doesn't support the security operations mission.

Getting started

All security operations teams have to start somewhere and have to select which tasks they believe will deliver the most value out of the gate. In this position it can be tempting to focus on what you don't have. For instance, 'we don't have a next generation firewall, we should deploy one', or 'we don't have a SIEM suite, that's the first thing we'll need'. Instead of doing this, it is strongly recommended that the focus turns to what you do have, and making sure that it's as secure as possible.

You may not have the latest firewalls, but are those you do have frequently audited and as secure as they can be? Do you know where all your IT assets are? Do you have logging enabled everywhere that it could be? Answering these questions does a couple of different things for you. First of all, it doesn't cost anything to tune what you already have. You aren't walking into an organisation and instantly demanding cash to pay for new toys in the name of security. This will help with your credibility. Once you've done the most you can with existing tools, then you can start to budget for and ask for those that you really need. Second, it helps identify existing weaknesses that should be addressed, and gives you the chance to clean up the environment before you encounter the 'how come security didn't catch this with their fancy new tools?' syndrome, which usually rears its ugly head at some point down the road. Finally, it prevents you from introducing complexity to an environment you might not fully understand. Indeed, it's a great way to learn a complex environment, which is key for a security operations team that may have a broad mandate to protect it.

Common initial tasks performed by security operations that follow this pattern include:

- firewall audits;
- vulnerability scanning and network discovery;
- user account audits;
- configuration management audits;
- software and cloud service audits;
- building processes to handle existing alerts and notifications.

Every item on this list can usually be performed with little to no operational or capital expense, and can instantly start to deliver value.

Giving priority

Once tasks have been identified the next step is to prioritise them. Rarely are we afforded the luxury of being able to serially work through things that are thrown our way, usually things come our way in an unrelenting parallel fashion. In order to assist your team in prioritising work, it's always a good idea to provide a framework for prioritisation. This framework should be applicable to all the typical functions performed by the team and should be broad enough that you don't need to update it every time a minor change to the team's responsibilities occurs.

Figure 2.1 shows an example of a security operations team priority framework. I created this for the first security operations team I managed, and it served us well for a number of years.

Everything the team worked on fitted into this framework. The highest priority item is life and family safety, which unfortunately in the era of doxing (the release of personally identifiable information with ill intent) can sometimes be a real risk for those charged

Figure 2.1 A security operations priority framework

Highest priority	
Your own life safety/That of your family	
Active incidents	
Things that impact external customers	
Things that impact internal customers	
Daily tasks	
Projects	Research and development
Lowest priority	

with going up against malicious actors on behalf of an enterprise. The next priority would be active incidents, which require immediate attention to ensure they don't become worse.

External customers refers to those customers outside the organisation; the people who pay to use our services. If they wanted us to investigate a potential unauthorised account access event for instance, we'd jump on it.

Next on the list would be work for internal customers, which are other teams within the organisation. Think priority access requests, or assisting a user who might be asking for advice on the most secure way to get things done.

Getting towards the bottom of the list, we find daily tasks. Most security operations teams have implemented a programme of things they want to check every day. After all, there's no point having various tools in place to monitor things if you don't check and respond to the events they detect on a regular basis. Even though the tasks are further down the list, it's important to remember that they are still pretty important, it's just that there are a couple of mitigating factors that mean it's usually okay if they get deprioritised on a given day. First of all, everyone on the team can be trained in how to do a given repetitive task, so if the person who is assigned the task cannot due to other priorities, there might be someone else who can. Second, if a daily task is missed one day, there is always tomorrow. Letting a daily task slide by 24 hours shouldn't be devastating, but in most cases it shouldn't extend beyond that. For each task, it is recommended a 'maximum number of missed days' rule is put in place.

Finally, we have the never-ending standard work that all organisations have ticking over in the background – projects, and research and development. If everything is complete, then by all means spend some time experimenting and developing new ways to do things. An advantage of having more people is that your team can reach this lowest point in the framework more frequently, which can lead to discovery of a better way of getting things done.

Defining procedures

Once your tasks and responsibilities are defined and prioritised, the next step is to make sure that they are ready to be conducted in a repeatable fashion by multiple team members. The start of this book covered the importance of scalability within security operations. Having well-defined procedures is the bedrock of scalability.

Let's use vulnerability management as an example of why this is so important. A typical vulnerability scanning tool will offer multiple scan options, such as an authenticated scan, which uses valid credentials to login to a system and take a deeper look at packages installed on that system, versus an unauthenticated scan, which probes and attempts to identify services running on a system from a purely external perspective. These types of scan can give very different results. You'll find far fewer vulnerabilities using an unauthenticated scan.

So, what happens if one day a team member runs an unauthenticated scan and then the following week a different team member uses the authenticated option? The risk level associated with a host will look very different week to week, and whoever is responsible for remediating the discovered issues will be in for a bit of a shock.

This is just one example of how having procedures in place can make a difference. If the procedure says all team members must run an authenticated scan, using a specific set of credentials, then the results will be consistent and it'll be easier to track remediation work.

This level of detail (settings, accounts) is required in procedures. There should be no room for ambiguity. All procedures should be tested prior to being put live by having two different people follow them while being observed, at different times. This will allow you to identify areas where extra details should be added.

Just like policies, procedures should be periodically reviewed and any updated versions circulated among team members. Then the most up-to-date version number should be recorded, so that team members can cross-check they are working to the correct version.

PUTTING IT INTO PRACTICE

As the people, the tasks, the priorities and the procedures start to become understood, the security operations team will soon find itself establishing an operating rhythm. It's not uncommon for there to be ups and downs in the early days. Perhaps a vulnerability scan will disrupt a sensitive host. Perhaps an overzealous analyst will panic and accidentally lockout the chief executive officer (CEO) while they really are on holiday in the Russian city of Petrozavodsk. It's important to remember that such things can and do happen; as long as we learn from them and adjust procedures where necessary, then things will work out. The ups will outnumber the downs, and value will be realised.

Security operations will start to be considered a trusted part of the organisation, and the victories will help enhance the team's reputation. As the business grows it's possible the team will grow too. Perhaps into multiple geographical locations, across different time zones, which is great news for those who were previously on-call all night.

There really is nothing more satisfying as a leader of a security operations team than seeing the team work together to deliver value, and having top-down support for their continued growth.

SUMMARY

In this chapter we've talked through the earliest days of a security operations team. We've covered the difference between events and incidents, which play a crucial role in our daily lives as security operations professionals. We discussed the importance of taking event noise and reducing it for our customers.

We studied the universal traits that all security operations professionals should possess, and the benefits of hiring people from diverse backgrounds.

Finally, we walked through an overview of establishing early responsibilities, prioritising them and defining procedures to ensure they are repetitive, and not susceptible to error.

The next chapter dives deeper into one of the primary areas of responsibility for a blue team: monitoring. Specifically, we'll look at how we monitor the networks that are the key to all communication in the enterprise, as well as new frontiers such as infrastructure-as-a-service (IaaS) environments and cloud-based applications.

PART I
BLUE TEAMS

3   MONITORING NETWORKS AND CLOUDS

When it comes to data, if it's going to move, there is a very strong chance it's going to move across the network. That's why monitoring the network is a key blue team responsibility, and one where a considerable amount of money, time and effort is expended. Most commonly, attention is focused at ingress and egress points between networks of differing security classifications, for instance, between the public internet and a private internal network. You'll often hear this referred to as monitoring north–south traffic. Implementing this type of monitoring is usually an organisation's first venture into the realm of network traffic monitoring for the purposes of detecting a security incident.

Organisations also have the option to implement network monitoring between connected devices that sit on the same network, or within the same classification of network. You'll often hear this referred to as east–west monitoring. The prevalence of east–west monitoring has increased in recent years, thanks in part to a number of network performance monitoring (NPM) tool vendors that have changed their focus to security monitoring. This pivot allows such vendors to take advantage of the fact that they already have monitoring capabilities in strategic locations on corporate and datacentre networks. The benefit of east–west monitoring is that you get to see a great deal more of what is happening within your network. That can lead to identification of indicators that an attacker is moving laterally from a compromised machine to the next target, or that a piece of ransomware is accessing and encrypting files on a file share. There is a negative too: you'll also get a lot more noise to manage, but, quite honestly, that is a small price to pay for the extra insight.

The monitoring of networks is traditionally achieved by plugging a monitoring tool into a specially configured network switch port called a span, or tap port. This type of port sends a copy of all network traffic traversing that switch to the tool where it can be analysed. These types of configuration are relatively simple to deploy with minimal impact on network performance and are widely used in datacentres and branch offices alike, thanks to span port capability being standard on most enterprise switch gear.

Enterprise cloud adoption, particularly in the form of a public cloud IaaS, is a bit of a game-changer when it comes to network traffic monitoring. If you've ever tried to configure a hardware span or tap port at an IaaS provider's datacentre, chances are you got as far as the car park, or maybe the reception desk, before the police were called. The multi-tenant nature of the public cloud means tapping at the hardware level is no longer a viable path for IaaS customers looking to monitor their network traffic, since you'd monitor everyone else's too. Instead, new approaches using virtual machines or instances, and traffic duplicating software agents are commonly used to replicate the work formerly done by enterprise switch hardware. While the implementation of network monitoring may be different between the traditional network and the cloud, the importance of doing it remains the same.

In this chapter, we'll be walking through the tools, techniques and procedures blue teams can use to monitor network traffic for events and incidents.

NETWORK FUNDAMENTALS

If you look at almost all of the major data breaches that have made the headlines over the last few years, the network has unsurprisingly played a central role. The same network, designed to interconnect and enable the business by facilitating high speed data transfer between those who are authorised to access it, was abused to maliciously exfiltrate data to those who are not. Sometimes it happens quickly, perhaps where an attacker is confident that their target is lacking the ability to detect them no matter how loud they are. Other times, a slower, more subtle exfiltration technique is leveraged to avoid tripping alarms and alerting the blue team.

No matter the speed or technique of the exfiltration, one thing is for sure. You have to be effectively monitoring the traffic traversing the network to stand even the slightest chance of finding a small clue that something is awry. With gigabit speed ethernet the current standard on most commercial and, in a lot of cases, residential switching and routing equipment, the volume of traffic soon adds up. In a large datacentre environment, it can easily become overwhelming. It's for these reasons that a strategic approach to implementing a network monitoring solution is required. First of all, the solution should be capable of handling the volume of data the organisation wishes to throw at it, and then some. To use a more technical term, it should be scalable. Second, collecting the data is only one part of the picture. The real value from network monitoring comes from the ability to analyse what you've captured and figure out what event and incident indicators lurk within it.

Like all security purchasing decisions, budget is usually the biggest factor. A large network commercial monitoring tool deployment that spans several physical office locations and a couple of datacentres will cost hundreds of thousands, if not millions, of pounds. To ensure you stay within budget, while not compromising on visibility, there are a couple of options. First of all, a number of open-source networking monitoring tools and intrusion detection systems (IDS) are available. The software portion of the deployment costs nothing to roll out and the features offered can very easily compare to their commercial counterparts. The trade-off with open-source solutions is that you're typically responsible for ensuring the solution is configured correctly and remains functional at all times. There is no support department for a community-maintained tool, aside from the community themselves, and they usually have day jobs. The second cost-saving idea is to take a risk-based approach to the deployment of the network monitoring solution. Do you really need a sensor on your guest network that provides isolated access to the internet only? How about skipping that and concentrating on the network segment where your databases reside? Sounds pretty straightforward, but there are a surprising number of 'all or nothing' mindsets out there. Complete coverage in critical areas is always better than partial coverage in all areas.

If your organisation has a dedicated network engineering team, it's crucial to the success of any network monitoring tool deployment that they are involved from the very beginning. There are of course tactical reasons for this, such as needing them to enable the span ports or tell you where to plug in your aggregation hardware. There are also more fundamental reasons key to the success of the deployment. First, they 'own' the network, and have the most in-depth knowledge of its layout and secrets. Corporate and government (especially government) networks are often spaghetti-like constructs that have been plumbed together over time. Through mergers and acquisitions, building moves and different phases in company history, the network is frequently a museum dedicated to the history of the organisation that put it there. The network team is charged with knowing how it all fits together, and having a good relationship with them is crucial in figuring out the best places to position your sensors. A co-operative approach to the project also prevents the sentiment creeping in that the security team is 'encroaching' onto the network team's turf, or otherwise keeping an eye on them. It's a fact of life for a network engineering team that they are usually among the first to be on the receiving end of a pointed finger when there is some unexplainable performance issue within an application. As the team working in their space, we'll want to make them comfortable that what we're doing isn't going to introduce a bottleneck that will result in even more frequent finger pointing.

There is another key reason to involve the network team early on, and it's one that is often overlooked. They likely already have a suite of monitoring tools, although one geared towards performance and uptime monitoring. A trap many security operations teams fall into is assuming that they have to use a product that is built for and marketed specifically at security teams. You can actually detect quite a few indicators of security incidents using 'standard' NPM tools. For example, an abnormal amount of data transiting the network off hours may well manifest itself as a giant spike on a chart that sticks out like a sore thumb. As mentioned earlier, be sure to make the most of what you have in place already, before adding additional bells and whistles.

Given the importance of the network in security operations, anyone working in the space would do extremely well to become familiar with some fundamental networking concepts. Network engineering is a full-time job, and unless you're working specifically as a network security engineer and given the time to specialise, it's unlikely that you'll ever learn every command that can be directed at a specific model of firewall. Instead, for security folks, understanding the underlying commonalities between all networks and how they implement various security concepts along the way is usually the best way to focus your learning.

Addresses, ports, packets and protocols

We're going to be talking a lot about these terms throughout this book, and they will be encountered on an almost daily basis by the security operations team.

Addresses
An address is an identifier of a specific host or interface on a network. Common examples of address types encountered by a security operations team include the following:

- A media access control (MAC) address, which is also known as the hardware address of an interface. MAC addresses are a 48-bit address, typically represented as 12-digit hexadecimal numbers, e.g. 01:AD:40:FC:55:97. The first half of the MAC address is known as the organisational unique identifier (OUI), and can be used to discover the manufacturer of the particular network interface. For example, the OUI A0:99:9B is assigned to Apple.

- An IPv4 address, which is a 32-bit address representing a host on a network. That host could be a single computer on a private (or internal) network, or it could be a routing device on the public internet, which through a technology known as network address translation (NAT), allows all devices connecting to the public internet through it to share a single public IP address. IPv4 addresses are typically represented using dot-decimal notation, which breaks the address into four 8-bit octets, each expressed by decimal numbers, for example 214.21.42.1. IPv4 has been the de-facto standard IP addressing scheme used on the internet since the 1980s. However, owing to the rapid growth in the number of devices connected to the internet, since early 2011, all available IPv4 public address blocks have been provisioned to the various regional internet registries, a condition known as IPv4 exhaustion. The solution is to make the jump from 32-bit IPv4 addresses to 128-bit IPv6 addresses.

- An IPv6 address, just like an IPv4 address, represents a host on a network; however it has a much larger, 128-bit address space. IPv6 addresses are typically represented as eight groups of four hexadecimal digits, with each group representing a hextet, for example 2601:600:c700:111d:31e8:aa34:3c2b:e4f3. The IPv6 addressing scheme is designed to overcome the problem of IPv4 exhaustion, and is already widely supported on the public internet; however, the transition to exclusive IPv6 usage is expected to take many years. Security professionals should become familiar with IPv6 addressing, as all modern operating systems support what is known as a dual-stack configuration, which essentially means support for IPv4 and IPv6 addressing simultaneously on the same interface. A lack of understanding around IPv6 could cause important indicators to be missed when reviewing logs, or otherwise monitoring network traffic.

Ports

The term port can have a couple of meanings depending on context. For the most part, when we use it in network security, we're referring to a specific Transmission Control Protocol (TCP) or User Datagram Protocol (UDP) port number, which, when combined with an IP address, represents an endpoint for a specific network conversation. The design of both the TCP and UDP packet header supports a 16-bit unsigned integer as a port number, which means valid port number values are between 0 and 65535. Commonly used network services, such as Hypertext Transfer Protocol (HTTP), have reserved, well-known port numbers assigned to them – in the case of HTTP, port 80. This convention allows clients to seamlessly find the services they're looking for. However, it should always be remembered that any service can listen on any port and the convention is applied as a form of governance, rather than a technical limitation. The Internet Corporation for Assigned Names and Numbers (ICANN) is responsible for this governance.

- Port numbers 0–1023 are defined as well-known port numbers. We already touched on TCP port 80 being reserved for HTTP, but other examples include port 22 which is reserved for the secure shell (SSH) protocol, port 443 which is reserved for HTTPS (transport layer security (TLS)), and port 53, which is reserved for Domain Name System (DNS) traffic.

- Port numbers 1024–49151 are known as registered ports. These ports are frequently used by proprietary services and technologies and can be registered as such with ICANN. Think of this as an official heads-up that a given service or application will leverage this port, and will be present in multiple networks. An example of a service running on a registered port is Microsoft Remote Desktop Protocol (RDP), which listens on TCP port 3389.

- Ports 49152–65535 are known as dynamic ports. These cannot be reserved, and are intended for ephemeral (short-lived) purposes. For instance, a source port on the client side of an HTTP request will be in this range.

Incidentally, the second context of a port commonly used in networking would be a physical port in a piece of hardware, like a RJ45 port in a network switch.

Packets

A formatted unit of data transmitted across a network at layer 3 (more on this shortly) is called a packet. Packets are structured to include a header and a payload. The payload consists of the actual data the user is transmitting, while the header includes control information, such as the source and destination address, sequence numbers and error checking features.

Protocols

A network protocol defines a set of standardised rules that determine how data should be formatted and transmitted between two hosts on a network, so that they may communicate regardless of their underlying operating systems. There are thousands of established network protocols, each with their own specific functions and conventions.

- The DNS protocol is responsible for translating hostnames to IP addresses so that connections can be established.

- TLS is a cryptographic protocol used to ensure confidentiality and integrity when data is transmitted between a client and a server.

- Simple mail transport protocol (SMTP) is the standard protocol used to transmit email.

As a security operations professional monitoring a network, you'll be exposed to a significant number of these protocols, albeit abstracted through the various monitoring tools and technologies that your organisation has deployed. While the tools will make it easier to digest what is occurring inside a given protocol, there really is no substitute for looking at the raw packet structures of the most common protocols and developing an understanding of how they are formatted. This will help further your understanding as to how protocols can be manipulated and used maliciously, which is knowledge that will have relevance throughout your information security career.

The OSI model

Foundational to understanding most networking concepts, let alone network security concepts, is the open systems interconnection (OSI) model. This conceptual model is intended to convey the standardised functions of a communications system, such as a computer network. It does this through a series of conceptual layers, stacked on top of one another. Each OSI layer serves the layer directly above it, and is served by the layer directly below it. There are seven layers in the model (Figure 3.1).

Figure 3.1 Layers of the OSI model

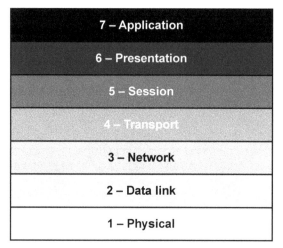

Layer 1 – Physical

At the lowest layer of the OSI model, we find the copper cables, fibre optics and electrical pulses concerned with transmitting the raw bits between networked devices. For security professionals, the vulnerabilities that we must address at this layer include:

- preventing physical theft and tampering (such as installation of unauthorised devices);
- environmental considerations, such as heat, water and power supply;
- human error, such as patching a cable into the wrong network or damaging equipment.

There is a chapter dedicated to physical security later in the book, and specifically how security operations teams can hook into physical security controls, including badge readers and surveillance systems.

Layer 2 – Data link

The data link layer defines how information is transmitted across the physical layer below it, and is responsible for making sure that the physical layer is functioning properly. At this layer, data is encapsulated into frames, and delivered to network interfaces by way of hardware (MAC) addresses. Some common security concerns at the data link layer follow:

- **MAC address spoofing.** While historically MAC addresses have been treated as 'hard coded', it is very possible to change them, and in fact, some devices purposefully use random MAC addresses every time they are connected to a new network. MAC spoofing can be used to bypass access control lists (ACLs) that use MAC addresses as an identifying element (which makes it a pretty poor control).

- **VLAN hopping.** Virtual local area networks (VLANs) are a traffic management technique that allow for the creation of isolated network segments at layer 2 across the same physical networking equipment. For instance, a single switch could process traffic for multiple VLANs, while the devices connected to that switch are only aware of the network segment they are associated with. VLAN hopping is a vulnerability in which an attacker is able to manipulate VLAN tags (used to indicate which VLAN a device belongs to) to escape one isolated segment and access another. For this reason, VLANs alone should not be relied upon as an effective security control.

- **Wireless attacks.** Wireless access points reside at layer 2 and, owing to poor configuration of wireless security and encryption features, are commonly the targets of malicious actors seeking to gain a direct path into a private network.

- **Attacks against switches.** If an attacker controls the switch, they control the traffic. There are an alarming number of switches configured with weak passwords, default Simple Network Management Protocol (SNMP) community strings (effectively well-documented passwords that permit the reading or altering of device configuration information) and clear text management ports that make them vulnerable to compromise.

Layer 3 – Network

The network layer is used to identify the addresses of the system on the network, and is responsible for the actual transmission of data between systems. On a Transmission Control Protocol/Internet Protocol (TCP/IP) network those addresses are of course IP addresses, which are frequently of interest to those of us in security operations, as they are used in IDS/IPS signatures, and can be leveraged as indicators of compromise. Security considerations at the network layer include the following:

- IP spoofing. In order to bypass IP-based ACLs, attackers may spoof, or falsify, the source IP address of a packet. Anti-spoofing measures are standard fare on most firewalls and should be enabled and properly configured to prevent the flow of spoofed source addresses into trusted networks.

- Attacks on routing protocols. Because of the trusting nature of the internet, very few internet service providers (ISPs) properly enforce checks on routing protocol updates and announcements, which can lead to route hijacking, or unintentional disruption to the routing of traffic.

Border Gateway Protocol (BGP) hijacking is a classic example of a vulnerability at layer 3. In the routing world, an autonomous system (AS), typically an ISP, is responsible for a group of IP network prefixes, and exchanges information about routing to those prefixes using BGP. The AS is said to 'originate' the prefixes it owns.

BGP routing announcements may not be filtered or authenticated by an AS, in which case it's possible for another AS to falsely claim it originates a prefix, or possesses a shorter route to a prefix than it really does. When this occurs, either maliciously with intent, or by accident, the condition is known as BGP hijacking.

There have been several highly disruptive cases of BGP hijacking over the years. A recent example occurred in April 2017, when Russian telecommunications company Rostelecom incorrectly announced it originated 50 prefixes from various financial institutions, such as Mastercard and Visa. For around 7 minutes, the traffic to these networks flowed through Rostelecom.

The nature of the prefixes impacted (financial) and the fact that the announcements from Rostelecom involved more specific prefixes than would normally be advertised has left many experts who studied the event convinced it was a deliberate attempt to hijack sensitive traffic.

Layer 4 – Transport

The transport layer is responsible for end-to-end communication between hosts, and provides the reliability services lacking from the network layer, although only for basic transmission services, and not for any application or service-specific functions. The transport layer is responsible for verifying that the network layer is operating efficiently, and if not, it requests a retransmission or returns an error to the above layer. TCP and UDP both operate at layer 4, and are examples of transport layer protocols. While TCP has mechanisms for ensuring reliable end-to-end communication, UDP provides only data integrity checking by way of a checksum,[1] and is frequently used in applications where some unreliability is acceptable, such as video calling. Security issues that manifest at the transport layer include the following:

- Port scanning. A port scan is a common technique leveraged by attackers and security operations teams to determine the identity or function of a host listening on a given IP address. The scan reveals which ports are open, and can be extended to include identification of the specific software services and version numbers running on those open ports. Although frequent port scanning of internet connected hosts is an expected occurrence, detection of port scanning events on internal networks can still be an important indicator.

- Denial of service. Although this type of attack is not limited to layer 4, a common mechanism used in a denial of service attack includes flooding a connected device with TCP Synchronise (SYN) packets to consume resources. This type of attack, known as a SYN flood, takes advantage of TCP's three-way handshake between both parties in the TCP conversation, to hold a connection half open. The target of the attack sits and diligently awaits an acknowledgement to complete the handshake, but that acknowledgement never arrives, because the attacker has no intention of sending it. If this happens with enough volume, the target cannot process genuine handshakes.

Layer 5 – Session

The session layer is responsible for establishing connections between systems, applications or users. The session layer may receive this request from a higher layer (e.g. an application), and then will negotiate a connection using the lower levels. Once a connection is established the session layer provides an interface to the network for the higher layers to communicate with. Once the higher layers are finished, the session layer is responsible for destroying the connections. Vulnerabilities at the session layer include:

- Session hijacking. A category of attack in which the attacker gains control of an established TCP session, fooling one side of the hijacked connection into believing it is still communicating with the other. In order for this to occur, the attacker must first identify the active session they want to target, which can be done through sniffing traffic. The next step is to guess the TCP sequence number associated with the session at that given time. The sequence number is one of TCP's end-to-end reliability features. After an initial sequence number is set during the TCP handshake, it increments by one digit for every one byte of data transmitted. In a modern implementation of TCP, the initial sequence number should be randomly generated to make it harder for an attacker to predict.

Layer 6 – Presentation

The presentation layer provides a consistent set of interfaces for applications and services to utilise when establishing connections through a session layer. The presentation layer is where tasks such as data compression, character encoding and, importantly for us security folks, data encryption takes place. Security considerations at the presentation layer include:

- Cryptographic flaws. Either not implementing encryption to protect sensitive information at all, or using weak cryptographic algorithms, can cause security and compliance issues.

- Encoding attacks. If an application was written to expect and handle user input encoded using one particular encoding standard, but another is used, and there are no checks or formatting mechanisms in play, this could result in a security vulnerability. For instance, an attacker may encode a URL sent to a web server using Unicode to bypass path filtering techniques and access files on the server outside of the defined web root.

Layer 7 – Application

Finally, the application layer provides the network's interface to end-user application protocols such as HTTP, email (SMTP, POP3 and IMAP) and SSH. Security operations teams may be responsible for the operation of web application firewalls (WAF), which operate at layer 7. Application layer vulnerabilities are a broad topic, but some examples include:

- The Open Web Application Security Project (OWASP) Top 10 (OWASP Foundation, 2019). These are the 10 most common web application vulnerabilities according to research conducted by the OWASP team. Cross site scripting (XSS), Structured Query Language (SQL) injection and broken authentication are some examples of vulnerability classifications that appear on the list.

- Backdoors. Supposedly hidden access points coded into applications by developers can be discovered and exploited by attackers.

- Misconfigurations. A broad topic, but a poorly configured application may expose information that could lead to a security vulnerability. For example, if an application logs sensitive information to a publicly accessible folder, this information could very easily be discovered and exposed.

If you were to trace a message through the model, for instance an HTTP request from a client computer to a web server, the request would originate in the application layer (layer 7), work its way down the model to the lowest layer (physical – layer 1), head back up and down a couple of layers as it makes its way through various networks, before finally heading back up to the application layer upon arrival at the destination web server.

TCP/IP

The suite of protocols leveraged on the public internet and, of course, many private networks, is commonly referred to as the TCP/IP suite. The concepts outlined in the OSI model are present in the TCP/IP suite, although the suite's communications model only refers to four layers, rather than the seven outlined in the OSI model. These layers are:

- The application layer, which is comparable in function with the application, presentation and session layers in OSI.

- The transport layer, which is comparable in function with the transport layer in OSI.

- The internet layer, which is comparable in function with the network layer in OSI.

- The network interface layer, which is comparable in function to the data link and physical layers in OSI.

It's important to remember that the OSI model is a conceptual model that protocols and standards can be based on, whereas TCP/IP is an actual standard that is widely used.

Networking gear

You can't have a network without some networking gear, which can be leveraged in the traditional hardware form factor, as software or a mixture of both. Let's go on a journey from the device to the datacentre and review the networking equipment that gets us there, and how it can be of relevance to security operations.

Network interfaces

For any device to communicate on the network, it must have an appropriate network interface controller (NIC) to allow it to do so. This could be a network card with a port for a copper cable or a wireless network interface, the end goal is the same – provide connectivity to the outside world. Every network interface has an associated hardware address, known as a MAC address. Under normal conditions this MAC address will stay pretty static once it's been associated with a given interface, and so it usually provides a relatively constant reference in a dynamic network. This is of considerable importance to us when trying to identify which device is the source of a possible incident, which can of course have an impact on how we choose to respond. Is it the CEO's laptop or the connected smart doorbell in shipping and receiving?

Switches

A network switch provides a foundation for the network by performing the packet switching required to get messages passed successfully between devices. Network switches keep track of the various network interfaces connected to them, by recording which MAC addresses are connected to which switch port and directing packets addressed to those MAC addresses accordingly. The most basic network switch is unmanaged, meaning you just plug it in. It will figure out what it's connected to and start processing packets with no configuration required. Such switches are usually geared towards the home or small office markets. In larger environments, network switches are typically managed devices, and offer an array of security, performance, monitoring, management and traffic shaping features. To the security professional working in an enterprise environment, the discovery of an unmanaged switch is usually a bad thing, as historically they are used to provide unsanctioned extra port capacity in a less than robust fashion.

Almost everyone who has worked in networking, support or security for some time has a rogue unmanaged switch story. Mine happened around 6 months into my first IT support job. I was sent to investigate why two network ports weren't functioning in a particular room. After writing down the port numbers, I headed to the patch panel to ensure they were connected to the appropriate switch. However, I was unable to locate the corresponding port numbers on said panel.

The next step was to physically trace the cables behind the ports, so back to the room I went, and dutifully climbed a ladder in order to open the false ceiling above the ports. As I lifted the ceiling tile, to my surprise, I felt a large thud on my head. That thud was caused by a 4-port unmanaged NETGEAR switch that had apparently lived in the ceiling for years. As it turned out, the power supply on the switch had gone bad and taken the ports down with it.

The next day we called for a cabling technician to run the cable all the way back to the patch panel, as should have happened when the ports were initially installed.

Managed switches on the other hand, offer features that are of tremendous value to us security professionals, and as such are seen in a much more positive light. We've already touched on monitoring, or span ports as an example of such a feature. These ports allow security teams to sit 'out of band' and get a look at the same raw traffic the switch is seeing. Other examples include the ability to implement 802.1X network access control (NAC), which is a topic we'll discuss shortly, as well as the ability to direct logging from the switch to a disparate logging platform via mechanisms such as syslog. Also, the ability to remotely shut down switch ports can be a great way to contain an incident.

You'll find most switches operating at the data link layer (layer 2) of the OSI model, and indeed the description outlined above relates to this type of switch. There are some types of switch that operate at other OSI layers. For instance, some switches include routing features, and as such operate at the network layer (layer 3). Others may operate all the way up at the application layer (layer 7), providing traffic switching based on a path contained in a URL, for example.

Routers

In order to get messages from one network to another you'll need a router to direct packets based on a destination address. Routers are connected to different networks through various interfaces and leverage a routing table to make a decision as to which interface is the correct way to send a packet so that it will correctly reach its destination. Routers operate at the network (layer 3) layer of the OSI model. Just as was the case with switches, routers can be implemented as either hardware or software.

In many cases routers will connect private networks to the internet, and as such may be bundled with firewalling capabilities. Indeed, many products that are primarily firewalls often act as routers. In a larger organisation a router may be used internally to connect different private networks. It's not uncommon for an organisation to use routing and firewalling to carve out a specific network segment for particularly sensitive operations, such as a payment processing network. This also helps them comply with specific security and compliance standards, for instance the Payment Card Industry Data Security Standard (PCI-DSS), by reducing the scope of any audit to the devices within that network segment. Of course, that may not always directly translate to better overall technical security at an organisation. If you lock everything away but leave the keys on the doorstep, you're still going to have issues.

Routers use routing protocols to share information about the current optimal path to reach a destination and dynamically update their routing table. The BGP is an example of such a protocol, and is used by ISPs to share information between their edge routers about the state of global internet links, and as such is often referred to as the backbone of the internet.

In May 2018, numerous models of small and home office router were targeted by a sophisticated malware strain known as VPNFilter. The malware, discovered by the Cisco Talos Group (2019), was found to impact 54 models of router built by various manufacturers, as well as some network attached storage (NAS) products. An estimated half a million devices were believed to be compromised by the malware.

The malware highlighted what can happen once a malicious actor gains control over a key piece of networking equipment, such as a router.

- It was possible for the actor behind VPNFilter to sniff credentials from traffic passing through the router.

- In many cases, the malware also allowed the attacker to pivot from the public internet into a private network, because the router was directly connected to both networks.

- Finally, the malware had destructive capabilities that could have rendered a device inoperable.

It's thought that a combination of incorrectly configured remote management features, known vulnerabilities in the victim router's operating systems, and weak or default passwords were exploited to facilitate the installation of the malware on the impacted devices.

Firewalls

If you're going to discuss securing a network, you can rest assured your conversation will include some firewall talk. A properly configured firewall will be instrumental in protecting networked resources by filtering the traffic allowed to access them. Firewalls achieve this by using ACLs to establish rules about what traffic is allowed and what traffic should be denied. Notice I used the term, a 'properly configured firewall'. That's an important call out, because firewalls require initial configuration, ongoing management and tuning to ensure they remain effective. Without these items, a firewall can be just another hop along the way for an attacker. We'll talk more about firewall management principles shortly.

Firewalls typically operate at layer 3 and layer 4, depending on their feature set. At layer 3, the firewall uses criteria found in a packet header, including source and destination IP addresses, as well as source and destination port numbers to make a filtering determination. It's for this reason that firewalls operating at layer 3 are known as packet filters.

When you mix in layer 4 features, including the ability to permit or deny TCP connections based on their current connection state (new/established/rogue or out-of-state), you're describing a 'stateful packet inspection' firewall. Most modern firewalls leverage stateful packet inspection, which allows the firewall to look beyond the header of a packet and into the payload to look for state indicators and keep track of the connection in a state table.

Application firewalls operate at layer 7 and inspect the content of application-specific traffic to make a filtering determination. For instance, a WAF inspects HTTP traffic to filter out requests that might be malicious in nature, perhaps including a string that would trigger an SQL injection vulnerability.

Firewalls can also be hardware or software based, and can be configured at the network or host level.

Modems

Short for modulator-demodulator, the modem is responsible for converting network data into electrical signals so that it may be transmitted across telephone or cable TV wires. In the world of residential broadband it's not uncommon for an ISP to supply a customer with a modem that also serves as a router, and may additionally include firewalling capability. For this reason, the single 'box' that the consumer may leverage to gain internet access is often referred to as the modem. However, technically the only part that is fulfilling the modem capability is the part that does the conversion into electrical signals as described above.

Modems are less likely to be encountered day-to-day in the enterprise security operations space these days, other than perhaps being used by remote employees to gain access to corporate resources. However, there are still plenty of companies that have dial-up modems hooked up to the management ports of switches and routers to facilitate remote management and troubleshooting in the event of a critical network failure. In this case, if you have them, security operations should be monitoring them for connection activity at all times.

Wireless

When considering the wireless technologies that the enterprise security operations team is most likely to encounter, we're mostly concerned with 802.11a/b/g/n wireless local area networks (WLANs), the wireless access points that broadcast the radio signals they rely on, and the WLAN controllers that allow the network engineering team to manage the access points from a central location.

From the security perspective, any time we take traffic out of the confines of a copper or fibre optic cable, and blast it through the air, we're markedly increasing the risk to the confidentiality of that traffic. The primary mitigation, in the form of wireless encryption technologies, including Wi-Fi Protected Access 2 (WPA2), like all security technologies, must be correctly configured, patched and monitored. WPA2 can be secured with either a single pre-shared key (personal mode) to encrypt all traffic between every client and access point, or leverage enterprise authentication technologies such as Remote Authentication Dial-In User Service (RADIUS) to generate a per session master encryption key valid only between the client and the access point. The latter option provides a greater degree of confidentiality because it does not rely on a single key that everyone has access to, which can be used to decrypt all the wireless traffic on the network.

If a pre-shared key is used on a WPA2 network, the length and complexity of the key plays an important role in determining how secure the network is. A WPA2 authentication handshake can be brute forced offline using a dictionary or other wordlist, a technique that will quickly expose weak, or short pre-shared keys.

In the second half of 2018, devices started to become certified as supporting WPA2's replacement, WPA3 (Wi-Fi Alliance, 2019). WPA3 will increase in prevalence in the next few years, and has a more secure handshake sequence that is not directly tied to the complexity of the user-defined pre-shared key.

Of course, the main driving force behind the use of wireless networking is convenience. It's convenient to be able to work in any room without having to worry about finding a wall socket to plug into. This convenience is what drives a common security risk, the so-called rogue access point. These pop up when an unauthorised user decides they'd rather connect wirelessly to a network, and either don't want to wait for a properly managed wireless network to be delivered, or don't know how to connect to the approved wireless network. They head on down to the local electronics shop, and configure and connect their own wireless network with direct access to the local area network (LAN).

Rogue access points present a potential risk to the enterprise, as they create a much wider entry point for potentially unauthorised users to sneak through. They can be mitigated through technical measures, such as the use of 802.1X (NAC) to limit port connectivity, or through specifically designed rogue access point detection hardware (such features are also commonly bundled in WLAN controllers).

Load balancers
Many service providers (SPs) pride themselves on the performance and availability of their services, and in fact, many are contractually bound to hit availability targets to ensure they get paid. One tool to help attain those targets is the load balancer, which, as the name suggests, balances load across multiple nodes in a redundant system to ensure that the failure of one node doesn't constitute a failure of the entire system.

Commonly, load balancers operate at layer 7, and sit in front of web servers to distribute HTTP requests from clients to a pool of servers. Web application load balancers are tremendously useful to security operations teams for a couple of reasons. First, since they are operating at the application layer, they're looking deep into the TCP packet to review the content of the HTTP request. While they're in there, we can ask them to look for things we might be interested in, such as XSS attempts or strings that might look like SQL injection and filter them out so that they never reach the target server. In effect, they can work as WAFs and many load balancers are sold with the ability to enable a WAF feature module. Of course, we should still address the root cause of such vulnerabilities in our applications, but having an extra layer of prevention or detection is rarely a bad thing. Second, load balancers commonly act as a termination point for a TLS connection from a client. They need to be able to see into encrypted TLS traffic in order to inspect the HTTP traffic as described above.

Modern TLS configurations, including the use of ciphers that support perfect forward secrecy (PFS), are great for confidentiality, but they can limit the security team's ability to monitor the encrypted traffic to look for malicious requests or evidence of data exfiltration. If the load balancer is decrypting and re-encrypting traffic before it is sent on to the destination server, it may be the only place where the traffic is accessible 'in the clear'. Given this, it's not uncommon for security teams to use the load balancer as a hook to get a copy of the traffic for monitoring by network monitoring tools.

Load balancers don't have to operate at layer 7. Some simply provide a pass-through for a TCP connection, and thus operate at layer 4. In these cases, traffic would not be intercepted and decrypted, and therefore, we'd need to look at another location to get our hooks in.

Bandwidth
The official definition of bandwidth in the networking context refers to the maximum data transfer rate achievable across a particular networking link. If you have a connection that can support the transfer of 100 megabits of data every second, you have a bandwidth of 100 Mbps. If more than 100 Mbps of traffic attempts to transit the link at a time, bandwidth will be exhausted, and the link will become congested, slowing the network down.

Bandwidth is an important concept to understand for the security professional, for a couple of reasons. The first is related to denial of service attacks. A denial of service attack might attempt to saturate a network link with so much traffic that the link becomes congested, as described above. Knowing how much bandwidth is available on a given link, as well as being able to understand typical bandwidth usage patterns, can help a security operations professional spot a potential problem. For a large-scale distributed denial of service (DDoS) attack, the volume of data being transmitted towards a target has been known to reach 1 terabit per second. In early 2018, GitHub – a source code management (SCM) SP – was hit by an attack that leveraged 1.35 terabits per second of traffic. At the time of writing, this is widely believed to be the largest DDoS attack on record.

The second reason it's important to understand bandwidth is also related to denial of service attacks, but with a slightly different spin. Sometimes, it's possible for a user, or even a security operations team, to create a denial of service condition accidentally. Vulnerability scans across the network are usually run off-hours to avoid the possibility of disruption during the workday; however, so too are other operations, such as backups and batch data processing jobs. It's important to ensure that these distinct bandwidth intensive jobs do not clash with one another, as they could bring the network to a grinding halt. Working with other teams to schedule scans at hours that do not disrupt their work is a great way to win friends during sociable hours, rather than having to apologise on an incident bridge at two in the morning.

MONITORING THE NETWORK

Now that we've covered the fundamentals of networking, we can begin to focus on how we can apply them in the security operations space, and in particular in our network monitoring strategy. When we talk about that strategy, it's important to remember that we're discussing more than just a single tool or product. While we'll leverage different hardware and software products that help us achieve the goals of our strategy, a product alone is not, and will never be, a strategy. A strategy is an end-to-end plan to achieve a specific aim, and will involve a combination of people, process and technology. An IDS might be able to detect and respond to a suspected intrusion, but it cannot drive the investigation into how the intrusion occurred in the first place; it can't lead enterprise-wide containment efforts and chair a follow up meeting to ensure that the source of the intrusion has been completely addressed. More critically, if there is no process in place to go from initial alert to incident response, we might deny ourselves the opportunity to ever go through all those phases.

Developing a monitoring strategy

The first steps on the path to developing a network monitoring strategy require you to ask yourself some introspective questions – 'yourself' being the organisation looking to deploy the strategy.

Which networked resources are we most concerned about, and why?
The answer to this first question depends entirely on the organisation asking it. If the future of the company is dependent upon a collection of files stored on a NAS device, chances are you'll be most concerned about monitoring for network traffic that could indicate those files are being inappropriately accessed, and potentially exfiltrated. Starting at the NAS and working backwards to the public internet might lead you through a series of different networks that would all provide a potential avenue for an attacker looking for an exfiltration path.

Perhaps the NAS is connected to a network segment dedicated to servers in a datacentre, and then, through a core router, clients in multiple office locations access the files from different network segments across the globe. Perhaps each of those network segments has its own gateway to the internet. Suddenly, you've got a lot of network segments and egress points to keep an eye on. That brings with it two challenges: increased cost and an increased number of potential alerts and events to triage.

In this particular case, if the files are so sensitive, a more secure approach might be to deny any host with the ability to connect to the internet access to them in the first place. Using a terminal server or bastion host (a hardened machine used solely for accessing sensitive files) would be a possible way to achieve this. Unfortunately, while that might make perfect sense from a security and risk perspective, it might not be an acceptable solution to the business. Like I said in Chapter 1, this line of work can be infuriating; you have to work around cases like this all the time.

What do I currently have in place?

So much money, time and effort is expended on deploying, or partially deploying, monitoring tools that add no or little value, simply because they are shiny new toys sold as a one-stop-shop for network security monitoring or because security operations teams and other teams are afraid to talk to each other about what monitoring tools are already in place. If a network engineering team has already deployed a comprehensive network monitoring suite, albeit one focused on performance monitoring, but a licence can be added to that existing infrastructure to provide security monitoring for a tenth of the price of deploying a whole new toolset, that is an approach at least worthy of evaluation. In a staggering number of organisations it would never even be considered.

Always ask about what is already in place. It may or may not be useful, but at least do the due diligence to make that determination. Budgets are precious things. I'd rather use mine to hire another set of human eyes for my team than to buy a tool to duplicate the functionality of one that is already in operation.

What can I purchase?

If you are in need of some tools and have the option to do so, then by all means, you should acquire them. Balance the answer to the first question (what am I most concerned about protecting?) with your budget, and get the best trade-off between suitable coverage and not having any money for other security initiatives.

The network security monitoring marketplace is awash with products that use a couple of different methods to make determinations about which traffic looks good and which traffic looks malicious. Make a list of the features that are important to you and your organisation, and take the time to evaluate the options when selecting. Network monitoring tools are not a small investment, both in financial terms and your time. After deployment, you'll want them to be in place for several years to come.

When making a purchasing decision, be sure to plan for the future. It's a pretty safe assumption that the networking monitoring solution will be asked to process an ever-increasing volume of traffic. With this in mind, a solution that can scale, both technically and financially, should be favoured. Be wary of licensing models that are tied to the volume of traffic processed, and factor in this growth when committing to the purchase.

Where should the events go?

Once the monitoring product is plugged in and listening to traffic, it's going to start generating alerts tied to observed events. Most monitoring platforms provide you with a user interface (UI) to acknowledge and close generated alerts. Some even allow you to do things like add notes and move the alert through various triage states. This may work quite nicely for the security operations team who use the product every day. However, working exclusively in a product that is leveraged only by one team can lead to a risk that is worthy of consideration: the risk that information within the tool can become 'siloed'.

This risk manifests when an issue is occurring across an enterprise: for example, we have an intrusion caused by an SQL injection vulnerability in a web application. All the various indicators of this issue might be there, but trapped in various siloed tools. Viewed in isolation these tools won't give anyone the full picture. Perhaps the application team have server logs in a log aggregation tool; perhaps the database administrators (DBAs) have database auditing and logging data in another; and, finally, the security operations team has a copy of the network traffic containing the malicious HTTP requests. To the database team, it might just look as though the application is talking to the database, like it does 10,000 times an hour. To the server team, the malicious requests might be buried in the noise. For the security operations team, the attack might be flagged and an alert created in the network monitoring tool. Without a way to quickly get this alert in front of other teams to cross-check their systems and report back, the whole thing might be missed.

If this particular event generated an alert in a centralised ticketing system that all the various teams use, perhaps we'd stand a chance of someone seeing the alert and responding in time to prevent the event becoming an incident. The ability of the tool to reach out to and fit into the enterprise ticketing and escalation process is critical to its success. Consider this when making the purchase.

How can I reduce the noise?

A network monitoring product is a lot like a newly landscaped garden. You'll spend a lot of money to have it put in and get it looking the way you want it to, only to have it stay that way for a very short period of time. These products require constant maintenance, pruning and trimming, to ensure they are still delivering the most value. False positives are common, especially in the early days. The question 'is this new, or new to us?' will be asked a million times over, as the determination of what normal background noise on the network looks like, versus something more nefarious. Security operations teams should be aware of this, and work to confirm that each escalated alert is truly in need of escalation, to avoid showering other teams with work that ultimately leads to nothing of significance.

Firewalls

While a comprehensive network monitoring strategy, complete with specific tools for the purpose may not be in place when you arrive on scene, it's highly likely that a firewall will be. These devices, which are of course network security devices that are actively blocking potential attacks, provide a good opportunity to get an initial look into what's going on in your network. Remember though, just because a firewall is there, doesn't mean it's doing its best work. Firewalls sit in common ground between network engineering teams and security teams and, quite frequently, the network team is more than happy to offload some of the governance work around firewalls to security. For these reasons, taking a long hard look at the firewall configuration can be a way to not only kick-start your monitoring strategy, but also to improve overall network security by hardening the device.

Firewall logs

Firewalls can generate a lot of logs, and in those logs are precious details that can help us understand the profile of the traffic that has successfully passed through the device, and conversely, the traffic that has been denied. We want those logs, and we want to be able to search through them at speed. This typically involves a couple of steps. First, we have to tell the firewall we want it to start logging. Most firewalls will not log every accepted and denied connection in their default condition. For some, it's a global setting; for others, it needs to be done on a rule-by-rule basis. Second, while firewalls will happily store logs locally in a log buffer, those buffers tend to fill up quickly and are overwritten by newer logs in very short order, therefore denying us the opportunity to access the older ones. It's best practice (for all logs, not just firewall logs) to offload immediately to a discrete logging platform. Commonly this is achieved using the syslog protocol, which allows logs to be streamed in real time to a syslog server, where they can then be searched, or loaded into a SIEM tool for rapid searching. This also helps keep our logs safe if a firewall becomes compromised at any point. After all, logs are a form of self-reporting, and if an attacker controls the self-reporting system, they'll want to cover their tracks.

Spanning the firewall

As previously mentioned, the most common place to find a firewall is at an egress/ingress point for a network. Therefore, they usually have to process traffic that is highly likely to include evidence of compromise, should one occur. Typically, the firewall will have connectivity between a core switch on the trusted side and an ISP router on the untrusted side. If we want to use that traffic for other purposes, such as installing a DLP tool or an IDS, asking the network team to span the switch port used by the firewall is a great way to get maximum insight with minimal changes to the network.

Next generation firewalls

Because of their strategic location in the network, firewalls these days do a lot more than simply filter traffic. So-called next generation firewalls can also do things like run an IDS/IPS, run a data monitoring tool, filter at layer 7, and even perform email and spam filtering. While this can work nicely, remember, the more features you add to a firewall, the more central processing unit (CPU) cycles you are going to take away from actually processing traffic. That can cause a performance impact, and since we're trying to stay friends with the network engineering team, might push us in another direction.

Intrusion detection/prevention systems

These devices have been mentioned multiple times already, and that's because they're a widely deployed network monitoring technology, and with plenty of open-source IDS/IPS solutions available, such as Suricata[2] and Snort,[3] you don't have to break the bank to deploy them. IDS/IPS solutions use signatures, essentially a set of rules around which indicators could signify potential malicious activity, to generate alerts, and if in prevent mode, deny connections matching those signatures.

The threat landscape is constantly evolving, which means that, for the operators of IDS/IPS systems, signatures should be kept up to date to ensure that the latest threats are detected. That's right; IDS/IPS tools are another part of your freshly landscaped garden that will require regular maintenance and watering to stay in tip-top shape. Usually, this duty falls to the security operations team, who must trade off enabling and disabling signatures to ensure maximum coverage while reducing unnecessary noise.

IDS/IPS placement

These solutions can give security teams a significant amount of information about what is occurring in network traffic, and if sitting 'out-of-band', in detection mode, can do so without negatively impacting network performance. Out-of-band simply means listening off a span or tap port, as opposed to being 'in-line', which means listening to the actual traffic as it passes in real-time. Of course, the trade-off here is that out-of-band detection relies on someone being ready to manually respond to an alert that represents an actual intrusion, whereas in-line prevention will automatically deny that malicious connection.

Usually the decision of how to use an IDS/IPS and where it should be placed is a business one, and like most information security decisions, requires a bit of compromise on either side. A hybrid approach, where IDS/IPS solutions can sit in-line, and prevent mode is phased in on specific signatures, is a good middle ground. If you're taking the time to validate that your new signatures aren't going to cause the network to shut down by using them in detect mode for a number of days prior to enabling prevent mode, you still have coverage and will have done your due diligence.

IDS/IPS events

Just as with firewalls, IDS/IPS solutions can spit out logs detailing the source and destination IPs of a connection, and which signature matched and generated the alert. The nature of most connections occurring across the internet can cause these alerts to fire multiple times per minute, which means the logs can soon pile up. As such, they'll need a large enough storage location and an interface that will allow you search through them in a timely fashion.

As with the IDS/IPS engine itself, there are open-source log aggregation tools available, such as the Elasticsearch stack[4] and Graylog.[5] While these might not offer the full range of features available in a SIEM tool, they do allow you to visualise and quickly parse your IDS/IPS logs.

Data loss prevention

The reasons for monitoring the network need not be limited to identification of technical attacks. DLP tools, such as Symantec Data Loss Prevention[6] and Forcepoint Data Loss Prevention,[7] leverage network traffic monitoring to look for data types that may be sensitive in nature, such as personally identifiable information (national insurance numbers), proprietary and confidential documents, and information subject to specific legislation, including healthcare data. Insider actions can also result in data breaches, whether those actions are intentional or unintentional. DLP tools are frequently used to ensure that insiders (employees) are handling data appropriately. For instance, it wouldn't be advisable to upload a file of personnel information, including bank account details, using unencrypted FTP. DLP tools can detect such activity and prevent it from happening by dropping the connection.

DLP systems generate events and logs in much the same way as the other tools we've already discussed, although the proprietary nature of most DLP suites might make hooking the logs into a SIEM system a little more involved than say, an IDS. When choosing a DLP system, compatibility with your SIEM or log aggregator is an important consideration, since any time you are working in a DLP tool, you're looking away from other systems that may contain correlating events.

Network-based DLP traffic monitors are typically supplemented by software agents installed directly on endpoint machines, so that they can work their magic in memory, and inspect data that might otherwise be encrypted on the network.

In order to be at their most effective, DLP tools must be configured to recognise the data types an organisation is most concerned about protecting. In many cases, this will involve choosing from a list of predefined data types, for example, bank account numbers and sort codes. In others, the tools should be configured to detect company-specific data classification tags, or code words.

Wire-data analytics

So far, we've been focused heavily on the content of network traffic, but there is another aspect that can provide valuable insight from a monitoring perspective. The 'shape' of network traffic is often an effective indicator that something may have changed, and that something could be worthy of our investigation. Of course, network traffic doesn't really have a 'shape' per se, so what I'm referring to is the appearance of network traffic when visualised in wire-data analytics tools, such as ExtraHop[8] and Versive.[9] This category of tool listens to the network traffic via a span port or tap aggregator, and compiles metrics based on the observed behaviour. These metrics include values such as traffic volume, protocol, errors detected, and source and destination addresses.

Commonly, these tools are placed to monitor east–west traffic, usually as a result of being purchased primarily to monitor internal traffic performance. It's not uncommon for an organisation hosting a SaaS application to need to monitor performance between the various tiers in their service. As security operations teams, we can leverage this data to great effect to get a tremendous view into the inner workings of our network. Wire-data analytics platform vendors have become wise to this, with many pivoting their marketing strategies to appeal directly to security operations teams.

As mentioned earlier, these tools also generate visualisations, which can bring to the fore anomalies in traffic that simply wouldn't stand out in log files. Graphs and charts that show spikes indicating a sudden increase in traffic between two hosts can be worthy of investigation and rationalisation. If that spike appears at the same time every day, for example, it could be a routine backup job. If it's truly a one off, that would be more suspect.

The use of machine learning technologies, applied to the traffic patterns observed by the wire-data analytics platform, can provide additional insight into deviation away from what is considered normal. However, the application of these technologies in wire-data analytics tools is still very much in its infancy and, as such, security operations teams should be cautious about relying on them exclusively.

NetFlow

Developed by Cisco in the mid-1990s, the NetFlow protocol allows switches and routers that support it to forward details regarding the connections they're seeing to a centralised NetFlow collector for analysis. These NetFlow records contain details regarding source and destination IPs, ports, the protocol in use, the number of packets and bytes observed, and timestamps for the start and end time of the flow.

NetFlow is widely supported by a variety of device manufacturers, providing a quick and easy way to increase visibility for security teams looking to monitor network traffic flows in all directions (north–south and east–west).

The drawbacks of relying on NetFlow include a lack of insight into the payload of a given connection and, like all device logging, it's a form of self-reporting that is vulnerable to modification. It's often said that NetFlow is like a call log provided by a telecommunications company, whereas wire-data is like an audio recording of the call.

Network access control

One of the least complex, but most effective methods of gaining access to a network is simply walking into a building and plugging a network cable into a wall socket. The overwhelming majority of networks are more than happy to welcome their guest by providing them with an IP address, and all the other interface configuration information they need to feel welcome. Clearly, physical security has a significant role to play in keeping unwelcome visitors away from the network, but when that layer of security is breached, there is a technical control that can assist. NAC or 802.1X to use the name of the underlying standard on which the technology is based, provides services to authenticate devices as they connect to networks, both wired and wireless.

With 802.1X enabled, a device connected to a switch port is not permitted to access network resources until it has been successfully authenticated, using a trusted authentication service. In most configurations, a server that supports the RADIUS authentication protocol performs this function. Authentication could occur based on a digital certificate, or a username and password combination. Once authentication has been successful, the authentication server instructs the switch to trust the device and permit it access to the network. This can be done by using a SNMP message to change the VLAN the switch port belongs to. Although not foolproof, it does provide a reasonable barrier to the casual drive-by plugger-inner.

To enhance basic NAC functionality, NAC products can also perform so-called posture checking. If these are in place, successful authentication to the network may not be enough to gain access. Through the use of an interrogation agent, NAC can assess a connected device to ensure it meets an organisation's compliance profile, including things like having up to date AV software, all the appropriate patches installed and full-disk encryption enabled. These controls can significantly reduce the chance that a compromised host will end up on an internal network. The reality is, however, that they are rarely deployed in full, since it can take a couple of minutes to ensure the device is completely compliant, and during that time period, the user will not be able to access the network, even if they ultimately are allowed to. The delay is just too much for some businesses to accept.

As with the other network monitoring tools discussed so far, NAC products can log and alert based on what they see, which when rolled in with other logging can be extremely valuable information for a security operations team.

Encryption in transit

Sending data 'in the clear', without any form of transport layer encryption, has long been frowned upon. Many compliance standards explicitly state the need to use strong cipher suites to encrypt traffic, and it's of course the right thing to do to ensure the confidentiality of information that passes across the network. It does, however, present security operations teams with a bit of a predicament when it comes to monitoring the network.

Modern TLS uses a technique called PFS to create an encryption key unique to each client–server session. This means that even if a server's private key is compromised, possession of that key wouldn't allow an attacker to decrypt traffic from a session that had previously occurred. For cipher suites without PFS, a compromised private key could be used to decrypt all sessions going forward, and if captured, sessions that had occurred in the past. In those pre-PFS days, security teams would simply load private keys onto their monitoring tools to decrypt the payload of encrypted network traffic. After all, we want to know what's in there to make sure it's not evidence of an attack, or data being exfiltrated.

In the days of PFS, this becomes a lot more challenging, but not impossible. Monitoring suites are adapting to the widespread use of PFS by developing agents that are installed on servers, and other devices that may terminate PFS connections. These agents provide session keys to the monitoring tool to facilitate real-time traffic decryption. However, support might be limited to a specific server platform, and that could lead to an unmonitored blind spot. Be sure to review current PFS support and the future PFS roadmap when picking a monitoring suite.

Baselining

Once the various tools that play a role in your monitoring strategy are in place, you'll likely be faced with an overwhelming body of information that you'll need to rationalise and react to. It can be tempting to jump in and start responding to every little blip and alert that you see, but as previously alluded to, perhaps a better way to spend your time at the beginning is to understand what is 'normal' for your network, being cognisant of the fact that 'normal' might include traffic associated with a previous successful compromise. The new perspectives afforded by monitoring tools can make it hard to decide what is worthy of immediate response. To overcome this, don't be afraid to enlist the help of other teams who may have a valuable perspective. You never know, they might also discover something they didn't know about their application or system, and empowering people with data is a great way to build trust, which comes in tremendously useful in this line of work.

Context and correlation

Throughout this chapter, we've discussed the SIEM suite and its ability to pull in data from different sources. Context really does matter, and having the ability to cross-reference what you are seeing in your monitoring data with a second source can add serious credibility to a claim that something doesn't look right. As soon as possible after getting one source configured, look for opportunities to correlate with others. It also works the other way around, and helps discount events that are benign.

Escalation

Finally, a highly important component in your strategy is having well-defined escalation paths for events that should be investigated further. This includes selecting the ticketing tools and systems used to track escalations, to ensure they go to the right people in an orderly fashion, and to avoid duplicate work. Nothing is worse than having done all the hard work of leveraging a tool to effectively monitor for events, only to have your efforts disrupted by a poorly executed escalation process. People will soon tire of it.

If there are multiple email and instant messenger threads involving multiple people all focused on the same event, something isn't right. The escalation process should be treated as a key part of the customer service experience; make it as smooth as possible and people will want to continue to be a part of it.

THE CLOUD

The shift to cloud-hosted infrastructure, platforms and software has driven more enterprise data, traditionally hosted in co-located datacentres and offices, to shared pools of computing resources accessible via the network. That network could be the public internet or private connectivity. In either case, security operations still needs a strategy to monitor that data. Ultimately, if customer information is compromised, the customer isn't going to care where it was compromised from, and nor should they.

Different cloud models afford us different levels of access to the underlying network traffic. For SaaS offerings that level of access is zero. For IaaS we can obtain an abstracted level of access to raw traffic through software agents installed on our hosted instances, or virtual machines.

Cloud access security brokers

To meet the needs of organisations leveraging SaaS products, vendors that fall into the category of cloud access security brokers (CASB) have emerged. The role of the CASB is to sit between enterprise users and their SaaS providers, to enable the enterprise to enforce policies when users push data to, and pull data from, the cloud. They can do this with application level hooks, such as published APIs, and the support of the SaaS provider, to enforce authentication settings. Another popular approach is to serve as a gateway to the application, using an internally issued and trusted TLS certificate to decrypt the traffic and inspect it in the same manner as a DLP tool. This approach can be extended to include features such as virus detection and services like tokenisation and file-level encryption, which render information unreadable to the cloud SP.

If a CASB is used to deploy file-level encryption, any access to the cloud service that occurs outside of the CASB gateway will result in the user gaining access to an awful lot of scrambled, useless data. Examples of CASB products include Netskope[10] and McAfee MVISION Cloud.[11]

Detecting shadow IT

Of course, not all cloud usage is sanctioned by an enterprise. Frustrated by enterprise IT and purchasing practices, users may find themselves tempted to simply go out and start using whichever cloud services they prefer. According to research conducted by McAfee MVISION (formerly Skyhigh networks), in 2016 the average enterprise used 1,427 distinct cloud services (Kohgadai, 2019). CASB products can also detect and alert unapproved cloud usage, also known as 'shadow IT', but this is also a function that can be achieved without specialised tools. Reviewing DNS logs often provides a means to discover what cloud services are being accessed from within an organisation, legitimate or otherwise.

Monitoring cloud networks

IaaS providers, such as Amazon Web Services (AWS),[12] Google Cloud[13] or Microsoft Azure,[14] allow us to carve out virtualised networks that will ultimately pass the same packets and protocols as their physical counterparts, but with one primary difference. That difference, of course, is that we don't have any access to the underlying hardware running the network. In order to monitor our traffic, we have to do so from an abstracted position via software agents.

Just as those NPM vendors have pivoted towards security, so too have they reacted to the increasing number of their customers hosting using IaaS providers. Virtualised instances of all popular wire-data analytics tools can be found within the marketplaces of any given IaaS provider. These instances are configured as listeners, but instead of being connected to a single span port, they are blasted with encapsulated copies of network traffic from the various individual nodes they'll monitor. It's a one-for-one setup. The target of the monitoring sends the actual connection to its destination, and then a copy of the same traffic to the monitoring tool. There are performance implications of doing this. The instance CPU will be using cycles to process twice as much traffic, unlike in the physical realm, where this function would be handed off to the network switch and its span port. Be sure to consider this, and size any virtualised hosts with an appropriate amount of resources.

Direct connections

Many organisations host using a hybrid model that includes both traditional datacentre connectivity and IaaS providers. To reduce the costs associated with transferring large amounts of data over the public internet, and to ensure as seamless an experience as possible for end users, organisations can elect to use private, directly connected network circuits to connect to their cloud resources.

In these cases, the direct connect circuits are typically terminated at routers in the organisation's datacentre, which provide a prime network tapping opportunity. From here security operations teams can monitor traffic flows between their internally hosted networks and IaaS infrastructure via physical span ports.

SUMMARY

This chapter has introduced the topic of monitoring the all-important networks that connect our enterprises. At the beginning, we looked at fundamental network concepts, including the OSI model and its various layers, TCP/IP – the protocol suite leveraged on the public internet, and the different types of networking equipment that make it all happen.

We then moved on to developing a network monitoring strategy, and took a look at the various tools and technologies we can leverage to implement that strategy, including firewall logs, IDS/IPS, wire-data analytics, NetFlow and NAC.

Finally, we touched on cloud and hybrid networks, and the tools available to us to ensure consistent network monitoring regardless of the underlying infrastructure.

The next chapter focuses on the devices that connect to our networks – endpoints such as laptops, tablets and smartphones. It considers how, given the ubiquity of these devices, a high level of assurance and monitoring can be provided, even when a device isn't connected to a network over which you have oversight.

REFERENCES

Kohgadai, A. (2019) '12 must-know statistics on cloud usage in the enterprise'. McAfee MVISION Cloud. Available at: https://www.skyhighnetworks.com/cloud-security-blog/12-must-know-statistics-on-cloud-usage-in-the-enterprise/

OWASP Foundation (2019) 'Category: OWASP Top Ten Project'. Available at: https://www.owasp.org/index.php/Category:OWASP_Top_Ten_Project

Talos Group (2019) 'New VPNFilter malware targets at least 500K networking devices worldwide'. Cisco Blogs. Available at: https://blogs.cisco.com/security/talos/vpnfilter

Wi-Fi Alliance (2019) 'Wi-Fi Alliance® introduces Wi-Fi CERTIFIED WPA3™ security'. Available at: https://www.wi-fi.org/news-events/newsroom/wi-fi-alliance-introduces-wi-fi-certified-wpa3-security

4   MANAGING ENDPOINT DEVICES

If you've walked the floor of any information security trade show, or perhaps caught the occasional subject line in a vendor's email campaign within the last few years, you've probably seen several plays on the theme 'the endpoint is the new perimeter'. The aim of this messaging is to suggest that, owing to trends such as a greater acceptance of remote working, the gig economy (i.e. use of contractors and freelancers), increased cloud adoption and more widespread mobile or personal device use, simply monitoring the traditional network perimeter with things like firewalls and IDS/IPSs doesn't cut it anymore. Instead, the focus should be on securing the endpoint device the employee is using to access enterprise resources.

The messaging does raise some compelling points and for some organisations an endpoint first strategy is probably a very reasonable way to go. However, for the vast majority of organisations it doesn't make sense to simply cast aside the network and leave it to fend for itself. Endpoint devices can become highly political topics, and ensuring a consistent set of controls on them can be tricky. It's far more likely that a well-intentioned helpdesk engineer will cave in and permit a one-off request to make a user a local administrator on their laptop, so they can install X, Y and Z, than a network administrator will make a firewall change at the corporate network level, for example. There is something nice about the blanket of uniformity the network provides, and it's much easier to notice a change on a single firewall than a change on one of two thousand laptops.

Securing the endpoint is all about balance. We want people to be productive, and we want people to be secure. In our quest to find that balance, we might find the pendulum swinging from one side to the other, and if we don't grab it and yank it back to the middle quickly enough, it might slip out of our reach forever. If we have an endpoint that is so locked down it becomes impractical for an employee to use it to fulfil their duties, that will force them down an alternative, unmonitored path, perhaps their own computer, or even a laptop purchased from 'an alternative budget', and kept off the enterprise IT asset list. In the other direction, if we have a device that is so permissive the user is free to overload it with whatever garbage applications and malware they desire, that could clearly present a risk to them, the data they're accessing and other such vulnerable devices that share the network.

Just as Chapter 2 talked about making friends with the network engineering team, this chapter covers working with the corporate IT team on the endpoint experience. This collaboration has multiple aspects to it. The first is to ensure that any 'base images', the standard operating system and software configurations deployed to company hardware, in use across the enterprise have a uniform set of security controls enabled.

This includes consistently applied operating system security polices and any endpoint security tools installed and configured (things like AV software, device encryption and DLP agents). Second, we'll want to work together on policy and governance of the endpoint. Although security operations might stay out of the actual creation of polices, they, along with IT support, will provide useful feedback and insights regarding how well policies are being adhered to in the real world, or how effective security tools really are, and can suggest any adjustments that should be made along the way.

IT support are some of the best placed people in your organisation to give security operations a much-needed head start in life. While folks will often hesitate before reaching out to security, they won't think twice about calling up their favourite IT support person to ask for advice or an opinion. It's this connection that can lead to IT support frequently becoming first responders in security incidents. They'll also have exposure to all of the applications and systems in use in an organisation, so will quickly be able to tell when something doesn't look right. No one will know their way around an enterprise issued endpoint device better than those who receive hundreds of queries about them per day. As security professionals, we should never make the mistake of dismissing those in IT support; we have a lot to learn from them.

This chapter looks at the various tools and techniques the blue team can use to secure the different types of endpoint device in use in the modern enterprise, even when they are not owned by the enterprise. It will also look at how we can take alerts and events generated by endpoints and mix them into our SIEM tools, to provide additional context and correlation to the network level events discussed in Chapter 2.

ENDPOINT TYPES

Let's quickly take a look at the various types of endpoint we'll likely encounter during the course of operations. For the most part, from our perspective, a computer is a computer, no matter what form it takes. However, there are a couple of important considerations that will play into how we plan on securing them.

Desktops

Although they're not as popular as they once were, there are still plenty of desktop machines out there. They tend to play a role in one of three use cases. Perhaps the employee using the desktop works in an environment where they don't need to move around much or access a machine outside of fixed business hours; think showroom sales staff or a cashier in a bank, for example. In another case, perhaps the employee is always moving and therefore requiring them to carry a laptop would be disruptive to their work. After all, if you're always on the go, it might be impractical to find the time to charge a laptop. In this case, a good example would be a nurse at a hospital moving between different wards and rooms in order to treat their patients. The third example would be cases in which the desktop machine is hooked up to specialist equipment, and connecting and disconnecting a laptop everyday would be too burdensome – think of a DJ running the board at a radio station or a scientist using specialist measuring tools.

Given that desktops are typically expected to remain in one place, some security organisations can fall into the trap of assuming they will. Shockingly, it is entirely possible for a human being of average strength to pick up a desktop computer, place it in the back of a Honda Civic and move it, with or without permission. I mention this because I have seen organisations that deploy full-disk encryption to every laptop they own, but neglect to do so for the desktop machines because of the assumption that they cannot be stolen, or that someone will notice the stealing occurring. I promise you, they can be, and people are very good at stealing them without people noticing. Endpoint encryption really does belong on all endpoints, not just laptops.

Conversely, another important consideration is what happens if those desktops do as is expected of them, and remain in a single location, and then that location is damaged by fire or flood? The enterprise could lose a considerable amount of its computing infrastructure in one fell swoop, and should be prepared with backups to get replacements up and running as soon as possible.

Laptops

A highly convenient way to get plenty of computing power into your employee's hands, wherever they may be, and at whatever time of day, it's no surprise that the laptop rules supreme at most organisations. The laptop and the employee can form an almost unbreakable bond, since a work laptop can sometimes be the only one people possess. This can pose quite the conundrum when one of them is asked to leave the organisation, and normally, it's the employee.

One of the biggest headaches for security organisations is dealing with the misconception that when an employer hands an employee a laptop, they are giving it to them. It's theirs, and will be theirs forever. Clearly, it's a tool primarily designed to enable access to enterprise resources to permit the employee to do their job, and, as such, after only a few weeks on the job it's typically awash with data that could be sensitive in nature. Another aspect to this incorrect assumption is 'since the laptop is mine, I can use it however I want', which is where friction between IT, security and the end user can come to the fore.

The portability of laptops makes them extremely vulnerable to theft, of course, and there are plenty of other physical threats, such as damage from dropping, or spills over the keyboard. These risks call for mitigation, including full-disk encryption and automated backup of local files, to be in place without exception.

Chromebooks

The name 'Chromebook' specifically refers to a device, usually in the form of a laptop, running the Chrome OS, a Linux-based operating system produced by Google. Unlike traditional laptops, Chromebooks are designed to be used primarily with online services and applications and, as such, can afford to slim down on local file storage, random access memory (RAM) and CPU. The result is a thinner, more compact device that often has a longer battery life than a traditional laptop. While Chromebooks are built for always-on internet connectivity, they do still permit the user to run applications locally, subject to having enough storage capacity on the device to do so. If you've been in information technology for a while, you'd be forgiven for thinking it could also be called a 'thin-client', because that's essentially what it is.

Chromebooks have seen tremendous growth in recent years, and are especially popular in educational settings. The low cost of the hardware, along with the highly available, configurable and subscription-based cloud services that back them, make them an enticing prospect for any organisation looking to provide their people with access to corporate resources via a highly portable device, while not wanting to splash out on a more expensive laptop and the management aspects that go along with it. As such, security operations teams should be aware of them, and how they can be configured to maximise an organisation's security posture.

Chromebooks break the typical enterprise IT model of a user being assigned a specific computer, since user data is stored away from the device, on a cloud service. Therefore, it is important to ensure that the team is capable of determining, through reliable audit trails, which user was logged onto which Chromebook at a given time.

Tablets

To further reduce the burden of carrying around a portable computer, we can ditch the keyboard altogether and use a touchscreen instead. Tablet computers feature screens that are 7 inches (about 18 cm) in size or greater, and will often be based on a mobile operating system, such as Apple iOS, Android or Microsoft Windows 10 S. These operating systems leverage official application store platforms to distribute the applications that will run on the devices, and with the exception of Android, purposefully restrict the ability of the end user to install applications from unofficial distribution channels. The benefit of doing this is better control over the quality of applications that end up on devices and a theoretical reduction in the opportunity for malicious software to creep onto the device. There are plenty of folks who object to being locked into one distribution platform, however, and will work to circumvent the technical controls that enforce this; this activity is known as 'jailbreaking'.

Tablets can be used effectively within an organisation, and they work especially well if the end users' duties can all be conducted in a single application. For instance, in a storefront setting to enter orders and process payments, or by a travelling security alarm installation technician to activate the system once the installation is complete. Many tablet operating systems offer special 'single application' modes to limit the usage of the tablet to just that application. In other cases, tablets may be used to access cloud hosted data, as either the primary or secondary device assigned to the end user.

The portability of tablet computers can be a curse as well as a blessing. They are very easy to steal and if left in public locations or handed to outsiders to complete a point-of-sale transaction, appropriate physical security measures, such as locking stands, should be deployed.

It's not uncommon for users with personally owned tablets to want to leverage them in addition to their company issued computers. Personally owned devices are covered below.

Smartphones

Smartphones are similar to tablets but smaller, and with a cellular connection in addition to the standard WLAN connection. Smartphones provide the most convenient (based purely on size) way to respond to emails and message on the go. That cellular connection can provide an unmonitored communications channel to a device that could easily find itself directly connected to an enterprise's internal wireless network. Given this, having a policy for which smartphones are allowed to connect to which networks, and ensuring that the policy is regularly enforced, is critical.

Smartphones can do other things besides messaging and email of course, and with the largest smartphones being only slightly smaller than the smallest tablets, it's pretty hard to make a clear distinction in terms of use cases. One thing we can say is that smartphones are ubiquitous and we simply cannot afford to ignore them. Later in this chapter we'll cover a tool available to security operations teams to manage both personally owned and enterprise-owned smartphones: mobile device management (MDM).

Payment terminals

Another common endpoint device, especially in front of house sales settings, is dedicated payment card terminals. These terminals read credit card data, contact card providers to gain transaction authorisation and facilitate electronic funds transfer. Payment card terminals can communicate over wireless networks, including cellular, or be connected directly to a wired network.

The industry is trending towards moving more payment terminal functionality to devices like smartphones and tablets, leveraging either a customised operating system or a dedicated application on a standard mobile operating system to work with card readers and ultimately process transactions. That said, there are still many examples of proprietary payment terminals out there, all with varying degrees of security in place. Given their proprietary nature, payment terminals can often be left exposed to known vulnerabilities for longer than devices running widely used operating systems.

If a security operations team finds itself with payment terminals in its purview, extra precautions should be taken, including network segmentation and having clear escalation paths to the terminal manufacturer in cases where security problems are suspected.

Internet of things

If something has an IP address and doesn't fit into any of the categories above, chances are it could be classified as belonging to the internet of things (IoT). The term IoT is used to describe connected devices of various types that leverage the internet to provide additional features or functionality; for example, an internet-connected security camera that leverages cloud storage and can send notifications when it spots a person.

The race to give all the things IP addresses has undoubtedly led to some pretty useful products, but alas, it's also given us its fair share of facepalm moments too, especially in information security departments. Ultimately, an IoT device still includes various input devices, is smart enough to use TCP/IP and can send messages across the internet, so can very easily be considered a computer.

Earlier, in the discussion on desktops and laptops, I mentioned the importance of uniformity in the build: having a consistent set of features to make management of them easier and to simplify detection of deviation from the norm. Well, I have bad news. There is little chance of being able to apply this philosophy to IoT devices. The sheer volume of different device types, operating system spins, attack surfaces and security features make for an anything but consistent experience. That's okay; it's what keeps things interesting in security operations.

Who owns the devices?

When we consider our options for managing these various device types, we must first answer this important question, because how we answer will have a direct effect on our approach. There are certain expectations that a device owned and configured by an organisation will be subject to monitoring and, if provided for work purposes, should be used in accordance with a given policy. Conversely, a personally owned device is private property, and any attempt to monitor or restrict its use will likely be met with fierce resistance, and in some jurisdictions, may even be illegal.

Like everything in security, we have to balance relative benefit with relative risk. If the employee is working exclusively in a SaaS application with non-sensitive data, and they have no reasonable way of rapidly removing data from that application, the use of a personally owned device doesn't seem that much of a problem. If that data were protected healthcare information, the risk changes somewhat.

Typically, the trade-off with personal devices is that an organisation wants to offer the employee the convenience of using a single smartphone for work, but hold on to some assurances about what can happen to any enterprise data that ends up on that device. MDM suites can help bridge this gap by carving out a sandboxed area of the device for enterprise data to reside, and shutting things down if certain security features aren't configured in accordance with an acceptable use or dedicated bring your own device (BYOD) policy.

Such policies are used to clearly articulate what is acceptable to the enterprise in regard to personally owned devices. Most frequently they offer a compromise between handing full control of the device to the enterprise and allowing certain actions to be taken. It's common, for example, that an enterprise will allow the checking of corporate email on a personally owned device, in exchange for the ability to remotely wipe the device if it goes missing.

For some organisations, the need to maintain complete control over every facet of their data means that personally owned devices are simply too risky to permit. In theory, this makes life a lot easier for security operations, but it means that we have to stay on top of enforcing this policy, and focus on keeping the devices out of our environment.

MINIMUM EQUIPMENT LIST

In the world of commercial aviation, the minimum equipment list (MEL) outlines the various systems on an airliner that absolutely must be in working order for the flight to proceed. The amount of redundancy built into the airliner means that not every instance of every system is operational 100 per cent of the time, but it can still be safe to fly. The MEL provides a clear cut-off point for when this is no longer the case.

The concept of a MEL can be applied to endpoint security. We can provide a list of control systems that must be functional for an endpoint to be used to conduct business (i.e. access data), and then we can come up with a mechanism to ensure compliance with that list. One such mechanism was discussed in an earlier chapter: the use of an NAC to restrict switch port connectivity to internal systems until posture checking has been completed. If a company doesn't have NAC available, or would find that control too restrictive, other less terminal approaches can be taken. Real-time alerting to inform the security operations team that a machine is out of compliance, followed by defined procedures for responding to that alert and performing remediation steps, for example.

Let's take a look at some of the items that may be on our MEL for endpoint devices.

Centralised authentication

One of the most fundamental needs for enterprise endpoints is the ability to set and maintain password complexity and other authentication requirements, and typically this is achieved through a centralised directory service. This directory service has responsibility for performing authentication and, as such, enforces the policies that govern it. Microsoft Active Directory is an example of a centralised directory service. The computer and user identities that are found within Active Directory are said to be members of the Active Directory domain. Enforcing that the endpoint is associated to the domain also ensures that the organisation issuing the endpoint has the ability to maintain access to the device, through accounts with administrative and other specific permissions. This access is used to provide end user support and perform other maintenance tasks on the device.

Given that the domain is so crucial in policy enforcement and IAM in organisations running Active Directory, domain membership is typically the foundational platform on which all other security controls sit. In other words, it's the most minimum you can get on the MEL.

Off domain

A common challenge for IT and security teams are users that remove their machines from the domain the second they receive them, usually by reimaging the machine to install a different operating system. The result of this is that the endpoint is also stripped of the security controls the security operations team relies on to enforce security policy, and without a way to authenticate to an off-domain machine, reinstalling them isn't an option. Software developers and network engineers are the usual suspects when it comes to this particular activity.

To address this particular challenge, security operations teams should first try to understand the drivers behind the user's decision to remove their machine from the domain. I have used a highly specialised technique, known as 'talking to the user' to do this previously. In some instances, the reason is plainly, 'I don't like the idea of being monitored', in which case you should refer back to the acceptable use policies the person signed when they agreed to take the job, and if that doesn't work perhaps ask human resources to intervene. In others, there can be a very specific technical reason, and this is where we can jump right in with that service culture I talk about throughout this book. 'I don't have permissions to do X, Y and Z, and that is preventing me from doing my job effectively', or 'The enterprise AV software is eating up 95% of my CPU', or even 'The DLP software blocks me from opening files with bank account numbers in, and I work in Finance'. All of these are valid reasons for a person to become frustrated by a security control, and our job is to intervene and provide a fix for the problem before the user is driven to take an action so drastic as rebuilding their entire machine from scratch.

Using a computer domain account to authenticate to an NAC solution is a highly effective way to keep non-domain machines off private networks, but, as already alluded to, NAC requires the business to be fully bought in and supportive to be effective.

Full-disk encryption

On my desktop I have a folder called 'Tidy'. Within 'Tidy' there is another folder called 'Tidy', and this cycle repeats itself around six more times before we reach the most deeply embedded 'Tidy'. This is a testament to the number of times I've been about to give a presentation, and I've thought to myself 'my desktop needs a tidy up before I share my screen with others'. Within each of those tidy folders are all the files I've been working on temporarily from the desktop at some point in the history of my laptop. There are snippets of code, email headers, IDS logs, firewall configurations and all manner of other random things of varying sensitivity. For all the truly important stuff, I'm comfortable that I have a copy backed up using cloud storage in a neatly organised directory structure, but locally, it's a free for all, and I know I'm not the only one who lives like this. This is why I, and everyone else, should have full-disk encryption on all their devices at all times.

If my machine gets stolen today, two things stand in the way of the person stealing it from pilfering through the multiple layers of 'Tidy' and finding something juicy. The first is the strength of my password, and it's pretty strong. The second is full-disk encryption. If my computer didn't have full-disk encryption enabled, the hard disk could simply be ripped out and connected to another machine, where it would be free to be explored by an attacker with zero regard for passwords or permissions enforced by my operating system. Full-disk encryption should be on your MEL.

All modern operating systems ship with native support for full-disk encryption, such as File Vault in Mac OS, and BitLocker in Microsoft Windows. Various commercial products exist to simplify centralised management of full-disk encryption for enterprises, by supporting features such as backup keys to gain access to a device even when a user finds themselves locked out.

While there are technical alternatives to full-disk encryption, such as folder-level and file-level encryption, from the perspective of an enterprise rolling out a technology to a wide variety of users of varying technical skill levels, there really is no substitute for the level of coverage full-disk encryption provides.

Removable media
The security afforded by full-disk encryption is quickly negated if a file is moved from a protected disk to one that is not encrypted, and the most likely opportunity for this to

happen is via removable media. Whether the root cause is the need for a quick way to exchange files between meeting participants, or a user diligently backing up important work, if the media is lost and unencrypted we have an incident on our hands.

Removable media also presents a significant data exfiltration risk. A 5 TB external hard disk costs around £150 at the time of writing, a small price to pay for a malicious actor looking for an extremely effective way to rapidly remove a large amount of data from a physical location.

To deal with the risks associated with removable media, many of the enterprise encryption tools discussed earlier can be used to enforce a policy that any removable media that comes into contact with a machine is also encrypted or used in a read-only mode. It's also possible to prohibit the use of removable media through policy tools such as Microsoft Group Policy and MDM products like Jamf.[1] When considering the security posture of an endpoint, removable media policies should be a major consideration. If there is no real business need for storage support to be enabled, an enterprise would be dramatically reducing their attack surface by restricting it.

If enforcing encryption on removable media, an organisation should make this policy extremely clear to both new hires and long-tenured employees. The majority of encryption tools that enforce this policy will prompt the user to encrypt any unencrypted storage devices that are attached to the machine so they can be used. Doing so causes the media to be formatted, therefore erasing any existing data on the drive.

I once had to explain this to a new hire who had inserted a personally owned universal serial bus (USB) drive to his corporate laptop, and clicked through various prompts that attempted to warn him of the impending mandatory encryption formatting. As a result, he lost quite a few personal photos and other documents. It was an awkward moment, and as I'm sure you can imagine, not one that endeared the user to the security team.

AV software

Malicious actors know the value of the endpoint as a landing spot. There are immediate rewards to be reaped upon arrival: credentials, sensitive documents, files of sentimental value, CPU cycles and network bandwidth to name but a few. These items would constitute a good haul, but the really juicy stuff comes later, when the actor is able to pivot to other networked resources from the newly compromised endpoint: a database containing 70 million user records, payment card information or protected healthcare information, for instance. Exfiltrating this data, holding it for ransom or selling it in bulk will definitely result in a better return on investment than selling the odd credential, or running a ransomware scheme against a single machine. While we can place many layers of defence between a database server and the public internet, we have to provide multiple direct paths to endpoint devices. Simply browsing the internet, downloading files, receiving an email and running software with an online component all provide opportunities for a malicious actor to gain a foothold on the device.

Up to date AV software, while not a silver bullet, provides a solid defence against a large chunk of these threats and, as such, deserves to be on your MEL. Yes, that also applies if you use Apple or Linux computers. AV works by scanning files at critical moments, such as when they are first introduced to the system, or as they are being loaded into memory when the user attempts to open them. Various elements of the file are then compared with a database of malicious files and behaviours, known as a signature database. If a match is found, the file is locked down before its payload can be unpacked by the system. It's a simple concept that has proven itself many times. That said, there are still instances where AV alone may not be enough. For example, in order to match a piece of malware to a signature database, that malware must have been captured, analysed, the signature created and delivered to the AV software in a timely fashion. If this process hasn't completed for whatever reason, perhaps the malware is simply too new, or there has been some other interruption to the AV updating process, then there is an exposure there. In another example, depending on the AV configuration, a user might have the option to ignore or bypass a quarantine warning. In this case, they could negate the protection that would have otherwise been afforded to them.

With many new variants of malware being released on a daily basis, the battle between the researchers writing signatures and the malware authors looking for new and innovative ways to obfuscate their malware is a never-ending cycle. In an attempt to stay one step ahead, AV tools also leverage generic behavioural detection techniques, which concentrate more on detecting patterns in application behaviour that may be associated with malware, rather than getting an exact signature match. This can work well, but can also lead to false positives, which, in turn, lead to user frustration.

Data loss prevention

I touched on the network elements of DLP in Chapter 3; now I switch focus to the endpoint agents that are frequently used to supplement the network coverage, which have become especially valuable when dealing with modern transport layer encryption and data being transmitted to cloud services. DLP may or may not be in your MEL, usually the determining factor will be if the organisation handles regulated data, such as healthcare information or payment card data. In order to demonstrate compliance with regulated data handling guidelines, DLP may form part of the strategy.

Endpoint DLP agents read data as it is loaded into memory and, if the data matches a given pattern or contains specific terms, have the ability to prevent it being uploaded via a browser, pasted into an email client or printed.

The more data types you ask DLP to look for, the more alerting it generates for the security operations team to review. In some cases, it can be very prone to false positives. Also it can pick up on a great deal of sensitive information that may not strictly fall under the purview of the security operations team, perhaps financial discussions about an upcoming business transaction or highly personal information related to an employee. These tools are powerful, and they serve as a reminder of why trustworthiness is an important trait for anyone working in security.

Application control software

AV software attempts to seek out 'known bad' by looking at a list of application signatures that shouldn't be allowed to run, or, to use another term, it takes a 'blacklist' approach. Application control software approaches things in the opposite manner, and allows only 'known good' applications to run; this is also known as a 'whitelist' approach. If it's not on the list, it's not going to run. Therefore, if your endpoints are only expected to need to run a small number of applications, this approach might work nicely. This is a highly restrictive method, of course, and may not work well in all environments. If you have a software development workforce for example, it's not going to go down well, as many developers like to use different toolsets based on personal preference.

You can also use application control to block specific apps or categories of applications, rather than going down the whitelist path. Organisations might do this to prevent the installation of certain games, or peer-to-peer file-sharing software, for instance.

As for its place on the MEL, the general consensus would be that if you've implemented it, you've done so for a specific reason and any attempt to remove it from the endpoint might indicate a security policy violation. In such a case, then it would very much belong on the list.

Asset management software

An endpoint represents an investment, and is an asset of the organisation that purchased it. Therefore, the organisation will likely wish to keep track of its asset. This is especially important when employees leave the company; the asset must be returned so that it can be reused.

It's not just the hardware either, software licence costs add up quickly. Knowing the exact number of licences in use, rather than having to make an educated guess, can allow for significant cost savings.

Asset management agents such as Samanage[2] and Microsoft System Center Configuration Manager (SCCM)[3] can run on machines and report back valuable information, such as which users are logged in, where they are physically located, IP addresses associated with network interfaces and which software products are installed. Removal of an asset management agent could indicate that the user is trying to install unlicensed software, or generally trying to dip under the radar. That's why it's a good candidate for inclusion on the MEL.

Configuration standards

Finally, we might require our endpoints to adopt specific configuration standards at all times to ensure they meet our security needs. For instance, perhaps we want them to leverage a specific DNS server, so we can monitor and filter DNS traffic. Perhaps we always want them to use a proxy server for internet access, so we can apply web content filtering. In these cases, a variety of methods are available to enforce compliance with these standards, including group policy or MDM tools.

ENDPOINT HARDENING

The items on the MEL are largely add-on items, meaning they are tools that typically require an additional purchase to be made above and beyond the standard features included with an operating system. However, a lot can be achieved by simply taking the time to leverage the features included with an operating system to secure it. One of the great tragedies of information security is that teams are so quick to run out and purchase security tools that they miss the features that are right there in front of them, which can maximise security posture without requiring further investment.

The term 'hardening' is used to describe the act of configuring a device in such a way as to reduce its attack surface. Building a hardened base image for enterprise deployment is usually a joint task conducted by IT and security operations teams, and can be a great project for building mutual understanding of each other's goals. Let's take a look at some commonly used endpoint hardening techniques.

Microsoft Windows

Despite a marked increase in the number of Apple computers making their way into the enterprise, the Microsoft Windows operating system still holds the largest share of the market by a wide margin at the time of writing. Tight integration with services such as Active Directory and the Exchange email and calendaring suite, as well as the ability to run on hardware built by a wide variety of manufacturers, makes usurping Microsoft a highly challenging prospect for anyone.

The ubiquitous nature of Microsoft Windows also means it's the prime (but not exclusive) target for malware, as it would make sense that a malicious actor would want to cast as wide a net as possible as they trawl for victims. Fortunately, the Windows operating system has a highly granular policy and permissions system that can help us dramatically reduce the opportunity for malicious software to do damage. We just have to make sure we use it.

User privilege levels
A configuration decision that can have a dramatic impact on the security of a Microsoft Windows endpoint is whether or not the end user should be a member of the local administrator group. Membership to this group gives the user complete power to install software and hardware on the machine, make system-wide configuration changes and create other user accounts. Given the power afforded by membership to the local administrator group, it seems odd that this is even up for discussion. However, in many organisations, membership is the norm, as it's seen as a way to dramatically reduce the number of tickets and service requests that come the way of the IT helpdesk. The fact that the administrative power is often limited to one specific machine is seen as a way to justify the additional risk incurred.

In February 2017, endpoint security firm Avecto, now a part of BeyondTrust, released an interesting study. They found that 94 per cent of all Microsoft vulnerabilities reported in 2016 could be mitigated if the active user did not have administrative rights (Patrizio, 2019). That's a staggering figure, and just goes to show the positive impact of choosing to strip users of overly broad permissions.

The balance, of course, is ensuring that we're not being too restrictive and preventing people from doing the things they legitimately need to do to be productive. A classic example is allowing the user to install a printer so that they can print a document at home, or while they're on the road. Adding a user to the local administrator group is often seen as the quickest, most hassle-free way to get the user what they need. As just noted, it actually gives them way more permissions than they truly need. This is where Microsoft's group policy engine comes in; with this, rather than allowing everything, we can make granular permissions adjustments to permit only specific actions. In this case, there is a Group Policy entry called 'Devices: Prevent users from installing printer drivers', which we could set to disabled, allowing our user to do what they need to, without having full administrative permissions.

Group Policy

I've already mentioned a couple of things that can be achieved with Group Policy in a Microsoft environment, but it's worth emphasising just how critical Group Policy settings can be when it comes to securing Windows endpoints, especially at a large scale. There are close to 5,000 configurable settings in Microsoft Group Policy. Not all of them have a direct effect on security, but many do.

A collection of Group Policy settings is known as a Group Policy Object (GPO), and they can be applied to computers at the Active Directory level, or locally to a single computer. GPOs can also be applied to users, rather than computers.

GPOs are inheritance based, meaning it's possible for an enterprise administrator to set a policy at the highest level of the directory structure, and for several other GPOs to be picked up and enforced at other points on the way down. An example would be a company that perhaps operates several subsidiaries. The parent company could set its global policies, and then each subsidiary company administrator could set their own policies in addition. In the event of conflicting policies (parent company says 'deny', but subsidiary wants to say 'allow'), the parent company's setting would win out.

In addition to directory-based inheritance, where the policy is applied can have a bearing on whether or not it actually gets applied. Policies are evaluated in the following order:

- Local, meaning any policy set on the specific computer.

- Active Directory site, which is an Active Directory grouping unit that is often used to group computers based on their physical location, for instance a branch office.

- Active Directory domain, which is the logical grouping of computers across the entire organisation.

- Organisational Unit (OU), which are grouping units within an Active Directory domain, used to organise and group users or computers. In the event that multiple policies are applied to a given OU, the administrator will select the order in which they should be applied.

Following this order, if a policy is initially applied at the local level, it could be overwritten multiple times, at the site, domain and OU levels. After all the policy inheritance and processing orders are factored in, the result is known as a 'resultant set of policy (RSoP)', and Microsoft provides tools to review this data, including the RSoP snap-in (Microsoft

Support, 2018) and the command line tool, gpresult (Microsoft, 2017). It's important for security operations teams who may be involved in configuring GPOs to harden Windows endpoints to understand these concepts, and to take the time to validate that a GPO that is enabled is actually being enforced in practice.

Examples of settings that can be applied via GPO, in addition to those we've already covered, include:

- preventing access to external drives (such as optical drives, or USB);
- restricting software installation;
- disabling the guest account on a machine;
- restricting access to the command prompt;
- disabling automatic driver updates;
- setting various logging preferences, including which activities to audit;
- enforcing wireless network security requirements;
- setting application control policies.

Sysmon

A free utility created by the Windows Sysinternals team, Sysmon (Microsoft, 2019), or System Monitor to use its full moniker, is a tremendously powerful tool. It can be widely deployed to Windows endpoints, and is installed as a Windows service and device driver. Its role is to monitor for various event types and generate a log entry containing information related to the event when it occurs. These events can then be ingested into a SIEM platform for correlation. This provides a great platform for blue teams seeking to identify malicious processes on Windows endpoints, such as those found in malware.

Sysmon is capable of detecting:

- process creation and termination;
- incoming and outgoing network connections;
- file creation timestamps and changes;
- driver loading;
- raw disk access;
- process memory access.

Sysmon requires a configuration file that defines which event types should generate log entries and which should be filtered out. Of course, not every process that is loaded is going to be malicious in nature, so without filtering, the amount of data collected by Sysmon could become overwhelming. It's possible to use a default configuration or build a customised one to meet the needs of your organisation.

If you've been around the information security industry for a couple of years or more, you may have come across the infamous @SwiftOnSecurity Twitter account, on which an information security-focused version of country-turned-pop superstar Taylor Swift dispenses high quality information security advice. If you are new to information security, bear with me. No one really knows who's behind the account, other than a pretty smart engineer who has tremendous Microsoft endpoint and Exchange management skills. Thankfully, the mysterious Taylor has crafted a high quality Sysmon configuration, which is hosted on GitHub for others to use and to contribute to. You can find this configuration at https://github.com/SwiftOnSecurity/sysmon-config.

While Sysmon can't prevent malware from executing, it can provide the blue team with early warning that a system may be compromised, and provide valuable data to assist in the analysis of a piece of malware.

MacOS

Apple MacOS devices, once the exception, are now becoming a more familiar sight in the offices of various types of enterprise. Many organisations share the same story when it comes to their relationship with the Mac platform. It started with one senior person, or perhaps a developer, requesting a Mac rather than a PC. An IT person was then tasked with joining the Mac to the Microsoft Active Directory domain, which is a process that has come a long way in the last few years. That gave IT some control over the Mac computer, but as more and more people started to ask for Macs, a better centralised management approach was required.

While this was all occurring, Apple was struggling to gain momentum with its own line of server hardware, known as Xserve, and its dedicated server operating system Mac OS X Server. This operating system included a variety of open-source tools to perform familiar server-type tasks, including operating a Lightweight Directory Access Protocol (LDAP) directory, acting as a DNS server, performing file hosting duties and acting as a web server. In 2011, the Xserve range of hardware was discontinued, and Mac OS X Server stopped being shipped as a dedicated operating system. Instead, the server capabilities of Mac OS X were moved into add-on application for the standard desktop version of Mac OS X Lion, and this model has been in place ever since. Without dedicated server hardware and few opportunities to legally run virtualised instances of Mac OS X due to licensing restrictions, it started to look as if Apple didn't really want to compete with Microsoft Active Directory. Instead, they sought to better integrate with it for directory services functionality, and introduced a more MDM-like approach to centralised endpoint management, known as Profile Manager. As a result, Profile Manager, or third-party MDM tools, are frequently the go-to tools for enterprises seeking to configure both company owned and personally owned Apple devices.

Profile Manager

A built-in MDM service in the MacOS server application, Profile Manager gives company administrators the ability to create and distribute configuration profiles, which are functionally similar to GPOs in the Microsoft Windows realm. Various mechanisms for distribution of configuration profiles are available to the organisation, including manual installation or automatic push. Typically, a manual install would be used where a user is agreeing to allow a personally owned device to be enrolled in an organisation's MDM programme, while an automatic push would be used to configure devices owned by the organisation.

A special profile, known as a 'Trust Profile' must first be installed on any device that is being enrolled with a Profile Manager configuration. This profile includes the digital certificates that will allow the device being managed to validate that the configuration profile they are receiving has been signed by the organisation.

Configuration profiles created with Profile Manager can also be applied to other Apple device specific operating systems, including iOS for the iPhone and iPad, and tvOS for Apple TV.

Security relevant settings that can be configured by a Profile Manager profile, include:

- password or passcode policies, including complexity settings;
- airplay (screensharing) destination restrictions;
- wireless networking settings;
- installation and trust of selected digital certificates, perhaps from an internal public key infrastructure;
- app installation restrictions;
- FileVault full-disk encryption settings, including setting of enterprise recovery key;
- host-based firewall configuration;
- Active Directory integration options;
- the ability to remotely lock and wipe devices.

Third-party MDM

Several third-party MDM tool vendors have built on top of the native Apple MDM ecosystem. Examples of such tools include Jamf Pro,[4] Mosyle Manager[5] and the open-source Munki.[6]

Although a great deal of the functionality afforded by these tools is possible while using just Apple's native features, the appeal of leveraging a third-party vendor is having (in many cases) a cloud-based solution for generating and distributing configuration profiles. This eliminates the need for an organisation to run a dedicated MacOS server host within its environment.

iOS

As previously mentioned, mobile devices running iOS can also be managed with configuration profiles created in Profile Manager. There are a series of configurable settings within Profile Manager that will only apply to iOS devices. Examples of these settings include:

- the ability to restrict the device to a single app, which can be effective in point of sale or self-service environments;

- web content filtering;

- enterprise SSO configuration;

- cellular access point name (APN) settings, which can be used to configure the manner in which the device connects to the public internet via a cellular network;

- lock screen message configuration.

Guided-access mode

An iOS device need not be managed by a Profile Manager configuration to be locked to a single application. A native feature of iOS is guided-access mode, which can be activated from the accessibility settings menu on the device. The person establishing the guided-access session enters a passcode that will be required to bring the device out of guided-access mode.

Android

Google's Android operating system has the largest chunk of the global smartphone market (around 88 per cent in the second quarter of 2018) and is also used to run various tablet devices. Android is a Linux-based mobile operating system and, unlike the Apple iOS approach of keeping everything as locked down as possible, it doesn't put up much of a fight when it comes to preventing users from accessing the inner workings of the operating system. Indeed, many manufacturers who build devices to run Android provide the ability for users to install their own operating systems and gain root-level access to a device. The act of modifying an Android device to gain this type of access is called 'rooting'.

Various methods can be leveraged to root an Android device, including the exploitation of known vulnerabilities in the operating system to achieve root access through software (sometimes known as soft-rooting), or leveraging the Android Debug Bridge, which is a command line interface used to execute commands on directly connected Android devices via USB. Of course, if rooting occurs through the exploitation of a security vulnerability, that also raises the question of what other, potentially malicious, processes could leverage that same vulnerability to compromise the device. However, various security and safety features that originally shipped with the device can be disabled by rooting, in the quest for absolute control of the device, which can be of concern for enterprises seeking to integrate personally owned Android devices into their environments.

MDM tools with support for managing Android devices often include rooted device detection features. However, as rooting techniques change and evolve with each new release of the Android operating system, the makers of these tools must account for these changes. If they don't, they risk failing to detect that a device has been rooted, which may lead to it receiving a different security configuration than intended.

There are several Android-specific security items that should be considered when establishing an Android hardening strategy.

Encryption

Devices should leverage encryption. From Android version 7 onwards, the platform supports a file-based encryption model. This model allows for different files to be encrypted leveraging a different encryption key. It also means certain services can access some content prior to the user authenticating to the device, which can enable critical functionality. Users can enable encryption via the security settings menu on their device, or be required to enable it via an MDM configuration profile. Additionally, email clients can be configured so that encryption must be enabled before a single email is received on the device, which is a setting frequently leveraged by enterprises.

Android also supports a full-disk encryption process, but support for this encryption model is being phased out in favour of the file-based approach mentioned above.

Require a strong PIN or passcode

Android can support a personal identification number (PIN) that is four digits in length or longer, or an alphanumeric passcode. Of course, a four-digit PIN doesn't really cut it in terms of having enough random combinations to keep an attacker out, so something longer should be enforced.

Sideloaded applications

Android applications are officially distributed through the Google Play store; however, it is entirely possible to load applications from other sources. This is called sideloading, and while there are legitimate reasons for doing so, there's always a chance that sideloading an application could introduce additional risk to the device. Sideloaded apps are not subject to Google's review process, and therefore might include bundled malware, or do things behind the scenes that aren't explicitly called out in the app's description.

Google Play protect is a service within Android that can look for suspect behaviours from all applications, sideloaded or not. It's highly recommended that this service be running at all times. Of course, another tip to avoid the risk of sideloading an application is not to do it in the first place.

Developer options

Android includes a number of options to support developers working on the platform. These options can create a larger attack surface on the device, and since most users aren't in the business of developing software for Android, they should be switched off if not needed. One such option in the developer options page includes disabling the Android Debug Bridge which was mentioned earlier as a vector for rooting the device.

Android Device Manager

A free service offered by Google, Android Device Manager allows a user to register their device so that it can be remotely erased should it be lost or stolen. Of course, devices need to be registered prior to getting lost or stolen, so that the service is ready to roll if needed, therefore it's a good idea to work with users to make sure this is done before they're allowed to access corporate resources.

In a similar fashion, many email clients, including Microsoft Outlook for Android, can also be leveraged to trigger a remote wipe.

SUMMARY

In this chapter we've reviewed the various types of endpoint devices found in an organisation, including desktops, laptops, tablets and modern thin-client-like devices such as Chromebooks.

I introduced the concept of a MEL for security tools installed on those endpoints, and reviewed examples of the types of tool that may qualify for inclusion on that list. Directory membership for centralised authentication and configuration management, full-disk encryption and up-to-date AV software can all make the case that they belong on the list.

Finally, we reviewed some of the features of the Microsoft Windows, MacOS, iOS and Android operating systems that can be leveraged to create a hardened configuration with a much-reduced attack surface.

So far, this book has covered protecting the mechanism used to access data (the network) and the devices that are used to access data (the endpoints), so now seems like the ideal time to focus on the data itself. The next chapter focuses on securing repositories of data, including databases, and the servers that run them.

REFERENCES

Microsoft (2017) 'gpresult'. Available at: https://docs.microsoft.com/en-us/windows-server/administration/windows-commands/gpresult

Microsoft (2019) 'Sysmon v10.41'. Available at: https://docs.microsoft.com/en-us/sysinternals/downloads/sysmon

Microsoft Support (2018) 'How to use Resultant Set of Policy logging to gather computer policy information'. Available at: https://support.microsoft.com/en-us/help/312321/how-to-use-resultant-set-of-policy-logging-to-gather-computer-policy-i

Patrizio, A. (2019) '94% of Microsoft vulnerabilities can be easily mitigated'. Computerworld, 26 February. Available at: https://www.computerworld.com/article/3173246/security/94-of-microsoft-vulnerabilities-can-be-easily-mitigated.html

5   PROTECTING DATA

Data is the lifeblood of the modern enterprise. The creation, exchange, analysis and storage of data are key components in countless business processes, so it's no surprise that there are plenty of opportunities for all of that data to slip into the wrong hands, become inaccurate, or perhaps become completely unusable. In security operations, and especially as part of the blue team, our job is to work to prevent data from meeting any of the fates listed above. When we do this, we're protecting data, but we're also protecting the enterprise and, most importantly, the lives and livelihoods of the people the data represents.

In the information age we run the risk of accepting that the occasional data breach, resulting in the exposure of sensitive personal information, is the price we must pay for the convenience of living our connected lives. It doesn't have to be this way. As information security professionals on the front line, we have the opportunity to make a fundamental impact on societal attitudes to this problem. Of course, we can't do it alone. We need the help and support of those developing applications, designing and deploying systems, legislating, and building companies that are fuelled by data.

One of the most commonly heard retorts in any data protection argument is, 'why would anyone want to hack us? We don't have anything interesting.' If you have data, any data, rest assured that someone else wants it. The reasons might not be immediately obvious, but data is a highly sought-after commodity for various malicious actors seeking to inflict harm or to influence a subject. That's why anyone handling data is morally and ethically bound to protect it, even before we consider legal, regulatory and compliance reasons for doing so.

That's not to say that incidents and breaches won't ever occur, because even the most diligent organisations and individuals have been caught out by circumstances and actors working in ways they could not have predicted. However, there have been plenty of cases where an incident and subsequent breach should have been prevented had basic measures and consideration for information security been in place. To compound things, in these days of heightened awareness, those cases are often prefaced by a clear and direct warning from an insider about the impending risk, yet those warnings often go unheeded. These are the incidents that are unforgivable, and should ultimately lead to people being held accountable. Legislation like the GDPR (EU, 2016) that came into effect in Europe in 2018, and the California Consumer Privacy Act (CCPA; California Legislative Information, 2018), which went into effect in January 2020, send a clear message that carelessness with data can lead to serious penalties.

The compromise of one person's personal data is a bad thing. The compromise of multiple people's information is an extremely bad thing. Of course, the nature of many enterprises' operations means they frequently stockpile large swathes of data, and frequently that data relates to multiple people. That's why when things go wrong, they can go extremely wrong. The servers, databases, cloud and other storage mechanisms that are used to store and process data are prime targets for malicious actors, and securing them requires a mixture of technical controls, governance and diligence.

In this chapter, we'll be taking a look at some key data protection concepts, and the tools and techniques we can leverage to apply them in the real world.

CONFIDENTIALITY, INTEGRITY AND AVAILABILITY

Three fundamental information security concepts, often visualised as the 'CIA triad', are as follows (see Figure 5.1):

- **Confidentiality**, ensuring that access to data is restricted to only those who are authorised to access it.
- **Integrity**, ensuring that data is accurate, and protected from unauthorised modification.
- **Availability**, ensuring that data is accessible to those who need to access it, at the times they need to access it.

Figure 5.1 The CIA triad

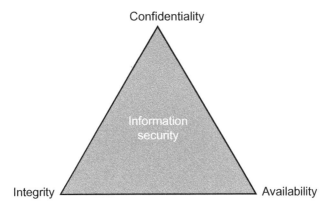

All information security programmes are built around these three concepts. In security operations, our job is to apply them at the technical level, and ensure that we're doing so in a way that aligns with business objectives and risk appetite. This becomes particularly apparent when we consider how we apply these concepts to protecting stored and processed data.

Confidentiality

Encryption, access controls and appropriate security training are all examples of controls that allow us to ensure that data is only accessible to those with a need to access it. Ensuring those controls are applied correctly, and managed constantly, is where we earn our keep. The truth is that many organisations are good at picking out technical controls, and crafting policies around them, but fall down when it comes to putting the theory into practice.

Ensuring confidentiality is an ongoing process. Authorised users come and go, and data sensitivity changes as elements are added and removed. Systems go in and out of production, but the data they hold on to still needs to be protected. For these reasons, when designing control processes to ensure confidentiality, we must remember they cannot be 'fire and forget', and must include elements of review and audit.

Confidentiality is also a core component of privacy, which has for a long time been seen as a separate, albeit overlapping discipline. In some larger organisations, for instance, it's common to have separate security and privacy departments. Privacy departments tend to be more focused on topics such as ensuring compliance with contractual terms and conditions, as well as the application of regulated data, and how that aligns with legislation, rather than being a technically focused team. Recently, owing to several high-profile incidents that have raised awareness of consumer privacy rights, a shift is occurring. Security operations and engineering teams are frequently finding themselves acting more like privacy operations and engineering teams. The key difference between the former and the latter is that privacy engineering is typically focused on creating features and deploying solutions that both protect consumer data from internal misuse, and provide avenues for consumers to request insight into how their data is being used by an organisation. For example, at a social media platform, a privacy engineering team may be involved in the development of features that allow users to see exactly how much information they are sharing with others, and how their data is exposed to third party organisations, such as advertisers, by the platform. I really like the overlap, as it provides yet another avenue for a security team to provide value, not just to the organisation, but to outside consumers interacting with that organisation.

In March 2018, a major scandal involving misuse of sensitive personal data stored in Facebook profiles by British political consulting firm Cambridge Analytica made headlines around the world. Former Cambridge Analytica employee turned whistle-blower, Christopher Wylie, worked with journalist Carole Cadwalladr. Together, they went public, and teamed up with major UK and US news organisations to reveal how Cambridge Analytica had obtained data relating to around 87 million people through Facebook. In the vast majority of cases this occurred without the explicit consent of those people. The data would later be used to build profiles that would be used to target political advertising.

Cambridge Analytica did this by leveraging a Facebook app called 'This is your digital life'. This application, created by Cambridge University researcher Aleksandr Kogan in 2013, was pitched as a personality quiz for academic research, and installed by around 270,000 people. Back then, Facebook's privacy model also allowed the application to access certain data from friends of those who had installed the app. This is how the jump from hundreds of thousands of users to tens of millions of users occurred. The data collected by the application was subsequently passed to Cambridge Analytica.

Upon discovering Cambridge Analytica had obtained the data in 2015, Facebook made requests for them to delete it. By this time, it appeared it was too late, and further journalistic investigation revealed that the data was never deleted. Through Cambridge Analytica, the data was leveraged by Donald Trump's 2016 United States presidential election campaign, and by Vote Leave in the 2016 Brexit referendum.

The scandal resulted in serious reputational and financial harm for Facebook, which issued apologies for its lax privacy controls, was forced to testify in front of the US Congress and to pay fines to regulators. It also signified the end of the Cambridge Analytica name. Perhaps most importantly, long term, the scandal raised general awareness of the misuse of consumer data, which could lead to the development of harsher penalties for future offenders.

Integrity

In order for data to be usable, it has to be accurate. Ensuring data has integrity involves preventing unauthorised or unintentional modification which, if it were to occur, would result in data becoming inaccurate and therefore unusable. Various controls are available to us to detect or prevent unauthorised or unintentional modification. An example would be an integrity hash, which can be used to prove that the contents of a file have not been modified in transit.

An integrity hash is generated by a cryptographic hashing algorithm, which examines the content of a given input, be it a file or message, and uses a mathematical process to output a hash value (or digest) based on those contents. If the contents of the file change, the value of the integrity hash also changes. The secure hashing algorithm (SHA) family of algorithms are commonly used for this purpose, with version 3 (SHA-3) being the most modern implementation at the time of writing. In security operations, our exposure to hashing commonly includes validating the content of downloaded files, such as software updates, to ensure they have integrity before they are applied. Integrity hashes of suspected malicious files can also be checked against various online services, including Virustotal[1] and the totalhash database,[2] to validate that they are in fact malicious, and to discover related malware samples. Hashing also plays an important role in evidence collection as part of incident response procedures and subsequently digital forensics.

Our old friend access control also has a big role to play when it comes to ensuring data integrity. If unauthorised access to data is granted and a malicious user leverages that access to modify that data, significant problems could result. Orders could be cancelled, payments could be made to the wrong accounts or, worse, industrial control systems could respond in incorrect ways.

There are also plenty of non-technical controls that can be employed to assist in ensuring data integrity. Even if an authorised user is the one inputting the data, they might not input the correct data. In this case, a process to introduce a second pair of eyes to validate their work might be required. This is known as a separation of duties control, and these are commonly used in financial processes.

I once investigated an incident caused by a data integrity issue. A malicious insider altered the contents of a file that included a series of financial transactions to be made via an automated system. The suspect started by replacing the recipient account information with their own bank account number and sort code. Next, they were able to use another user's credentials to upload the file to an online processing service, which resulted in payments being redirected to their bank account.

It wasn't long before the discrepancy was noticed by the finance department, and an investigation ensued. Fortunately, the system that output the original file kept a log which included an integrity hash, and the modified version file was found on the suspect's laptop. There was no question that the integrity of the data in that file had been lost from one system to another, and there was no question of who was responsible.

Availability

In this era of always-on services, availability is a key consideration for a SP or business that needs to keep data accessible to users or customers. Keeping data accessible through thick and thin is an important part of an overall security programme. Service level agreements commonly outline the maximum acceptable downtime for a SP, and dipping under those agreed numbers can often lead to financial penalties.

Availability controls include backups, redundant network circuits and high availability installations of key hardware components, such as firewalls. Fully redundant datacentres in geographically diverse locations can also be employed as a part of a business continuity or disaster recovery (DR) plan.

Of course, if you double up on switches, routers, servers and even entire datacentres, you should also be doubling up on security controls. If you have a highly secured and monitored primary datacentre, but skimp on those controls in your backup datacentre, guess where your exposure is? Having multiple copies of the same data for DR purposes is commendable, but you should be protecting that data with the same rigour in both environments, otherwise you run the risk of a compromise occurring while you look the other way. Unfortunately, many DR environments are created as a shell of the primary environment, and security controls are often missed. It's important to remember that today's DR could be tomorrow's production.

In our role in security operations, we may find ourselves responsible for ensuring data availability in some tricky situations. An example could be during the compromise of a single server in a pool of servers, where we might be called upon to identify and contain the compromised host, while allowing the clean hosts to continue processing.

While it's true that the actual responsibility for business continuity and DR might be 'owned' by a group outside the security team, perhaps an operations team, or a site reliability engineering team, in reality it's a shared function that several teams will have a say in. Frequently, in our unique position to view the enterprise, both up close in all its grimy detail and from above looking down on the various interconnected applications, networks, endpoints and users, we truly have some of the best insight when it comes to implementing an availability strategy.

SECURING SERVERS

With the vast majority of data processing activity occurring on server instances, it's no surprise that they're a high value target for our adversaries, and therefore should be a high priority from our defensive perspective. Servers, of course, are computers that perform activities on behalf of other computers, and they do that regardless of their form factor. Hardware server instances, in both rackmount and tower form, are familiar sights in datacentres and offices respectively and provide the foundation for other non-physical forms of server to operate. Virtual machines, IaaS instances and containers are all examples of server technologies that leverage logical boundaries crafted in software to enable various management and resiliency features.

The ability to shift a virtual machine from one set of hardware to another seamlessly, auto-scale based on load and demand, and restore an entire server instance from a snapshot are just some examples of the advantages afforded by virtualisation. Even the latest cloud trend, known as serverless computing, runs atop servers! Granted, those servers are abstracted from the end user via software, but, of course, the provider offering the serverless model will still need to secure and operate the underlying server resources that are running it.

Server hardening

A day in the life of a server should be a lot more predictable than the day in the life of an endpoint device. While the endpoint is driven in all directions at the whim of its user, a server is typically repeating the same tasks day-in day-out, using a much smaller subset of applications. In theory, this makes hardening servers (the practice of configuring them to be as secure as possible by reducing the potential attack surface) a relatively simple task, but as with all things in this field, there is sometimes a void between theory and reality.

Server hardening frequently involves limiting the number of services running on the server and, as a direct result, the number of open ports listening on that server. For instance, why would a host used only as a network file server need to run web server components? Closing ports and disabling services that are not required will reduce the attack surface significantly.

Similarly, whitelisting services and applications that should be allowed to run on the server will have a dramatic impact on its overall security posture. When it comes to installed applications, servers should be kept as pure as possible. No additional web browsers, for example, as servers aren't a place for internet browsing.

CIS benchmarks

The Center for Internet Security (CIS), a non-profit organisation which works with the IT community, has created a series of benchmarks[3] to assist with hardening servers (and other types of device). The benchmarks are free to download, and walk through optimal configuration settings for enhanced security. Benchmarks exist for all major server operating systems, including Microsoft Windows and various flavours of Linux including Amazon Linux, the AWS native Linux distribution.

By following the configuration standards in the CIS benchmarks, it's possible to take an off the shelf (also known as 'vanilla') copy of a server operating system, and tighten the screws to harden the operating system as much as possible. Additionally, thanks to the increased usage of virtualisation technologies, it's possible, and often more effective, to do it the other way around. Pre-configured operating system images that adhere to the CIS benchmarks are available for download and deployment into an environment. Starting with the most secure configuration and working backwards, perhaps making a couple of concessions on settings to enable the business along the way, will often put you in a better place than attempting to retroactively apply enhanced security.

Strengthening authentication

As part of our overall effort to keep servers as pure as snow, we can make several enhancements to authentication and access control through procedural and technical controls. One such control would be mandating user accounts separate from those used for accessing resources and endpoints day-to-day, to be used to access servers for the purposes of performing administrative tasks. These separate, administrator-only accounts could then be subject to more stringent password complexity requirements, or better, require the use of multifactor authentication (MFA) to gain access to the server. This protects against the risk of daily use credentials becoming compromised, perhaps through phishing, and subsequently being used to access a server.

Another benefit to the separate credential model is that it makes it much clearer to determine who is actually using their server administrative level access on a regular basis. We'll talk about this more in Chapter 6 on IAM, but frequently people request more access than they truly need. Having a policy stating that administrative accounts that aren't used once in any 30-day period are disabled, or removed completely, is another effective way to reduce exposure. The fewer accounts with access, the fewer accounts that could potentially be compromised.

From our vantage point in security operations, having a smaller subset of user accounts that have deep-level administrative access to servers to monitor for anomalous behaviour or other signs of compromise, helps us to more effectively prioritise our response to any alerts relevant to credential use.

Logging

Of course, to get alerts regarding credential usage on servers, we have to be logging all related events. This is typically achieved by first ensuring that all of our servers are set to log all of the events we need, and then those logs are sent (as always) to a disparate logging platform for collection and analysis.

In the Microsoft Windows Server world, these log entries are recorded in the Windows Security event log. Each event type comes with its own event ID, and there are certain event IDs that we can key off for relating to credential usage.

Some examples of high priority Windows Security event IDs are shown in Table 5.1.

Table 5.1 High priority Windows Security events

Event ID	Description
4624	An account logged on successfully
4625	An account failed to log on
4648	A logon was attempted using explicit credentials (A user attempted to use another credential set to perform a task like mapping a network drive)
4672	Special privileges assigned to new log on (Denotes when an administrator-level account has logged onto the server)
4698–4702	These events are related to the creation, deletion and modification of scheduled tasks
4720	A user account was created
4722	A user account was enabled
4723	A user attempted to change their own password
4725	A user account was disabled
4726	A user account was deleted
4732	A user account was added to a security-enabled local group
4733	A user account was removed from a security-enabled local group
4740	A user account was locked out
4776	Successful login recorded by a Windows domain controller
4777	A failed login attempt was recorded by a Windows domain controller

On Linux-based systems, we'll find credential usage activity logged in /var/log/secure (for Red Hat-based Linux distributions), or /var/log/auth.log (for Debian-based distributions). Event type descriptions are recorded in plain English, with one log entry per event. Example descriptions include:

- For successful login activity, 'accepted password' and 'accepted publickey'.

- For failed login activity, 'authentication failure', 'rejected password' or 'failed password'.

- For privileged (sudo) account usage, the term 'sudo' along with the command executed with sudo permissions.
- For account creation events, the term 'new user'.

Knowing the specific event types and formats of the platforms you're tasked with monitoring will allow you to create rules in your SIEM or log aggregation tools to alert on those that are the most relevant to your enterprise.

Network profiling

It's not just what's happening on the server (running applications and services) that should be easier to profile than an endpoint, but also which hosts the server is talking to via the network. In a multi-tiered application, for example, we might expect to see network communication between a middle-tier application server and a backend database server. We might also see communication between a DBA's laptop and the database server. What we wouldn't expect to see is the database server communicating, or attempting to communicate, with an endpoint being run by a customer service agent in the field, or even to a destination outside the organisation's private network.

Profiling the expected network activity of a server, and then alerting on deviations from that baseline, can provide a very reliable measure of determining if a host is compromised. Once again, wire-data analytics tools can help flag this, as well as firewalls and NetFlow logs. Host-based firewalls can also be used to lock down the communication flows as much as possible.

Physical security

There's a saying in information security that goes 'if they can touch it, they can compromise it' and it relates to physical security of hardware devices, including servers. While we might automatically think of servers as being correctly racked in highly secure datacentres, the truth is, there are plenty out there that aren't. I've personally observed mission critical file servers balanced precariously on chairs in random closets, stored in an unlocked outdoor shed, used as the IT administrator's desk chair and plugged in within a few feet of a water main. In all of these cases the physical wellbeing of the device was clearly not the first consideration, and compromise of the device by human or environmental factors was highly likely.

Physical compromise of a device by a malicious actor could be achieved through theft and subsequent removal from the location, or perhaps by leveraging a local port to connect directly to the server, for instance, using a USB drive to install malicious software, or boot into an alternative operating system to bypass permissions and access data. Technical measures used to defend against such attacks would include full-disk encryption applied on server hard drives, disabling local USB and other diagnostic ports, and unplanned reboot and power outage monitoring.

An incident that became the catalyst for several technical and physical security hires (including myself) involved the physical theft of several corporate email servers. It occurred during the Thanksgiving weekend, a 4-day holiday period in the United States. In accordance with city code, my future employer had diligently fitted a so-called 'Knox Box' to the outside of their office building. The Knox Box contained all the keys required to access every single part of the building in the event of a fire. The fire department had a special key to enable them to access the contents of the box.

On the first day of the long weekend, two suspects visited the deserted office building and took a sledgehammer to the Knox Box, knocking it to the ground. They then removed it from the site, presumably so they could work on it with a greater array of tools, and were able to obtain the keys contained within.

The following day they returned with their newly acquired keys and had the run of the still-empty building. At some point in the day, an IT technician received a page that company email wasn't working. After failing to access the email server remotely, they dutifully headed into the office. Upon arrival in the server room, it soon became obvious the problem wasn't one that could be solved quickly. A selection of servers that ran the company email were gone completely. The next few days were spent acquiring new hardware and rebuilding everything from backups.

The suspects were eventually caught; they had targeted multiple businesses and were also engaged in a wireless wardriving scheme (driving around looking for poorly configured wireless networks). Interestingly, the corporate email servers were targeted specifically. They wanted access to company secrets and other sensitive information, which they then planned on using to commit financial crimes. The suspects were charged by the United States Secret Service and are currently serving jail time. The Knox Box was replaced, but installed in a more secure fashion.

Environmental concerns such as temperature, proximity of water pipes, types of fire suppression systems in use and the overall physical security of the space occupied by the server are also important considerations to those of us in the blue team. If we're so hyper-focused on the technical security measures we're building out and operating, we might miss some of these less technical, but equally important factors.

Those who wish to compromise the assets we're trying to protect do not play by a rule book. They'll also take the path of least resistance to get to what they need. As we move around the enterprise, auditing the environments that we're familiar with at the technical level, it's important to remember that a motivated malicious actor would be more likely to smash a window and grab a server in order to compromise the data on it, than chain together a series of complex technical attacks to achieve the same goal.

Redundancy

Although likely in the domain of the server administration or IT operations teams, server redundancy has a direct effect on availability, and therefore is of interest to us. Additionally, server redundancy features can have other impacts on our daily operations, which we'll discuss shortly.

Given that we want to keep our servers ticking over nicely, it's not uncommon for them to include redundancy features such as dual power supplies, multiple NICs and a redundant array of independent disks (RAID). In security operations, understanding how these features are employed by a given server will help us make sense of certain aspects of our monitoring, as well as better prepare for a security incident involving a highly redundant server.

Redundant network interfaces

Let's start with redundant NICs. Each physical NIC has to have its own MAC address, as discussed in Chapter 3, although multiple NICs may be 'teamed' or 'bonded' to create one logical NIC for high availability. This can be in either an active/active or active/standby configuration. In the case of active/active, the NICs are both receiving traffic at all times, and in the event that one goes down, the other just carries on the work as before. From an addressing standpoint, active/active configurations typically implement a pseudo interface, which is a logical interface with its own MAC and IP addressing that is virtualised on top of the two physical interfaces.

Hosts trying to connect to this logical interface don't need to know about the underlying physical interfaces, and so, if a path to the logical interface changes because a link is physically broken, traffic will just take the alternative switch port connected to the 'good' version of the logical interface.

When traffic shifts due to the failure of a single NIC in an active/active redundancy configuration, this can manifest itself in network monitoring tools as a spike in traffic on a switch, or across a link, which can (and should) raise some alarms with the blue team and likely the networking team as well. This is where knowing what redundancy features are implemented and what they look like when they're activated is highly important. If equipment goes down, chances are the team responsible for fixing it will want to know so they can make the required repairs, and won't want to be distracted by any misplaced 'security incident' talk.

In an active/standby configuration, one physical NIC does all the work, while the second sits idle, monitoring the first. In the event that the active NIC goes down, the standby NIC assumes control of the IP address that was previously on the active one, and uses an Address Resolution Protocol (ARP) broadcast to announce the changing of the guard, in terms of the underlying MAC address associated with the IP. In some cases, when this happens it can trigger host-based IDS or AV software alerts because a long-standing IP/MAC association has been changed, and ARP poisoning is suspected.

Redundant array of independent disks (RAID)

A RAID is a grouping of physical hard drives to form a logical disk that has fault tolerance and redundancy features. The term 'RAID level' is used to describe the configuration of those physical disks and the types of fault tolerance they afford. RAID 1, for instance, is a RAID level that provides disk mirroring, a one-for-one copy between two disks, in which everything written to the primary disk is simultaneously written to a backup disk. If the primary disk fails, your backup disk is ready, willing and able to take over.

Perhaps the most commonly used server RAID level is RAID 5, a configuration that requires at least three physical disks to implement. RAID 5 leverages a technique called striping with parity to store blocks of data and parity information across all the disks in the array. Block parity information is stored on an opposing disk to the one containing the actual data block it references. In a three-disk RAID 5 configuration, this means the array can survive the loss of any single disk. Importantly, most RAID hardware will allow the failed drive to be hot swapped and rebuilt, with minimal impact on performance.

Although knowing the RAID layout of a specific server isn't too high on our priority list in security operations, there is a situation where it might be useful to us. In the event of a security incident that is evolving into a digital forensics investigation, security operations engineers might serve as first responders and be asked to collect hard drive images for further investigation.

Imaging a single hard disk is a fairly straightforward task. Imaging multiple hard drives found within a server is also pretty simple; it just takes a bit longer. However, in order to make sense of the data found on those hard drives, if they are part of a RAID, the digital forensics examiner will be required to do a bit of rebuilding work. Providing the examiner with information about the RAID, such as its RAID level and the make and model of the RAID controller, will be a great help in this situation. The more information available to the examiner, the quicker they'll be able to work and, therefore, the quicker they'll be able to deliver results.

CLOUD STORAGE

In the IaaS era, data storage responsibilities are moving away from individual file server instances and into the realm of dedicated storage platforms. The sheer scale of the data requiring storage, the need for data to be accessible by multiple hosts and services, as well as security and compliance features, such as encryption at rest, audit logging and lifecycle management, are all factors driving this change. Of course, the underpinnings of these platforms are the same physical disk drives that we've used for years, but now they're being abstracted from us by SPs who are taking care of tasks such as hardware maintenance, redundancy and backups behind the scenes.

It's not just a change in technology. The shift to dedicated, cloud-based storage platforms requires a shift in the way of thinking for those responsible for administering the storage. It only takes a couple of clicks to expose the entire contents of a storage platform to the public internet, intentionally or not. Similarly, when you don't have access to the physical disk, deletion of a file really means deletion of a file. There can be no carving through a filesystem to recover lost data.

Amazon S3, part of the AWS suite of offerings, is a widely used IaaS storage platform. Throughout the last couple of years, a number of high profile S3 misconfigurations have led to damaging and dangerous exposures of sensitive information. In most cases, the data exposures are caused by users of the platform accidentally permitting anonymous access to the objects (i.e. files) contained within S3 buckets (a 'bucket' being the term for the container used to store files and folders).

Security company UpGuard has done a great deal of research on accidentally exposed S3 buckets, and reported several cases throughout 2017 and 2018. One such case involved ISP, Pocket iNet. In October 2018, UpGuard uncovered around 73 gigabytes of sensitive data relating to the Pocket iNet network infrastructure. This data included passwords used to access firewalls, routers and switches, network diagrams, device configuration information and photographs of infrastructure.

Given the company's role as an ISP, including to some sensitive clients, this exposure was a particularly worrying occurrence. After disclosing the finding to Pocket iNet, UpGuard reported it took a full 7 days before the exposure was addressed.

You can read more about this particular case on the UpGuard blog, https://www.upguard.com/breaches/out-of-pocket-how-an-isp-exposed-administrative-system-credentials.

When it comes to our role in security operations, the shift to cloud-based storage platforms brings both risk and reward. The risk, as we've just covered, relates to the speed at which files can be accidentally exposed to a potentially unlimited audience. The reward is that we get a consistent set of features, enabling us to monitor for things like permission changes or even simple access to files, across the entirety of our storage environment (as opposed to having multiple storage platforms in use, each with their own logging formats).

The key to success in securing cloud storage is knowing; knowing which platforms are in use, how they are being used, for which purposes and by which teams. As a security operations team, getting our hooks into the cloud storage platform early is key. We don't want a nasty surprise down the road, when we're suddenly made aware that sensitive enterprise data has been stored in a cloud location for months, or even years, without proper governance and monitoring. At a surprising number of companies, the unofficial use of cloud services for data storage is a major issue. This covers everything from development teams spinning up IaaS accounts and running components of their applications in an environment backed by a random developer's company credit card, or simply folks picking their favourite cloud storage provider to use as a backup service for the contents of their laptop.

Setting expectations for cloud storage use, working with teams to implement the appropriate monitoring and controls, and searching for deviations from anything that has been agreed upon should be part of our daily routine in security operations.

Securing cloud storage

IaaS providers who offer cloud storage solutions are hyper-aware that we, meaning security teams of businesses moving to the cloud, are also hyper-aware of the risks and changes associated with doing so. They understand that our security, regulatory and compliance needs do not go away simply because we're moving our data out of a datacentre into a cloud environment. So, to help us out, and primarily of course, continue to be able to win our business, IaaS providers are offering security features that we can leverage to make sure our cloud storage solutions are in the best possible shape.

Identity and access management
Of fundamental importance in any data storage environment is knowing who exactly has access to what, and what they can do with that access. While traditionally we've relied on operating system and file system permissions settings models to implement access controls, cloud platforms offer new ways of doing so, and it's critically important that we understand them to avoid the most significant risk to our data, accidental exposure.

Amazon S3, for example, has made the headlines when users have set permissions incorrectly, and has gone to great lengths to clarify how their permissions model works, providing new global options to prevent accidental exposures like the one covered in our case study. S3 buckets are not publicly accessible by default; someone has to make them that way. Updated UIs in AWS now place a giant yellowy-orange label next to any publicly accessible S3 bucket, to make it very clear when this configuration has been applied.

Fundamental permission levels haven't really changed with the jump from on-site to cloud storage platforms; we'll still find such standards as read, write and browse, which can be applied at the folder or file level. What has changed, however, is the scope and dimensions in which those permissions can be applied, and the roles and responsibilities of the people applying them. This is what catches people out. Permissions can be given at the user-level and on the actual storage resource, with a union of all the permissions being applied to determine the final effective permission set. For example, an administrator might want to give a specific user full access to a folder, but the person managing that folder might want the user to only have read-only permissions. These permissions are going to clash, and it's up to the specific cloud platform to determine which permissions truly apply.

Given that a move to an IaaS provider is often coupled with a move to a 'DevOps' operating model, in which the developers who build the applications are responsible for configuring and running various infrastructure components, it's likely that those developers-turned-operators are going to be the ones applying permissions to the cloud storage environment. So, we have the perfect storm of new permissions models that can be applied against storage locations, individual users or groups and a new type of user applying those permission models. It's easy to see why things can, and do, go wrong.

As the security operations team, we can lend a hand. We can configure alerts to notify us when permissions are adjusted, and review those changes with the teams making them; at the very least, we should do this when a bucket is made public. We can also make it part of our operating rhythm to audit our cloud storage location permissions on a regular basis, to look for files and folders that have slipped through the cracks. We can also ensure that any access afforded to internal users is governed by our overall IAM strategy. This is especially important when access to our IaaS platform isn't fully integrated with internal directory systems, as we'll lose the ability to revoke access by simply disabling an enterprise user account.

Encryption

'Who has access to my data?' is a question that is coming up with increasing frequency from customers, in the form of other businesses, or individual consumers. If you're hosting data in a cloud environment, the answer could very well include the IaaS or SaaS provider hosting your data. After all, they have superusers and administrators, too. In order to protect sensitive data that is hosted in a cloud environment from unauthorised or unexpected access by the provider, encryption is frequently the go-to technology. By using encryption keys that the provider does not have access to, we allow continued use of the IaaS platform for storage, while providing a level of assurance around access control. If the provider attempts to access our data, all they'll see is a bunch of encrypted garbage, without that all-important key.

Most storage platforms offer encryption at rest, usually based on the Advanced Encryption Standard (AES), and in some cases, even enabled by default without user intervention. The ability to leverage customer-controlled encryption keys usually requires some configuration and, of course, key management. In security operations we may find ourselves custodians of those all-important keys, in which case we'd need to build procedures for key management, rotation and destruction, and ensure that we have the appropriate tools ourselves to do all of these things.

Of course, it's the burden of key management along with other storage-related management work that drives many organisations to IaaS providers in the first place. So, moving but still having to do key management can be off-putting to businesses attempting to leverage all the features the SP can offer. Usually the decision to use customer-owned and managed keys is a business one that comes down to specific customer or regulatory requirements for data handling.

Encryption should also be used to protect data as it moves across the internet, or private links, from the enterprise into the storage platform. Typically, this is achieved through technologies such as the SSH protocol or TLS. Although the SP might very well offer access 'in-the-clear' to data in specific cases, perhaps for files being used to back websites that only offer plain text HTTP front ends, we should be driving towards 100 per cent encryption-in-transit at all times. Our network monitoring tools can help us find cases where encryption-in-transit is not being correctly applied.

Logging

All of the major IaaS providers offer us the chance to produce highly detailed logs about every action that occurs on their storage platforms, and they then all offer us the chance to send those logs directly back to those same storage platforms for 'safe-keeping'. Can you see the issue there? Aside from the fact we're going to be paying more for storing data and then storing data about access to that original data, we really should be getting those logs off the platform and into an isolated system to eliminate the risk of them being tampered with.

I shouldn't be so harsh on cloud providers, this is the same model used by server operating systems out of the box, after all. Just as we need to schlep file system audit logs off servers as quickly as possible into a disparate logging platform, where they can be correlated across the enterprise, we should do the same from our cloud storage providers.

Given the widespread usage of these IaaS providers, most commercial SIEM tools, such as AlienVault USM[4] and Splunk,[5] offer integrations with the major providers for ingesting their specific log formats (Figure 5.2). These integrations will typically include dashboards that can provide insight into how data is being accessed from those cloud data storage platforms.

In security operations, we should work with the relevant teams to ensure that appropriate logging is applied to all cloud storage locations, those logs are delivered to our centralised log aggregation tools, and routinely review the configuration to ensure that we're not missing newly created storage locations.

Lockdown

Earlier, I briefly touched on using unapproved cloud storage providers as a backup location. Commonly, users are leveraging tools such as Google Drive, Microsoft OneDrive or Dropbox to back up personal data from home, so it seems like a natural extension to use those same services to back up work data. The challenge this creates is that the data is owned by the enterprise, and if the employee leaves the organisation, the data goes with them. The solution to this problem is twofold.

First, enterprises should offer an approved storage location. It may be hosted internally, or it may be hosted in the cloud. It doesn't really matter; it just needs to be somewhere that is accessible by all employees. Having a consistent platform on which everyone can store files and collaborate will help address one of the fundamental reasons why people go rogue and take their files to other platforms.

Second, we should work to lock down or restrict access to any cloud storage solution outside that approved solution. This seems aggressive, but it's the only reliable way of keeping data out of unapproved platforms. Personally, I'm not usually a fan of throwing up the barriers in such a dramatic fashion, but to deal with this particular problem I've found the only way to be effective is to be aggressive.

Access restrictions can be applied at various layers. URL filtering tools can block browser-based access to unapproved cloud storage platforms. Application controls can prevent the client applications associated with those cloud storage platforms from running. Likewise, IT asset management suites can detect those applications and trigger their uninstallation. DLP suites can prevent files being uploaded to certain providers. There are a multitude of options available to us; which ones we ultimately leverage will depend upon the enterprise.

Being aggressive in restricting access to these tools is likely to be met with fierce resistance by the business. There is always some argument about needing to access those alternative tools that we're planning on blocking. Most commonly, an approved file storage and sharing platform in our enterprise might be prohibited in another, so sharing files between organisations becomes problematic. It's best to tackle these

Figure 5.2 Splunk integration with AWS logs

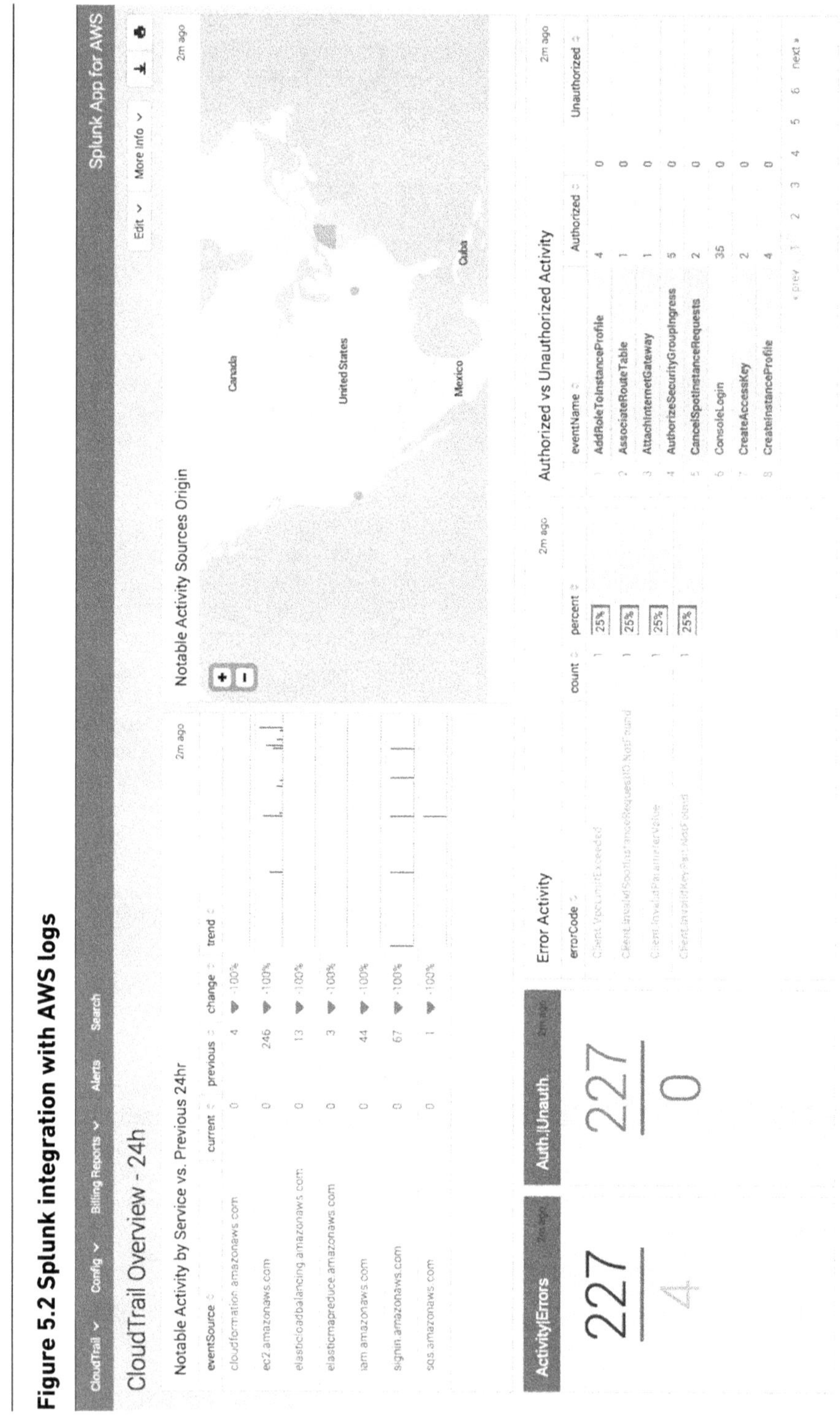

issues in a case-by-case, exception-based manner. The exceptions can be tracked, and governed accordingly. In many cases this is preferable to the alternative: a free-for-all in which files can be stored anywhere, with only a policy standing between the end user and storage of files in an unapproved location.

If we can't lockdown through technical measures due to business objections, the next best thing we can do is look for evidence of unapproved cloud storage usage, through network and endpoint monitoring. Upon detection, have in place a plan to address this usage with the end user, and redirect them to the approved solution.

DATABASE SECURITY

Databases allow organisations to quickly derive value from the data they've collected by adding structure to it, and allowing it to be queried and exposed to end user applications. Databases contain tables, which in turn contain rows of individual records. Columns within the tables provide labels and data type constraints for each field. The result is an easily navigable, consistent dataset that is an extremely high value target. Not only would compromise expose the data within the database, we'd also be giving up a full set of instructions of what each field represents and how it relates to other tables.

In the modern enterprise, databases are typically hosted on servers running relational database management software (RDMS), or hosted on cloud-based platforms in which the underlying infrastructure is managed by a SP. IaaS and platform-as-a-service (PaaS) providers offer database endpoints for enterprises to connect to and use without having to worry about management tasks such as monitoring disk usage, running backups and patching RDMS software. Given that database operations are typically performed by full-time, highly specialised DBAs, leveraging a SP is frequently seen as a way to reduce associated staffing costs.

For security operations, the underlying infrastructure powering the database is of secondary concern compared with considerations such as ensuring the data in the database is being accessed from expected locations, is transferred in the expected volumes, that appropriate safeguards (including encryption) are in place, or that we have the correct insight to fully audit each query being made. All of these considerations align with two core objectives. The first is protecting databases against unauthorised access. The second is ensuring legitimate access is not being misused.

Mapping out databases

The first step in developing a database security programme is understanding as much about the databases in the environment as possible. Where do they reside? What database technologies are in use? What type of information do they contain? The answers to these questions will help shape our strategy. For instance, if I have 100 databases in an environment and five of them contained highly sensitive or highly regulated data, then there are no prizes for guessing which ones I'm going to prioritise protecting. As always, the approach should be to trust but verify. Asking a DBA to provide the structure of all databases in the environment can give you the best picture of what types of data you can expect to find in a given database, and that way there can be no hiding behind an individual's interpretation of what 'sensitive data' really is.

With the list of databases and their contents in hand, the next step is to figure out where these databases are logically hosted. In a number of organisations, a dedicated database network subnet is in place, and perhaps even segregated behind a firewall. In others, databases might be co-mingled in whichever subnet was available at the time they were created. It might even be the case that a database resides on the same server as the application it's serving, meaning there will be no insights to be gleamed from network traffic between the two components, as that network traffic won't exist. Once the logical hosting locations are mapped out, it helps us narrow down our options for monitoring activity in the database.

Finally, understanding the underlying database technologies, and the security features that they afford, will help us determine where we can hook in our suite of security operations tools. Database engines such as MySQL,[6] Postgres,[7] Microsoft SQL Server[8] and Oracle[9] are commonly found in enterprise environments. In some organisations, one database technology will be leveraged exclusively; in others, a mixture of these engines will be leveraged. Different engines will return different logging formats and run on different ports, and, therefore, we'll need to be aware of these differences when integrating them into our SIEM, network monitoring and log aggregation tools.

Monitoring database usage

Once we know what we have to monitor, we can start to monitor it. When it comes to databases, regardless of underlying technology, there are always a couple of consistent sources of information we can leverage, providing they're correctly configured and enabled.

Authentication and access logging

Access to databases should be achieved through the use of valid credentials, just like any other system in the environment. Depending on the database engine in use, these credentials could either be tied back to a centralised directory, which is ideal, or may be locally maintained within the engine itself. Accounts leveraged to access databases typically fall into two categories: user accounts used by individuals to access data and perform administrative or operational duties on the database, and service accounts used by applications or other machine-driven processes to access and manipulate data. A situation we always want to avoid is the use of service accounts by individuals, as that can create a serious gap in auditability.

Regardless of the type of account, the principle of least privilege should be applied. The absolute minimum level of access should be afforded to any given account to reduce the risk of that account being misused should it somehow become compromised. In the case of web applications that talk to backend databases, separate service accounts for read and write operations should even be considered to truly meet the intent of the principle of least privilege.

All database engines offer the ability to log which accounts are being leveraged to access them, and from which source IP addresses. Our first hook should be these logs. We can use them to do things like confirm that a service account assigned to a given application is originating a database session from that application's servers, rather than a developer's laptop. We can alert on access from an individual's user account at times outside regular business hours. These kinds of abnormalities should be investigated by the security operations team, even if they're ultimately found to be benign.

Query logging

We can also go a step further and enable query logging, which lets us know what the user is doing, or attempting to do within the database post-authentication. Query logs can alert us to attempts to escalate permissions beyond those that are assigned to the account, by way of access denied messages in response to specific queries. They can also be used to discover database level attacks, including SQL injection attempts, which, without inspection of the queries, might otherwise appear to be wrapped within perfectly normal traffic between a web server and a backend database.

Having just read the paragraph above, you're probably thinking that query logs are a no-brainer, and would be enabled in every engine and by every enterprise by default. That's not always the case. In high traffic environments, the volume of data generated by query logs soon begins to add up, and can become hard to manage. There can also be a performance hit associated with enabling the logging, and DBAs are the kind of people to whom milliseconds make all the difference. If you're meeting resistance when it comes to enabling query logs, a good strategy is to concentrate on enabling logging where it matters the most, perhaps on those tables that contain sensitive or regulated data.

Finally, a word of caution. Because query logs include full copies of database queries, including elements of the query that come after the 'WHERE' element in the statement, the logs themselves are potentially sensitive in nature. For instance, in an electronic healthcare environment, they could contain protected healthcare information. Make sure to protect those logs as if they were the original data, because they'll often contain chunks of it.

Network traffic

In cases where the database is stored on a remote server, away from the clients that are accessing it, network traffic between the client and the server can provide a highly valuable insight. A sudden, rapid increase in network traffic between a database and a client could mean that data exfiltration is under way, and having network monitoring tools in place that can detect and alert on these types of event is incredibly valuable. Monitoring based on traffic volume allows us to sit out of band, without impacting server performance. We won't get the level of insight that query logging affords, but in environments where those logs are not available it's the next best thing. Having both sources to tell different parts of the story is the ideal scenario. A query log that allows you to quickly determine which query resulted in the sudden increase in data being transmitted helps you clearly differentiate between cause and effect.

Hardening databases

To put them in the best possible position from a defensive perspective, there are proactive steps that can be taken to harden databases. Security operations will unlikely be the team involved in implementing the following features, but we'll be one of the teams that will benefit the most if they're implemented. Hence, it's in our interest to push for them to be implemented sooner rather than later. Additionally, regulatory and compliance standards, as well as customer contracts, may require some of these features to be in place.

Network access restrictions

Limiting the sources that are allowed to communicate with the database via the network can make monitoring it a much easier proposition and, more importantly, help prevent compromised credentials being leveraged to gain access. Earlier, the idea of a separate database subnet with a firewall to enforce segregation was mentioned. This is exactly the type of network access restriction we're referring to here, providing it is properly configured and maintained.

Encryption

There are various layers at which we can deploy encryption in our database infrastructure. Encryption in transit between client and server is a must, especially in highly regulated environments, and with all major database engines supporting it, there really isn't an excuse not to.

Additionally, encrypting the disks used to store the database is highly important to protect against physical theft, or to prevent an IaaS provider from accessing your data (if encrypting using a key that is owned and managed by the IaaS customer).

Finally, encryption can be applied within the database itself, at the table, column, row or field levels. Granular permissions can then be leveraged to determine who within the organisation should be able to access the encrypted content within the database. These types of encryption can be highly useful in regulated environments, for instance in databases that contain credit card data, to mask payment card information from exposure to internal users.

Objections to the use of encryption within the database include the negative impact it has on the ability to query encrypted data elements.

Redundancy

Databases are often critical pieces of infrastructure within a computing environment, so it makes sense that we'd want them to be highly available. Database servers can of course leverage the same hardware redundancy features as other types of server, including multiple NICs and RAIDs, but there are additional things we can do to keep the database up and running at all times.

Replicas of databases can be built on alternative hardware, and kept in sync via the network. In the event that the primary database server goes down, a failover to alternative hardware running the replica can be handled by the RDMS. The larger and busier databases become, the more bandwidth is required to keep them in sync. In some cases, dedicated links between two physical locations are used to keep primary and replica as close as possible to completely in sync at all times.

BACKUPS

Sensitive data doesn't become any less sensitive when it is transferred to backup media. One of the most common security mistakes made in an enterprise environment can be traced back to forgetting this basic truth. If you spend time applying encryption to a server's hard disk arrays and then back up data from that server to removable storage media in the clear, you don't need me to tell you that your server encryption is useless at that point.

Some organisations consider themselves as having a successful backup programme in place if they are performing regular backups of key systems. Well, they might just be patting themselves on the back a little too soon. There are at least two additional elements to a backup programme that have to be in place for it to be considered effective, and both of them are of interest to us in security operations.

Restore testing
A backup isn't a backup if it can't be restored. Instead it's additional, useless data. At least once a year, test restores should be performed from backups of key systems. Yes, it's a lot of work, but I'd rather be doing a test in a controlled manner than doing a live backup for the first time with one ear pinned to the phone listening to a stressed-out executive asking for updates on an incident management phone bridge.

In security operations we can facilitate this process by acting as guardians of the backup/restore testing cycle; raising an exception if a particular system falls out of compliance with this standard.

Consistent security controls
If data is encrypted in the live system, it should be encrypted on the backups. If credentials are required to access the data in the live system, they should be required to access the backup. A backup programme can only be considered successful if this is the case.

In the blue team, we can proactively check these controls are applied, and issue correctional advice if required. We can also ask our friends in the red team to grab a backup drive and see what they can do with it.

SUMMARY

This chapter opened by discussing three fundamental information security concepts, which are perhaps easiest to understand when considered in the context of protecting enterprise data. Those concepts, which are confidentiality, integrity and availability, are the foundation of everything we do in this field.

We then reviewed several of the common storage locations for enterprise data, including servers, cloud storage platforms and databases. Next, we discussed various tools and techniques that we can leverage in security operations to ensure that these locations are part of our overall enterprise security strategy.

For servers, we discussed hardening the server instance to reduce its attack surface, using tools like the CIS benchmarks, and enabling detailed audit logging to capture all credential usage.

As we moved to cloud storage platforms, we discussed topics such as establishing an approved cloud storage solution, ensuring that IAM concepts are applied correctly to that environment, and then restricting access to as many unapproved storage locations as possible.

As we focused on databases, we discussed techniques such as query logging, replication and applying appropriate user permissions.

We've also discussed the importance of both creating and correctly handling backups of all these sources. Ultimately, our users won't really be concerned with whether their data was stolen from the primary location or from a backup of that location; they'll just be riddled with worry that their data is in the hands of someone it shouldn't be.

In the next chapter, we'll jump fully into a topic that we've dipped our toes into during this one: IAM. IAM has a key role to play, not just in protecting data, but in protecting the reputation of an organisation. In many organisations, the security operations team is finding itself establishing and running an IAM programme. This may not have been anticipated or expected a few years ago, but, given the evolution of insider threat risk, it is something that has become increasingly necessary.

REFERENCES

California Legislative Information (2018) 'SB-1121 California Consumer Privacy Act of 2018'. Senate Bill No. 1121. Available at: http://leginfo.legislature.ca.gov/faces/billTextClient.xhtml?bill_id=201720180SB1121

EU (2016) 'Regulation (EU) 2016/679 of the European Parliament and of the Council of 27 April 2016 on the protection of natural persons with regard to the processing of personal data and on the free movement of such data, and repealing Directive 95/46/EC (General Data Protection Regulation)'. *Official Journal of the European Union*. Available at: https://eur-lex.europa.eu/legal-content/EN/TXT/HTML/?uri=CELEX:32016R0679&from=EN

6   IDENTITY AND ACCESS MANAGEMENT

At the beginning of my information security career, if you'd asked me which area I'd spend the most time on over the next decade, IAM wouldn't have been anywhere near the top of my list. Looking back now, it's a strong contender for the very top spot. There are multiple reasons why this turned out to be the case. IAM projects are complex, time-consuming affairs. Information security compliance standards place large emphasis on the area, and increased awareness of insider threats has driven security operations teams to be more introspective; these are but a few of those reasons. Knowing who can access what, and what they can do once they've accessed it, is important when monitoring an environment, and increases significantly in importance when responding to a potential security incident.

IAM has always been important, but in recent times, the growth in the usage of SaaS applications has given the discipline renewed impetuous. SaaS applications often leverage per-user licensing models, so the vendors of those applications want to get as many users into those platforms as possible, and they want to make sure they keep coming back. Enterprises want their users to use the SaaS apps they've invested in, and not a shadowy, unapproved competing application. To achieve this common goal, SSO through technologies such as Security Assertion Markup Language (SAML), Oauth and LDAP directory integrations are leveraged to ensure that end users are led down the correct path, and that path is as frictionless as possible. SSO allows users to leverage their existing enterprise identities and sessions to authenticate into SaaS applications, which makes jumping from app to app a seamless experience.

SSO isn't without risk, however, given that compromise of a single set of credentials can lead to the compromise of any data in any application that uses those credentials. Given this, all good SSO rollouts should include implementation of controls such as MFA, centralised logging and the ability to rapidly deprovision users who leave the organisation.

SSO, and IAM responsibilities in general, are often split between corporate IT and security operations. This split stems from the fact that IT is typically charged with purchasing and configuring applications (either SaaS or hosted internally), and security has a vested interest in keeping an eye on what is occurring in those apps, and who is using them. In some cases, additional teams may 'own' the applications we're looking to govern through our IAM programme. A good example of such an application would be the Human Resources Information System (HRIS). This type of system is used to track employees, their holiday time, payroll information and other personal data. HRIS systems have complex permission models that in many cases mirror the structure of the organisation. In larger organisations, administering the HRIS is a full-time job and, as such, we'd need to involve the HRIS administrator in any integration work we did between the HRIS and an SSO provider.

In this chapter we're going to look at the goals of an IAM programme, how we can make our IAM programme effective, and some of the tools we can leverage along the way.

IAM TERMINOLOGY

Before we start, let's take a look at some commonly used IAM terminology. These terms will be used throughout the chapter.

- Subject – a person, for example, a user in our enterprise who needs access.
- Service provider (SP) – the application or service the subject is requesting access to. Using the term SP rather than 'application' or 'service', keeps things consistent regardless of where the application is hosted.
- Role – a permission level in an SP that permits a given level of access (e.g. administrative level permissions or read-only permissions).
- Authentication – the process of validating the identity of a subject.
- Authorisation – the process of determining a subject is permitted to access a given SP.
- Identity provider (IdP) – a centralised authority that can authenticate user identity, and vouch for that user to the SP.
- Approver – a person who can approve a subject's request to access an SP.
- Requestor – the person requesting the subject be given access, which could be the subject themselves, or someone else.
- Provisioning/deprovisioning – the process of creating/removing accounts in a given SP to enable/disable the subject's access.

GOALS OF IAM

A common misconception is that an IAM programme exists solely to prevent employees from gaining access to systems that they have no business need to access. While that is *a* goal, it's not *the* goal. For an IAM programme to be successful it also has to be effective in getting people the access they're entitled to as quickly as possible. It has to be easy to engage with, meaning there should be a single entry point to the process for every single application and role in the organisation. If the IAM programme does not fulfil these objectives, subjects will be compelled to circumvent it, a behaviour that will place the enterprise at significant risk. Like any change in an environment, the creation of accounts without an audit trail means that it's harder to work backwards and remove the stealthily provisioned access when the subject no longer needs it, perhaps because they changed jobs or left the organisation altogether.

IAM as an opportunity

One of the least documented aspects of IAM, but one of the most valuable in my opinion, is the opportunity a high quality IAM programme affords a security operations team from a relationship building and user trust perspective. This is also one of the reasons I like security teams, not just IT teams, to be at the forefront when it comes to implementing an IAM programme.

Most security controls, think AV software, policies or web content filtering, are seen as barriers. They stop things from flowing. They get in the way. We all know those 'things' are malicious for the most part, but we have to concede that sometimes they can be perfectly legitimate false positives. While we, in security operations, might be exposed to 1,000 filtered or blacklisted web page access attempts across the enterprise every day, for a typical user who runs into one a month, and it just so happens that this month it's a false positive, the experience can be quite frustrating.

IAM provides us with an opportunity to deploy a security control that is seen as quite the opposite of a barrier. Instead, done properly, an IAM programme that is pleasant to interact with, and provides access in a consistent fashion, such as through an enterprise IdP, will be viewed as an enabler. Users won't even realise that the process and platform they're engaging with is a security control, and that is a pretty good measure of success. It's like putting on a seatbelt automatically when you sit in a car. We all know the reasons why we do it, but we don't think of those reasons every time we get in the car. We just know, subconsciously, that it's part of the overall process of getting into a car.

Least privilege

In the context of IAM, the principle of least privilege states that a subject should be afforded the minimum level of access needed to perform the functions required as part of their daily work. We wouldn't want everyone in the entire company having access to payroll information, for example. It's a solid principle, and one that most organisations attempt to align with. The benefit of doing so, other than making it easier to ensure confidentiality, includes reducing the damage that could be done should a set of credentials become compromised.

It seems pretty straightforward, but as with all things, there are challenges associated with implementing this principle. Every application is different, and teams like IT and security need to rely on input from application specialists to determine what the correct permission set looks like in a given application. Some applications, like the HRIS mentioned earlier, have incredibly complex permission sets that are applied and inherited in proprietary fashion. In far too many organisations the default response when a subject is unable to access a specific feature in an application is to 'give them admin'.

In these cases, having a centralised IdP with the ability to pass various attributes for evaluation by the SP so that it can make an informed decision on the permitted access level gives security operations teams a huge advantage.

Role-based access control

The concept of RBAC is another goal that an IAM project can work towards delivering. As you can probably guess, in an RBAC implementation, the idea is that access levels are related directly to the person's position in the organisation. All people with the same role should have the same permissions on the same systems. Any access that falls outside of the RBAC model is considered an exception.

There are a couple of challenges associated with getting RBAC in place. The first is that a lot of organisations don't do a great job of defining roles consistently. For instance, I've worked in an environment where out of just over 1,000 employees there were 680 distinct job titles! This is not a unique situation. I should explain that the root cause of such organisational inconsistency in this particular case was a company that had grown from multiple acquisitions over the years.

Consistency in job titles and roles within an organisation isn't a security problem to fix by any means. It's a business problem, and there are many other reasons why an organisation would do well to make sure they've performed some kind of 'levelling' exercise to group employees who are essentially doing the same job. It becomes easier to set expectations for the role and measure performance, for example. While it may not be our problem to solve, if we get wind of someone attempting to solve it, we can certainly latch on to the process. Personally, I've been through a handful of levelling exercises, with a heads up from human resources (HR) on upcoming job titles and descriptions, which have then been used to map to an RBAC model as part of the same wave of activity. As an aside, HR absolutely loves this because it helps give them an extra justification for commencing what is typically not a very popular exercise, especially for those employees who get 'levelled' down.

In some environments, access levels may not just be influenced by role, but by other subject attributes, such as security clearance level, citizenship status or physical location. A software developer in the Paris office might not be permitted to access data regarding a US customer, but a person holding the same position, on the same team, in the New York office, may be good to go.

The success of an RBAC model can be measured by how many access exceptions exist. The ultimate goal should be to reduce exceptions as much as practicable. Permissions should be applied to groups of subjects, with a common attribute (or attributes) used to generate those groups, rather than individuals. Of course, the reality is that exceptions do occur. Special projects require special permissions. Jane's job role just changed, but she'll still need access to X to train up her replacement for the next couple of months. Exceptions are okay, but only if they're managed properly. That starts with documentation; we should have a record of where and why an exception was granted, as well as when, and when it could be removed. In Jane's case, we should follow up to make sure that we remove her exceptional access after that month is up.

Separation of duties

An IAM programme can also be leveraged as a mechanism for implementing separation of duties rules on highly sensitive processes. Separation of duties is used to prevent a single person from having complete, end-to-end responsibility for a process that, if manipulated or otherwise performed incorrectly, could have damaging results.

In some highly secure environments, separation of duties rules can extend to network engineers who must work in pairs to install new connectivity. One to do the work and the other to validate and record that it has been done properly. This prevents innocent, or not so innocent, mistakes that can lead to cross-connections between environments of differing security classifications. They are also common for people responsible for executing and approving financial transactions, to avoid the risk of fraud or embezzlement.

Thinking back once again to the example discussed when considering data integrity in Chapter 4, where a malicious insider manipulated the contents of a text file to influence bank account transfers in their own favour. A separation of duties requirement in the process would have prevented the incident from occurring.

It should not have been possible for one person to both generate the list of money transfers to be made and then press the buttons to set those transfers in motion. Unfortunately, in this particular example, the process was an old, one-off, inherited one that wasn't widely documented, so the opportunity to implement this was missed.

In the era of DevOps, which brings with it trends such as continuous integration and continuous deployment (CI/CD), the separation of duties concept can find itself with renewed importance. It's long been an accepted security principle that developers of software applications, especially in the case of SaaS applications, should not have access to the code that is running in production. The idea being that those developers cannot make changes in production that would alter the way the code is running, perhaps by introducing a backdoor or otherwise adding a hidden function for nefarious purposes. When we ran in a world of monthly (or perhaps even less frequent) releases and deployments, there was plenty of opportunity for us to place gating steps as code was added to the release. Peer reviews, change controls, security review of sensitive changes and leveraging dedicated deployment engineers to promote code from staging environments to production are all examples of mechanisms that were available to us.

Through CI/CD, we could be releasing multiple times per day, and in the DevOps model, developers are expected to both write and operate their code, so some degree of production access is a must to enable this to happen. Most organisations simply do not have the resources to review every one of these rapid-fire deployments in the same level of detail as they might have done previously, and with developer access to production now an essential business need, security teams might feel rightly nervous about the state of their application security processes.

To allay some of these fears, there are separation of duty steps that can be introduced, even when a DevOps model is in use. These steps have significant tie in to IAM. First of all, no *single* person should be able to both write code and push it to production. Peer review of code should be mandated, and this is frequently performed at a couple of different levels. First, a peer should review the code as it is initially committed into the staging, or feature branch. Second, the master branch that is ultimately deployed to production should require some additional approver input. Production branches should be protected, and a limited number of people should be able to permit code to be added to them.

SCM tools such as GitHub[1] and BitBucket[2] support different roles per development project to enable this type of separation of duties. Security operations should be heavily involved in ensuring that these permissions are appropriately applied and are used to enforce the organisation's policies around software deployment.

Even if a DevOps operational model has been implemented, it's rare that a developer will need full production access at all times. Therefore, a second layer of security can be applied to enhance security post-deployment. A general level of access to production, perhaps to monitoring tools and selected non-sensitive hosts could be afforded to the developer for day-to-day use; then, having a process in place for the developer to temporarily elevate permissions to that of an administrative-level user, to permit detailed troubleshooting and fully gain access to data in the environment. All such elevations should be logged, sent to the SIEM suite and stored as events. As these events are correlated with other events involving the developer's activity, they may be correlated with others that could raise alarms and trigger a response.

Leveraging frequent deployments and allowing developers into production may be modern approaches, but they still rely on good old-fashioned security principles, like separation of duties and least privilege, to be done in the most secure manner possible.

Multifactor authentication

No corporate system containing any amount of non-public information should be exposed to the internet without MFA enabled. The risk of compromised credentials being leveraged to gain unauthorised access to that system is simply too great. Significant numbers of user credentials become compromised daily, through activities such as phishing, compromise of authentication databases and malware infections, to name but a few. Password reuse is a habit that many are guilty of, which introduces the risk of credential stuffing, an attack in which the attacker leverages credential sets from a compromised application to login to another.

To counter these risks, MFA, also known as two-factor or two-step authentication, is the go-to control. MFA requires the user to supply two or more of the different types of authentication factor, which are listed below.

- something you know; a password;
- something you have; a one-time password, authentication code, smart card or universal second factor (U2F) device;
- something you are; a biometric identifier like a fingerprint.

In security operations, we're frequently charged with deploying and maintaining the enterprise MFA strategy as part of the overall IAM programme. When initially deploying MFA, we'll need a little help. Teams like our old friends in IT and network engineering will have a significant role to play in ensuring the success of the deployment. We might even need the support of internal training and development professionals, to create materials that educate our users on how MFA works.

Priority should be given to systems that afford remote access to private networks, such as virtual private networks (VPNs), as well as externally accessible browser-based email clients, and any other exposed applications that may permit access to non-public information. But, ultimately, the goal should be to enforce MFA on all systems that are accessible via the internet. There should be no path of least resistance for a malicious actor.

Services like email may afford different mechanisms for accessing the same data, for example, a browser-based email client, or a protocol such as IMAP. It's important to ensure that all avenues to the same data are protected with MFA accordingly.

Selecting a second factor

One of the most important considerations to be made when deploying MFA is which second factor type(s) will be supported and how they'll be implemented. For instance, a one-time password could be delivered via an SMS message or it could be generated on a dedicated hardware token; a smartphone authenticator application could also be an option. The decision on which route is taken usually comes down to budget, and consideration of any specific regulatory or legal needs for a given implementation. In this particular example, SMS would likely be the cheapest option to implement, since most people would already have a device capable of receiving an SMS message; yet concerns about the security of SMS as a delivery mechanism for authentication codes, and outright restrictions on it in some guidelines and standards, might push an enterprise towards the smartphone authenticator instead.

Through 2016 and into mid-2017, NIST was busy preparing a document named *Digital Identity Guidelines: Authentication and Lifecycle Management* (Grassi et al., 2017).

In July 2016, early drafts of the document caused headlines when NIST declared that the use of SMS as a second-factor delivery mechanism was 'deprecated'. Many in the industry picked up on the declaration, and spun up stories about how SMS was no longer an acceptable mechanism for second-factor authentication. The result was that NIST had to issue clarifying statements a few days later, softening their stance. The language that made it into the final version of the document was also toned down.

The reasoning behind the message to move away from SMS-based two factor authentication includes on-the-record exploitation of Signalling System 7 (SS7) vulnerabilities in cellular networks to intercept SMS messages. SS7 is a set of protocols developed in the 1970s that are used by telecommunications providers on private signalling networks to set up and tear down calls. Unfortunately, the protocol suite itself doesn't have any built-in security features, since, when it was conceived, the idea of people leveraging the internet to obtain access to those private signalling networks and manipulating the signalling calls wasn't on anyone's radar. If a malicious actor gains access to a provider's SS7 system through a misconfigured firewall or weak administrative username and password, they stand a very good chance of being able to manipulate it into disclosing information on a subscriber which can be used to reroute calls and messages.

Additionally, the fact that many SMS integrated messaging platforms, such as Apple's iMessage product, allow an SMS message to be delivered to multiple devices, increases the possible exposure of any authentication code. Social engineering attacks against mobile network carriers, in which an attacker tricks a carrier into associating a given mobile phone number with a different SIM card, are also a widely acknowledged risk.

While these risks, and NIST's initial stance, prove that SMS can be a flawed mechanism for MFA, especially in high-security situations, it's still better than no MFA at all. The fact that SMS allows any mobile device, smartphone or otherwise, to be leveraged as an authentication mechanism, still makes it a compelling option for many applications and enterprises.

U2F

U2F is an authentication standard supported by a number of hardware authentication devices that leverage USB or near field communications (NFC) connectivity, without the need for specific device drivers. By not requiring device drivers or any other specific software to be preinstalled for the authentication hardware, U2F tokens such as those made by Yubico (Figure 6.1) work seamlessly across a wide variety of platforms, dramatically reducing the complexity of any deployment.

The U2F standard was developed by Google and Yubico, but is now maintained by the FIDO alliance.[3] The standard leverages public key cryptography in a challenge-response authentication pattern to authenticate the user. While typically leveraged as a second factor in addition to a traditional password, the standard is also being leveraged as a password replacement in some organisations.

Figure 6.1 Yubikey U2F hardware (Lightning and USB form factor) (Source: Yubico Press Room Images & Logos. https://www.yubico.com/press/images/)

Maintaining MFA

Like any user-facing process, an MFA deployment will require ongoing support and maintenance work. Depending on the specific organisation, these tasks may be performed within security operations, or in some cases delegated to IT support. Obviously, the size of those respective organisations plays a role in that decision, and security teams tend to be smaller than IT support teams.

Tasks that fall into this category include resetting a user association with an MFA device (if you leverage smartphone apps, this can be a daily task as people upgrade and change devices) and troubleshooting synchronisation issues between the MFA device and the IdP. Security operations will typically take charge of monitoring MFA activity for abnormalities (such as a spike in failed attempts) that may indicate an attempt to gain unauthorised access to an account.

IAM TOOLS

Beyond MFA, there are a variety of technologies we can deploy in support of our IAM strategy. Tools exist that support access request and approval workflows, automate account provisioning and deprovisioning tasks, provide centralised identity management and SSO, and perform regular auditing of permissions levels assigned to users.

The identity management industry is sizable, and a variety of cloud-based solution providers have popped up in recent years with product offerings capable of performing some or all of these tasks. Given the complexities associated with managing IAM, in even a relatively small organisation, an IAM tool is usually high up on the list of desired security purchases.

Cloud-based identity

OneLogin,[4] Okta[5] and Auth0[6] are three examples of cloud-based identity SPs competing with each other for the affections of security operations and IT teams around the globe. All three of their products allow for various features to be enabled and disabled in a modular fashion. These features include the following.

Single sign-on

Identity management tools enable enterprises to extend their centralised identity directories, such as Microsoft Active Directory, beyond the boundaries of the corporate firewall. SSO functionality can then be easily bolted on to existing user identities, through protocols such as SAML.

SAML is a mechanism for exchanging authentication and authorisation information between the IdP and an SP. To get this working, the administrator of the SP and the IdP administrator must first get together and share some initial information. The IdP administrator will provide an X.509 certificate that will be used by the IdP to sign incoming assertions. That certificate will be stored by the SP for later evaluation. Other information exchanged at this stage includes a globally unique entity ID, which allows the SP to uniquely identify the IdP, and various redirection URLs to control user entry and exit points for both the SP and IdP. Once both sides have shared the requisite information to configure SAML, the application is ready for SSO.

When it's time to login using SAML, the user can trigger an authentication request through the SP or the IdP, a flow known as SP-initiated or IdP-initiated SAML respectively.

In an SP-initiated flow (see Figure 6.2), the SP determines that the user is associated with an IdP and redirects the user to their IdP. If the user has an active session with their IdP (say they logged in to the IdP when they logged into their machine) and the user is authorised to access the SP requesting the login, the IdP will build and send a SAML assertion to the SP. The assertion is an XML document containing the user's information, including their name, user identifier and other attributes. The assertion is signed using the certificate exchanged between the IdP administrator and SP administrator previously.

Figure 6.2 An SP-initiated SAML flow

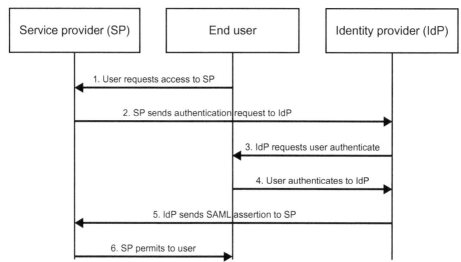

In the IdP-initiated flow, the user will typically click on a link within the IdP (since they're already logged in), which will generate the assertion and redirect the user to the SP.

The security advantages to SSO include the ability to enforce consistent authentication requirements (such as password policies or MFA) across a multitude of applications, even when they're hosted outside the enterprise's private environment. SSO also means that it's possible for security operations teams to disable a subject's access to all enterprise applications with a single click. There is no more reviewing the list of user accounts associated with each SaaS application and manually disabling the account, which is a huge time saver, and reduces the opportunity for accounts to be missed.

Provisioning and deprovisioning
The first couple of weeks at any new job are stressful. The change in environment, the new faces and the pressure of trying to fit in to a team that may have been together for years all take their toll. To make things worse, orientation and access provisioning processes are often slow-going affairs, which means it can take a couple of weeks

before you get the access you need to be successful in your new position. In some cases, it can take a few days just to find out who you need to talk to, to request access to a specific system. It's for this reason that cloud-based identity management tools make automating provisioning and deprovisioning tasks a major selling point.

These processes might once again sit somewhere between IT and security operations, but security operations have a vested interest in making sure they're automated, and automated well. Automation leads to consistency, and also enhances the orientation experience for the new employee. If your first experience with a corporate security team is to ask for access to a system, and it is provided to you in a timely fashion through a well-run process, you're probably going to be a very happy customer of that security team. This builds trust between both parties, and in security we know how valuable that trust is down the line.

Every SP will have its own set of provisioning and deprovisioning flows, and they'll be triggered in different ways. Perhaps a series of APIs can be called to create a new account and later remove it, or maybe a just-in-time model is used to create an account upon receiving the first SAML assertion for a new user from the IdP. To differentiate themselves, cloud-based identity management suites are constantly in a race to build integrations that make provisioning tasks as simple as selecting a check box for a given SP. The most popular SPs are frequently integrated first, given the size of the potential audience, while less widely used applications might need to be integrated in a manual fashion.

Birth-right access is a term used to describe a level of access granted to a person upon their 'birth' into the organisation. In other words, no approval is required, you just get access to the particular system. Birth-right access can be truly global (i.e. everyone in the organisation gets it) or based on a RBAC model (i.e. everyone with a particular job title gets it). Active Directory accounts, soft phone numbers and email mailboxes are common examples of birth-right assignments in many organisations. A cloud-based IdP will allow the assignment of such roles through a rules engine. Attributes associated with the user will allow the IdP to evaluate which birth-right provisioning tasks should be performed by the IdP.

Automated deprovisioning of access is just as, if not more, important to get right. People come and go from, or simply change roles within an organisation, on a continuous basis. Adjusting permissions to align with a person's current role in a timely fashion is a critical security control, but one that is often overlooked. It's not uncommon to find the highest tenured employee is the one with the most privileges on a given system, as permissions have been added to roles, but never removed.

In the majority of cases, a departure is on good terms, and the person leaving just wants to move on to the next chapter of their professional life. In others, the departure may not be so cordial. It's in these cases where it's vital to make sure that an aggrieved former insider's access is removed as soon as possible.

All of the cloud-based IdPs discussed above offer integrations with several popular HRIS systems, and are aware of the different types of termination that can be applied to a given user. This means that access can be appropriately removed, and accounts can be deprovisioned on a timeline appropriate for the termination. For instance, in the case of a voluntary termination, where an employee is moving on and working a notice period, the HRIS administrator will enter the employee's last day into the HRIS. Access will remain in place until the end of that day (this can be configured), and then deprovisioning activities will commence.

In the case of an involuntary termination, in other words, the employee is being told that today is going to be their last day with the company, the HRIS can trigger a real-time termination notification to the IdP, as long as the HRIS administrator updates the employee record. That real-time notification can begin the process of removing access immediately.

Of course, the reason we want to remove an ex-employee's access as quickly as possible is to prevent the continued use of that access beyond the period of their employment with the company. A former insider that is not deprovisioned quickly enough is now an outsider with insider access, and that is a situation we strive to prevent on a daily basis.

Access request and approval
While birth-right access and RBAC should take care of the overwhelming majority of access needs, there are going to be cases where exceptional access is requested, or perhaps there is another business reason to request access on a case-by-case basis. For example, perhaps an organisation has a limited number of user licences for a particular application, and wants to stay within that limit. In such cases, IdP can track the request, approval and assignment of the associated access. Many of them use an 'app-store' like model, in which the user can 'shop' for applications that are relevant to their position, and either self-serve, or request permission to install the application.

These tools also record a highly important audit trail, which lists all the approvals a person requested and got before they were provisioned into an SP. In the case of sensitive, perhaps financially relevant systems, this is an important investigative tool, and may even be required by applicable regulatory and compliance standards. The audit trail proves that the appropriate oversight was performed before access was provisioned, and means that we can quickly tell which systems a person has access to in the case that their account becomes compromised. We will not have this ability without an audit trail.

In far too many organisations, the way access is granted to a system is what I like to call walk-up provisioning, where a person walks up to an identified system owner and asks for access. Most people in that situation want to be helpful so provide the access, but don't record that they've done so. Having a well-defined and well-managed set of IAM processes and tools empowers those system owners to say, 'just put a request in with security and it'll be done pretty quickly', which can avoid serious issues later.

Contextual authentication
IdPs have been delegated the responsibility of taking care of authentication for a wide variety of SPs, so they're a very good place to apply traditional authentication policies. Contextual authentication takes this a step further and allows us to dynamically evaluate an authentication request, based on factors such as: the device type the user is attempting to authenticate from; the geo-located source location of the authentication event (down to the country, or even city level); or perhaps whether this is the first time a given user has been seen on a particular IP address.

This is tremendously powerful stuff. We can apply additional rigour to authentication events occurring from newly seen IP addresses, perhaps requiring three factors instead of two. Leveraging a tie in with our MDM solution, we could deny access to a particular application if it comes from a personal device rather than a company-owned one.

Plugins exist to take this level of integration down to the endpoint and server level, meaning our IdP could be used to apply MFA to internal systems, a very good idea in the case of database servers, for example.

No clouds allowed?

It would be naïve to think a cloud-based solution works for all environments, and due to the security requirements of some, there just isn't a workable path to leveraging a cloud-based IdP. On-premises versions of these tools, including Microsoft Active Directory Federation Services (ADFS), are also available, which offer some of the features described above.

Identity management is a space where I think the SaaS model makes complete sense, since new updates and integrations can be added at a pace that is just not possible in an internally hosted product. Of course, there are drawbacks to cloud too. Throwing all your identity eggs into one cloud-shaped basket can cause major problems if the SP goes down, leaving you without direct insight into how quickly the problem can be resolved.

Inverse logging

In Chapter 5 we talked about logging credentials on server platforms for the purposes of flagging anomalous access events relating to a given subject's user account. What can be equally valuable, from a preventive control perspective, are the logs that aren't generated. This may seem a bit off the wall, but bear with me.

If access is afforded to a person, but a period of time, say 60 days, goes by without that access being leveraged, it seems reasonable to ask whether they really need it. The majority of SPs allow you to track the last time an account was used. Having a policy around so-called 'dormant' accounts and a process to handle them is highly recommended. If an account isn't used for 60 days, notify the user it will be disabled within the next 48 hours. If they really need it, they'll object. In my experience they won't, and they won't even remember that they've had the access assigned. This reduces the overall attack surface in a given SP and can even save money on licence costs. Anytime security operations saves an organisation money is a good time to be in security operations.

CHECKS AND BALANCES

Even the most proficient organisations with the most mature IAM processes in place can still be victims of things like drive-by provisioning, and people working outside defined processes. It's a fact that most people come to work to do a job and want to break down perceived barriers to doing that job as quickly as possible.

For this reason, a series of checks and balances should be in place to ensure what is being reported to the security team reflects reality. This can be done in a couple of technical and non-technical ways.

First of all, security operations should be on the lookout for shadow-IT-type usage of new applications that might not fall under existing IAM policies. We're monitoring the environment, so, just like any other type of threat, we should be able to detect an increase in usage of a such tools. We can then respond and work with the people using those tools to get them into the right processes if appropriate, or prevent future use of the particular application.

Second, each application should be reviewed on a given schedule to ensure that the people who actually have access to the application tally with those that security is aware of through IAM audit trails. This task is usually performed by an internal compliance team (as quite frequently it's a requirement to ensure compliance with a given standard), but, depending on the size of the organisation, it might fall to security operations. Any discrepancies should be investigated as security incidents (recall that an incident is the act of violating a policy). A good rule of thumb is that sensitive systems are audited on a quarterly basis, but every environment is different and subject to various rules and controls.

This two-pronged approach, driving people to obtain access in as easy a manner as possible, and owning the IAM process, while still checking our working on a defined schedule, is truly some of the most important work security operations can do. Throughout this chapter, I've talked about how these tasks might traditionally fall between IT, security and compliance. If you're not happy with the state of IAM at your enterprise and another team is primarily responsible for it, my advice is to attempt to seize control of the process, or at the very least offer to improve it. This will help the enterprise to be more secure in a very measurable way, and it will help with other more security operations-centric tasks, such as incident response and day-to-day event monitoring.

SUMMARY

At the start of this chapter, we looked at the increasing relevance of IAM in the world of applications that reside outside the corporate network, such as SaaS products. I introduced some common terminology associated with IAM programmes, including SP and IdP.

We then reviewed some of the key IAM concepts that are the goals of any IAM programme, including applying the principle of least privilege, leveraging RBAC and deploying MFA.

We talked about cloud-based IdPs that offer multiple features to make IAM processes as effective as possible, including SSO, automated workflow provisioning and contextual authentication. We discussed the importance of knowing when provisioned access is not being leveraged, so it can be removed.

Finally, we talked about applying checks and balances to identify any access that has been provisioned outside IAM workflows, and the importance of detecting application usage that is not approved by the organisation.

The next chapter focuses on a topic that in many cases is directly related to IAM, security incident response. As discussed above, common causes of security incidents include compromised credentials, and how well we've performed the IAM work discussed in this chapter can have a direct bearing on how quickly we can respond to a security incident. That's why IAM is so important to do well, and forms a major part of the modern security operations team's responsibilities.

REFERENCE

Grassi, P.A., Fenton, J.L., Newton, E.M., Perlner, R.A., Regenscheid, A.R., Burr, W.E. and Richer, J.P. (2017) *Digital Identity Guidelines: Authentication and Lifecycle Management.* NIST Special Publication 800-63B. Available at: https://pages.nist.gov/800-63-3/sp800-63b.html

7   INCIDENT DETECTION AND RESPONSE

Key objectives of the blue team, through all the daily work discussed in the opening chapters of this book, are preventing security incidents from occurring by enforcing security policy at a technical level, detecting conditions that might indicate an incident is occurring, and investigating and responding accordingly when those conditions occur. Prevention is the primary objective, of course, and if we're able to successfully prevent an incident occurring, we've really earned our keep that day. However, it's a truth that many in our industry will attest to, that just when you think you're on top of everything, something new pops up and seeks to catch you out. It's on these occasions that the ability to detect and respond become just as important as the ability to prevent.

Incident response should never be seen as an indicator of failure. Yes, it's a high-pressure situation, and things have probably not gone entirely as we'd like if we're at the point of having to respond to a security incident, but it should still be considered an opportunity to get things right. Security incidents can go from 'less than ideal' to extremely bad if the response portion of the situation is not executed properly.

This is why executing well-defined plans and procedures that are in place, that outline exactly what constitutes a security incident, testing those procedures frequently, and generally being ready to respond at a moment's notice are perhaps the most critical functions of the blue team.

In this chapter we'll review the role of security operations as it relates to incident detection and response. We'll look at tools such as SIEM, which are some of our most effective detection tools, if they're correctly configured. We'll talk about non-technical indicators and the ways that incidents may manifest themselves to the security operations team, other than via a computer screen. Next, we'll consider different organisational structures, including how the security operations team would align with a dedicated incident response team if one is present. Finally, we'll talk about the transition from security incident to digital forensics investigation, and the role the security operations team can play in aiding that process.

SECURITY INCIDENT BASICS

As I mentioned in the early pages of this book, incident response is a complex topic with many components that can, and have, filled many pages of many books. This chapter focuses on how security operations teams fit in to the incident response process, since a lot of the time we'll be the ones triggering, and following it. With that in mind, let's jump into the security incident basics: a quick overview of what a security incident is, some common incident types, the phases of a security incident response and the role of the incident response playbook.

Security incident overview

In Chapter 1 I referenced the NIST definition of a security incident, which as a reminder, was 'the act of violating an explicit or implied security policy'. As technologists, we can sometimes scoff at the importance of policies. I've heard, from others, and admittedly myself at certain points during my career, the expression, 'policies aren't going to stop someone compromising us'. I get that mindset. No malicious actor ever stopped to read the login warning banner before they attempted to brute force their way into an internet accessible machine running RDP. What policies do is give us a baseline from which we can classify deviations, and the NIST definition of an incident is a perfect example of that.

It might be an incredibly bad idea for an employee to store a copy of database credentials in a personally owned Google Drive account and share the file with others via an open link. Negligent, even, and perhaps something worthy of dismissal. Unless there is a policy in place stating that this type of activity is strictly against the rules, it's hard to guarantee that any corrective action can be taken.

Policies will differ from one environment to the other, which means an activity that constitutes a violation in policy at one organisation will not necessarily be classified as such at another. This is yet another reason why policies are so important. If those credentials in the example mentioned above were for a database containing protected healthcare information, then the person sharing them so recklessly would very likely be in violation of several policies (and definitely regulatory requirements). If, however, the database contained only public information, then that changes the context significantly.

In security operations we might not be the people writing the policies, and we probably are more than okay with that. However, we should have input into them, since we're on the front lines and more likely to see exactly what activities are going to lead to problems.

Internal vs. external

Classifying security incidents by their origin is a decent place to start when considering how to detect and respond to them. When you ask people to think about security incidents, most automatically conjure up thoughts of hoodie-clad hackers sitting thousands of miles away attempting to hijack connections, break through authentication layers, or otherwise compromise web-facing servers to get at sensitive data within an organisation. These would all be examples of incidents with external origins; an unauthorised individual on the outside seeking a way in through the use of phishing, malware, exploitation of a web application vulnerability or looking for misconfigured infrastructure.

Conversely, an incident with internal origins begins with an insider who, intentionally or unintentionally, completes an action that results in an incident. Inappropriate handling of credentials (such as in our earlier example), violations of acceptable use policies, attempting to gain access to resources to which they're not authorised, and inappropriate data handling are a few examples of internal incident types. Internal security incidents, if not detected and addressed promptly, can be far more damaging than those with external origins.

To detect incidents with internal origins, security operations needs a lot of insight into internally sensitive materials. This is why trustworthiness is such an important trait for anyone who works in this field. Through DLP alerts you could be among the first to know about an impending acquisition of your company. You may become hyper-aware of an executive's internet browsing habits through log files. You might get to see compensation data for the entire company as it is passed between payroll and HR in email. To be effective at achieving our core objectives of incident prevention, being exposed to this stuff is a side effect. It's a highly privileged position, and one we can't afford to lose.

Incident response process

Security incidents pass through a number of phases during their life cycle. Different security and compliance standards label these phases in different ways, and the exact number of phases may vary, but they generally align with those found in the NIST document SP 800-61 (Kent et al., 2008).

Identification
Before you can respond to a security incident, you must first identify that it is occurring. This is the phase that security operations will likely be involved in most frequently, given that we are tasked with identifying potential security incidents. This phase may also be known as the detection phase.

Containment
To prevent a bad situation from becoming worse, actions should be taken to limit the potential scope of the incident, for example, by disconnecting an infected machine from the network. Depending on how the organisation is set up, security operations might be directly involved in this phase or might direct other teams in support of it.

Eradication
Eradication is the act of removing the source of the incident from the network. Examples of eradication activities include applying a patch to fix a web application vulnerability, or reissuing a set of credentials after they become compromised. Typically, this phase of work will be performed outside security operations by teams that have direct responsibility for the affected systems.

Recovery
Next there is the recovery phase, in which teams work to return to a state of 'business as normal'. Again, the work in this phase will likely be conducted by teams outside security operations, but we might have overall responsibility for declaring that an incident has been officially resolved.

Post-mortem
Following the completion of the recovery process, an incident is considered closed. Still, it's always a wise move to hold an incident 'post-mortem' meeting, to discuss what transpired, how things could have been done better and spin up any additional work that may be required in order to prevent a reoccurrence of the incident. Such meetings are

typically held within a couple of days of the incident being closed, to ensure all relevant information is fresh in everyone's mind.

The playbook

The security incident response playbook is a document that details the company-specific steps that align with each of the phases just discussed. The primary audience for this document includes the individuals and teams that are likely to be involved in running the response. Security operations, as a team at the forefront of any security incident response work, even if not directly involved in the creation of the playbook, should be at least consulted, and even better, have direct input to the document.

Typically, the incident response playbook is collated by a senior or founding member of the information security team, or perhaps those dedicated to incident management work within the organisation. The playbook is built up in an iterative manner over time, and built to align with business-specific processes as much as possible. The goal of incident response (and security in general) is to be slotted in, in such a way as to align with the goals and objectives of the business, not the other way around.

The playbook should be kept up to date to reflect changes in key contacts at the company, updated or new business processes, and any changes to applications and systems in use. It should also be appropriately accessible from a well-known location.

Prior to use in response to a real incident, the playbook should be reviewed and tested. Peer-review, table-top walkthrough exercises, and then scenario-based testing, all form part of this particular life cycle. The involvement of security operations in such reviews is critical to ensure the success of the incident response process, and it also serves as a great training opportunity for analysts.

ORGANISATIONAL STRUCTURE

Just as the seating plan of the security operations team varies from organisation to organisation, so too does the exact role and responsibility of the team during an incident response scenario. In some cases, security operations is the primary security incident response team, in others, we may serve as the first responders who trigger escalations to dedicated security incident responders. Finally, there may be a unified incident response team that is responsible for all incident management, not just security incident management.

It's important to get an understanding of where exactly the team fits in to the overall security and wider organisational structure, because this will have a direct impact on everything from hiring to security tool purchases and the content of procedures that detail how security operations operate. Let's take a look at some common ways security operations may slot in to the organisational structure.

As the dedicated security incident response team

In this model, the security operations team is responsible for the monitoring of the environment, triage of events, escalation and management of security incidents as they occur. In other words, an analyst can own the entire life cycle from detection, through response and driving the resolution.

The advantages of this model are that it exposes the analyst to the various elements of the incident response cycle, and therefore makes the job more varied and interesting. This may allow for better retention. The downside to this is that it is less likely that the analyst will be a specialist in any one aspect of either operations or incident response, which may not align with their career aspirations, or the goals of the security operations team. In which case, having differing roles within the security operations team is a valid option to counter this problem; it just means that you will likely have to employ a greater number of people, which obviously has a budgetary impact.

Another challenge of the model is that if an analyst is working an incident, they're not going to be triaging events for a few hours, or possibly even a couple of days. Building this scenario into your planning and procedures would be necessary to ensure that things aren't missed. The desire to get the analyst back to the front line will have to be countered actively, to prevent key incident details being overlooked in the desire to not allow the next incident to sneak by.

Alongside a dedicated security incident response team

Having a clear distinction between analysts who process events and escalate suspected incidents and the dedicated team of incident responders to whom the events are escalated has many advantages. It allows the incident responders to take over when a detailed investigation is required, allowing the analysts to remain free to work new events as they come in. After all, a security incident occurring does not mean that the potential for another incident automatically diminishes at that same moment.

There are disadvantages to this model too, though. The relationship between the security operations analysts and their counterparts in incident response requires ongoing maintenance. Humans are emotional creatures, and there are a couple of reasons why one side might start to get frustrated with the other. For the security operations analysts, the fact that they hand off the work just as it starts to get very interesting can be a kick in the teeth. For the incident responders, they might feel that the analysts are escalating too much to them, and simply shifting the noise to a different part of the organisation. To overcome this, having a defined career path for those who want to transition from security operations to incident response is a great option for those who wish to follow it. Additionally, having incident responders train and shadow those in the security operations team about what is and isn't worthy of investigation can help build relationships.

Alongside a dedicated incident management team

In some organisations, all incident management may happen through a dedicated incident management team. The scope of that team is not limited just to security incidents, but to network outages, server and application incidents too. Typically, these types of team are embedded in an operations group, which has responsibility for things like change management and problem management also.

In such cases, the most critical aspect of the arrangement is working with the incident management team ahead of time to ensure that all the correct procedures are in place, for escalations and for how security incidents specifically are handled. Generally, in incident management, you'll want to notify as many stakeholders of the incident as quickly as possible, so that they can respond accordingly. When it comes to security incidents, this is less likely to be the case, owing to their sensitivity. This needs to be made very clear before an incident is escalated from security operations. The last thing a security incident needs is information being broadcast too widely before all the facts are known.

Often these types of arrangement require cross-functional work, so having a clear distinction of who is responsible for what is key to setting expectations. A good option is to propose that in the event of a security incident, a security operations team member can assume the role of incident manager, or incident lead. This gives us the best of both worlds. We get to leverage the infrastructure and reach of the incident management team, while maintaining a degree of control over the response.

Ultimately, there is no right or wrong answer here. Every business is unique in terms of priorities and available resources. The structures we've just covered all have advantages and disadvantages. The best advice is to go with the approach that you think makes the best sense, and if you're not happy with it, change things around. This is all part of the learning curve of building out a new function.

SECURITY INCIDENT IDENTIFICATION

Throughout this book I've talked through the various tools and techniques in place to collect events occurring in our environment. As we go about monitoring networks, endpoint devices, servers, applications and identities, the events will start to stream in. While the vast majority of those events will be routine occurrences, there will be those that indicate that something abnormal and unexpected may be occurring. Such events will require investigation, correlation and, if warranted, escalation to 'incident' status.

The best weapon in your arsenal when it comes to knowing what is everyday background noise and what is suspect, are the highly trained analysts. Security products can help these folks work and detect things quicker, but ultimately the human brain and its experiences are without equal.

Security incident and event management

SIEM has been referenced multiple times throughout the book, so it's only fair that we explain exactly what it can and cannot do for us when it comes to incident detection.

The job of the SIEM is to analyse signals from our other tools – network traffic flow data, log files, IDS/IPS alerts, or data from IaaS vendor APIs. Using defined rules and signatures, or perhaps even applying a machine learning algorithm, cross-correlation of these individual events can lead to the creation of security relevant events. Most SIEM tools then attempt to rank these events in order of severity on your behalf.

Next, the SIEM will typically include escalation and incident management workflow features, allowing an analyst to 'claim' a particular event as their own, and promote it to an incident within a few clicks. Using such workflows allows for highly specific tracking and generation of metrics such as time to respond and how long a particular event was investigated before it was resolved. Metrics like these provide hard data that can be used to make staffing and budgetary arguments. So, although the process might seem a bit long-winded if your event count is high, there is plenty of value in using it.

Integrations with other ticketing systems allow relevant information to break out of the SIEM and be exposed to other teams who may need to become involved in the incident response.

The main selling point of the SIEM is that it provides a 'single pane of glass' for analysts who otherwise might need to jump from one system to another, thus, saving time, and reducing the opportunity for correlating events to be missed. The expression 'single pane of glass' comes from overhyped marketing terminology, but in this case it does actually reflect the goal of the product in quite a nice, memorable way.

What the SIEM vendor salesperson or marketing department won't tell you, is that the overwhelming majority of SIEM deployments are never fully completed to the extent that they should be. Effective SIEM tool deployments require interaction with a wide variety of other teams, including IT, networking, application teams and perhaps even HR if identities are added in real time. Deployments take time, and the longer it takes to deploy any tool, the more likely it is that the deployment will fail.

SIEMs require constant maintenance and updating to stay relevant. A change to a particular log format here and there can totally throw a SIEM off the trail if it is not expecting a field to be adjusted. Similarly, if a logging source stops sending data for any reason, perhaps because a system was shut down, or rebuilt, the result is gaps in data that are hard to recover from. Ensuring that SIEMs are configured to alert when they don't receive data from an expected source within a few minutes is a key control to prevent this situation. Staying on top of new logging formats and tuning SIEMs to detect new event types can make up a significant chunk of work for the security operations team.

SIEMs can be particularly expensive too. Many enterprise security tools come at inflated cost, as there is an assumption that security teams have a massive tool budget. Software and support are significant recurring expenses. The hardware resources required to run said software can also be extensive. It takes a lot of RAM and CPU to crunch the numbers, and it takes a lot of disk to store all those chatty log files. As the logging and monitoring needs of an organisation only tend increase over time, so too do these processing and storage needs. This growth should be factored in and considered when signing up with a SIEM vendor.

The reason I mention the negative aspects of SIEM solutions is not some personal vendetta against the SIEM industry. Instead it's to point out that SIEMs are not silver bullets that you can plug in one day and expect to get instant results. They can certainly make our lives easier, allow us to detect and investigate things more quickly, but cannot detect every security incident with complete certainty. Also, as the expression goes, 'garbage in, garbage out'. You have to be confident that the data you're feeding the SIEM is high quality and reliable, because if not, the data you get out of it won't be either. It's for this reason I consider SIEM tools to be a 'secondary' purchase, once the core network, endpoint and server monitoring and protection tools are in place. I'd even place an IdP solution higher on the list of priorities. There is no doubt though, once these foundational components are in place and producing actionable data, having a SIEM to wrangle it all is a tremendously valuable asset.

Building detections that fit

One of the most effective ways that a security operations team can deliver instant value to their organisation, and deliver a good service, is to build custom incident detection mechanisms that are directly relevant to the business we're supporting. We can find ourselves spending a lot of time concentrating on indicators of compromise, network traffic flows and attempts to find vulnerabilities in our applications through scanning; but, some of the worst, most damaging security incidents from a customer perspective can hide in plain sight, embedded deep within legitimate traffic that is accessing our services.

I'm referring to incidents that occur within the business logic of our applications. Things like fraudulent transactions and the general misuse of our services for purposes that weren't intended. For example, leveraging storage space provided for documents to host illegal images or using chat features to abuse and harass. If we, as a blue team, can develop hooks into our applications to detect these kinds of events, and pull them into the SIEM alongside all the technical events, we start to offer a whole new level of value.

One of my favourite examples of building a custom detection right into an application occurred when I was managing security operations at a US company that ran a travel booking application. We were called in by our customer support team for assistance on an incident in which a couple of customers found themselves being billed for travel they'd never booked. The customers, based in the United States, had been charged for tickets issued for travel between two cities in Africa.

We began by looking at the activity logs for the user accounts that had actually been used to book the travel, and within a few minutes we could very easily tell that something was suspicious. Having logged in from a single US-based IP address for the past couple of years, suddenly, the user had a login event from an IP in South Africa. This pattern repeated itself on our second user that had reported the same behaviour. Further review of the users' sign-in configuration revealed that they were using a corporate SSO portal, which provided access to our application via SAML.

Working with the customer's security team, we were able to determine that the user had been phished a couple of days before the bookings were made. Unfortunately, since the customer was not enforcing MFA, the password was all the attacker needed to gain access to not just the victim's account, but all the applications connected to it via SSOs.

While we were investigating these initial cases, another popped up, and then another. All followed exactly the same pattern. We provided guidance to our customers to enable MFA on their SSO portals as soon as possible, but we wanted to do more. That's when we saw the person booking the tickets always followed the same URL pattern to book the travel, and always logged in from a particular range of IP addresses.

We used the authentication event from that range of IP addresses, combined with the URL pattern and a custom application log that our development team was able to put together for us to generate a very specific event type in our SIEM. If we saw authentication success from the IP range, combined with access to the booking flow, combined with an origin city in Africa – we'd get an alert instantly. We could then jump in and shut down the booking. Eventually, we even automated that part.

Within the first 12 months, we'd blocked around $125,000 worth of fraudulent bookings using this method. Our customers liked us, and so did our executives.

Non-technical detection

Not all incidents show up as events or incidents in logs or SIEM tools. In many cases, as in the anecdote above, they're brought to us by the end users of our systems, who've noticed something strange, or want to run something by us. Of course, there are also cases when they are sure they've fallen for a phishing scam and need to know what to do next. Throughout the opening chapters of this book, we talked about building trust and rapport with our users. This is exactly why that is so important. We need them to be our extended eyes and ears, and having a user base that is unafraid to come to security for help is a very powerful thing.

HR giving you the heads up that they're investigating some possible misconduct or the police or other government agency showing up at the office, are other examples of non-technical incident detection.

Events and incidents will come to security operations through these channels, which means we need to be prepared when that happens. Do we have a well-publicised contact for internal and external folks to report things to us? A surprising number of organisations do not. Who is on point to work with government agencies or law enforcement? Do the folks who monitor company social media accounts know how to recognise, and respond to, a security incident report? What happens when we receive such a report or visit? These are all examples of questions that should be fully answered, with those answers baked into security operations daily procedures, and included in the incident response playbook.

In January 2019, Grant Thompson, a 14-year-old from Arizona, made a shocking discovery. He identified a major flaw in Apple's widely used FaceTime video calling service that allowed eavesdropping on a device owned by a call recipient, even if that recipient hadn't answered the incoming FaceTime call.

When Grant, and his mother Michele Thompson, attempted to report the issue, they ran into a common problem. While Apple had a bug bounty programme that permits security researchers to submit discovered flaws to Apple in return for financial compensation, the programme and reporting mechanism were geared towards those who had enrolled with Apple as developers, and not everyday members of the public.

Leveraging a number of different avenues, Michele Thompson attempted to let Apple know about the serious vulnerability. Emails to Apple product security, Twitter and Facebook posts were all sent Apple's way, but for a week she struggled to get any sort of response. She was told to register as a developer (a privilege that costs $99 a year) to leverage the formal reporting structure.

Ultimately the right person at Apple became aware of the flaw about 1 week after the initial report was made, and saw that it was prioritised to be fixed. The full fix took a couple of weeks; however, through an incident response process, Apple was able to contain the flaw by disabling the 'Group FaceTime' feature that had introduced it.

This is a great example of a non-technical incident detection type, and something that occurs with more frequency than you'd probably expect. Apple had a lot of the right things in place, including the bug bounty programme and a defined reporting path. However, by not making it as easy as possible to leverage that reporting path, they were doing themselves a huge disservice, and missed an opportunity to quickly address a critical software vulnerability.

ON-CALL

Security incidents don't always occur during business hours. This is a truth both I, and my wife, who doesn't work in information security, can attest to. Unless you have a security operations team working shifts to provide 24-7 coverage, a luxury many of us don't have, then this typically means an on-call rotation is established.

Having on-call responsibilities is a pretty significant undertaking for any information security professional, and one that requires a level of planning, training and expectation setting from both the employee and the employer that can sometimes be overlooked. To put this another way, if the extent of a security operations team's on-call procedures is to include the line 'must partake in an on-call rotation' in an analyst's job description, then a few pieces of detail are missing that are extremely important.

Employers need to recognise that asking someone to be on-call, all day every day, for a prescribed period, usually a week, causes significant disruption to their life. This is why we should be setting expectations around this, and documenting things like 'how frequently will I be on-call?', 'when should on-call be activated?', 'what event types warrant an on-call response?', 'how soon should the on-call person be expected to respond?' and 'who is backup if the primary on-call person cannot respond quickly enough?'

It is also important to define the paths to activate the on-call resource: for instance, a dedicated phone number that forwards to a mobile phone, or a paging application that triggers SMS messages by automated means, such as an integration to initiate a page when a SIEM sees a particular type of event. You can't allow a barrage of messaging, email or phone calls from anyone in the company who decides that what they're doing at that moment warrants immediate response. The on-call person will become overwhelmed and less effective, and might even want to leave altogether.

Worse than a poorly defined on-call process is what I like to call a 'stealth on-call' process – the notion that there is an unwritten expectation to respond out of hours within a certain time. Personally, I'm the type of person who is checking emails at a regular interval at all hours of the day (unless I'm making a conscious effort not to), and typically responding as soon as I've read the email. If that's my choice, then that is fine. However, it's not fair to expect everyone in security operations (or any other team) to respond quickly at all hours, every day. People need to be allowed to switch off, and as a leader of a security operations team, one of the best things you can do for your team is make this explicit. Ensure your on-call procedures include the statement, 'there is no expectation to respond out of hours, unless you are on-call and following the on-call procedures and guidelines'.

FIRST RESPONDERS

Owing to the nature of our position and responsibilities within the organisation, security operations analysts are likely to find themselves serving in the role of first responder to a security incident. That's a very good thing, and something that we want to be the case. Anyone in an enterprise can find themselves acting as first responder, and we should prepare them for that eventuality, but the level of training and expertise that an analyst brings to the role will of course surpass that of a non-technical user.

The role of the first responder can be summarised as collecting the appropriate information and notifying the correct people. Of course, there is a bit more to it than that. Being an effective first responder involves knowing what *not* to do when responding to a security incident. For example, we wouldn't want our first responders taking actions that could potentially impact our ability to fully understand what has occurred and therefore respond appropriately. A common example of this is panicking after a malware infection is detected and deleting files in an attempt to remove the infection, rather than isolating the host from the network and enabling time to be taken to understand the full extent of the damage caused by the malware.

As an incident evolves into a digital forensics investigation, the actions taken by the first responder can have significant impact on the availability and reliability of evidence available to the digital forensics investigator. Whenever we begin responding to a security incident, we should be of the mindset that it might evolve into a digital forensics investigation, and that the investigation might one day have to be defended in a court of law. It seems a little dramatic, but adopting this mindset will encourage behaviour such as documenting steps taken during the incident, and the rationale behind taking those steps.

One of the greatest traits of any first responder, whether they have a technical background or not, is knowing when to stop and ask for help. Often, especially in this industry, there is a hesitation to admit that you might not feel completely qualified to complete a given task, or to ask for guidance because of concerns regarding how you'll be perceived. Well, the truth is that it's a lot more dangerous and damaging to proceed when there are doubts, than to raise them. In information security and incident response everyone is continually learning. If you're in a leadership role in security, you should be working to create an environment in which people are comfortable asking questions and seeking advice.

THE SECURITY OPERATIONS CENTRE

I talked briefly about the SOC at the very beginning of this book. The SOC is a dedicated room in which the security operations team goes about its business. The SOC is frequently adorned with large monitors that allow analysts to keep monitoring data around crucial systems in their eyeline at all times. Depending on the nature of the organisation, the type of environment being protected, budget and, of course, physical constraints of the buildings that house the teams, we may or may not sit in a SOC.

I've worked in environments with and without a dedicated SOC. There are advantages and disadvantages to both approaches. Perhaps the most significant advantage of a dedicated SOC comes when an incident is detected and the response begins. Incidents are sensitive occurrences, and care must be taken to ensure that information related to the incident is carefully controlled and disseminated as needed. When the responders are working together in a specific room or section of a building, they can talk more freely without fearing that information will be exposed to the wrong people.

The disadvantages of the SOC include the fact that they're typically access controlled, for the reason we just described. They put up very real barriers between the security operations team and others in the organisation. Since we're trying to be a service-oriented, user-facing team, this can be somewhat counterproductive.

Ultimately, the factors described above will all be considered when deciding upon the physical housing of the security operations team. Whichever setting is in place will have a bearing on the incident response playbook, and the mechanisms used to ensure all parties are communicating effectively during a response.

DIGITAL FORENSICS

Incident response and digital forensics investigations have a tricky relationship. One often leads to or from the other, and they share a lot of common goals; however, there is one key difference. Incident response is all about eradication and getting things back to normal. Let's blow away this server and restore it from backup as quickly as possible, for example. Digital forensics, on the other hand, relies on evidence preservation and a meticulous scientific process to ensure that the findings of any investigation are reliable, and admissible as evidence. In the era of always-on services, the desire to get things running again can often usurp the need to preserve things in a manner that will allow us to investigate with the level of rigour we'd like. Being first responders in security incidents, we should be aware of this balance, and take appropriate steps during the response to ensure we don't lose forensic opportunities. If an employee causes an incident by violating an acceptable use policy, for instance, we'll need to collect evidence to support any disciplinary actions that are coming their way.

Security operations analysts are likely not going to be the ones performing an in-depth forensic analysis of digital evidence, but as first responders, they can play a significant role in the success of any investigation. Sometimes, a savvy first responder, or analyst on the phone bridge, can be all that stands in the way of losing an important preservation opportunity. Once again, we should review our environment and our procedures, and consider how we might build in hooks and opportunities to preserve evidence for forensics once the dust has settled.

Unlike incident response, where for the most part, organisations are free to define and adopt their own procedures, the rules of admission around digital evidence are strictly governed by the law of the land. Having someone involved in the incident who is aware of these rules and the steps that must be taken to ensure they are followed is hugely advantageous, whether or not they are attached directly to security operations. If you have a dedicated incident response function within security, it seems logical that the members of that team would be trained in digital forensics techniques as a minimum.

SUMMARY

In this chapter, we focused on how security operations can play different roles in the security incident response process, depending upon organisational structure. We examined an overview of the incident response process and the different types of incident that may occur during the course of daily operations.

We talked about the SIEM, a primary example of a technical detection tool that is leveraged by many security operations teams. This included adding value by building enterprise-specific detections that hook into the business processes associated with the enterprise. We then touched on non-technical ways in which incidents may be detected.

Next, we covered on-call procedures, the importance of the first responder role and the difference being housed in a SOC can make to how a security operations team handles an incident.

Finally, we introduced some basic digital forensics concepts, and the importance of ensuring that we don't lose out on the opportunity to conduct a digital forensics investigation once an incident has been addressed.

The next chapter concentrates on a blue team task that can have a direct and significant impact on the likelihood of a security incident occurring in the first place, vulnerability management.

REFERENCE

Kent, K., Grance, T. and Masone, K. (2008) *Computer Security Incident Handling Guide*. US Dept. of Commerce, National Institute of Standards and Technology, Gaithersburg, MD.

8 VULNERABILITY MANAGEMENT

In defensive security the term 'vulnerability management' is used to describe the function of identifying, classifying (usually by severity), tracking and remediating various software vulnerabilities, so they can no longer be exploited by a malicious actor. Those vulnerabilities could have been introduced at the code level, or caused by a misconfiguration during deployment. Vulnerability management is typically driven by security operations teams but requires the support of multiple teams to be done correctly.

I once interviewed a job candidate who worked for one of the biggest technology companies in the world. For 3 years his sole responsibility was to manage vulnerability scans against millions of external IP addresses owned by that company. Scans would run constantly, reports would be generated and he'd track the remediation efforts where needed. As he put it, 'I was promised a job in information security, but I don't think that is what this is'. I felt his pain and could relate to what he was saying, as I'm sure could many other IT security professionals.

Vulnerability management is a very important process which, if done correctly, will have a marked impact on the overall security of an organisation. The downside is that all the automated scanning, reporting and tracking is, for most folks, a highly monotonous affair. Additionally, it feels like you're constantly generating work for other teams, because you're opening tickets for things to be patched or reconfigured on an almost daily basis. To compound things even further, given that you're frequently having to chase teams for updates on remediation, you can develop a reputation as someone who is overly negative, or constantly nagging and whining. This is a very real perception problem, to the point where I've seen people cut out of after-work social events as a direct result of the bad blood that has built up during 'remediation ticket comment flame wars', which is extremely disheartening.

As I mentioned in the introduction to this book, this stigma around vulnerability management usually means it's a task given to the most junior member of the security operations team. Once they've built some tenure, the next person comes in and is handed responsibility for the task. And repeat. The new person sits down and watches the other members of the team busily respond to security incidents, while their job is to chase down Steven for not applying a patch to update the minor version of Java on some random test server.

All of this means we've got a bit of a challenge on our hands. On the one hand, we've got an extremely important task to complete, from a regulatory, compliance and purely technical security perspective. On the other, it's a task that can wear people down to the point where they're miserably looking for other job opportunities because they're so fed up with managing it. In this chapter we'll talk about how to overcome the 'vulnerability management blues', and build an effective vulnerability management programme. We'll also dig into the tools and technologies we'll leverage to make this happen, including the aforementioned vulnerability scans. Finally, we'll discuss the evolution of vulnerability management, to the point where those scans might actually become less critical.

BUILDING A PROGRAMME

Like many aspects of information security, vulnerability management requires the construction of a programme to support it and to make sure it's executed properly and achieves all the right goals. A vulnerability management programme is about more than running scans. It's about making sure that the results of those scans are digested by the correct people, and that they understand the expectations for what they should be doing with those results. It also means having top-down support for the work you will ultimately create. This is critical because having this support can allow you to position the work of ensuring vulnerabilities are patched as a part of the background machine-noise of the enterprise, which is exactly what it should be.

Usually, at the very top of the organisational chart there is very little resistance to a vulnerability management programme. To the C-level executives, fixing vulnerabilities to prevent security incidents, and potentially data breaches, is a complete no-brainer. Added to the fact that it's generally a good idea, there are frequently contractual, regulatory and compliance reasons for doing so. In the PCI-DSS for example, requirements 6.1 and 6.2 call out the need to classify and remediate vulnerabilities in software, based on severity. The most critical software security vulnerabilities, according to PCI-DSS, should be patched within a month of a patch being made available by the software vendor.

Where the resistance typically likes to rear its head is at the mid-to-high levels of technical leadership within an organisation. Those who are responsible for delivery of a service, hosting an application or building software generally have other pressures placed on them by stakeholders in the organisation, so can sometimes push back a little harder than perhaps we'd expect. The key to overcoming this resistance is to build your programme around them, the people who you will rely on the most to perform the actual remediation work. After all, detection and classification of vulnerabilities is a great first step, but if you cannot do anything about them that's a bit like going to the doctor, getting a prescription and throwing it away.

Setting up for success

Let's examine some steps we can take when establishing a vulnerability management programme, to build rapport with our colleagues in that tricky technical leadership layer, and overcome any early attempts to resist working with the programme.

Working the way technical teams like to work

'What ticketing system do you folks use to track issues?' A critical question, and one that is sadly often an afterthought. It's a question that should be asked extremely early in the process, because you'll want to ensure that you have a way of getting tickets opened in that system as autonomously as possible from whatever vulnerability scanning engine you elect to purchase. It's probably unsurprising that the features that are of most concern for security professionals when considering a scanning solution are things like scope of supported targets (operating systems and software), how frequently new vulnerability signatures are added and the size of the team writing vulnerability signatures. However, it's just as important to consider the reporting and ticketing features available, since they'll be the features that will save us the most time, and help reduce the tedium associated with the vulnerability management blues discussed earlier.

Depending on the team you're working with, even within the same organisation, it's possible that multiple ticketing systems might be in use. For instance, an IT or operations team might use helpdesk ticketing software, whereas a traditional development, or DevOps, organisation might use bug tracking software, which allows them to better assign tasks to their release cadence. It's worth taking the time to understand and integrate with both, even though it might require a little extra work up front.

Although a common strategy for security teams is to pick a single ticketing system to use, and ask teams to join them in it, or simply manage the remediation tracking through the vulnerability scanning product itself, it's always better to reach out and fit in with the established pattern. Not only does this convey that the security team is making the effort to build the programme around the way other teams like to work, but it genuinely helps other teams to schedule remediation efforts in line with other commitments.

When working with DevOps teams where there is a combined emphasis on software development and operations, how does vulnerability management fit in to their work cadence? Should vulnerability remediation tasks be added to a backlog and dealt with as time allows, or should the security operations team work with a technical product manager to prioritise the workload and add it directly to a given agile sprint?

Be mindful of other business pressures when prioritising vulnerability management work. Is there a massive system deployment occurring this month? Are the teams fighting another ongoing, non-security incident? By taking these time-consuming occurrences into consideration and using judgement on which patches really should be prioritised, you'll build credit with stressed and overworked teams. Of course, critical patches should never be allowed to slide, however.

Understanding the true risk associated with a vulnerability

In Chapter 1 the importance of security operations as a filter, rather than an amplifier, was discussed. While in that particular case we were focused on events rather than vulnerability scan results, the same concept rings true here. Vulnerability scanners like to err on the side of caution, and prepare the person receiving the report for the worst-case scenario. They might detect for instance, that a vulnerable version of software is running on a host, but they might not be able to attempt exploitation of that vulnerability to validate it, because it could lead to system instability or cause the vulnerable component to crash completely. Scan results can sometimes include theoretical vulnerabilities, but the reality is that other mitigating factors are in place to actually prevent the vulnerability from being exploited. For instance, if you leave your car unlocked, it's technically vulnerable, but if you do so in a locked garage, it's not quite as vulnerable.

This is where extra human eyes and expertise can really come to the fore. Rather than blindly relying on scan results to open tickets, if we can apply a layer of interpretation to the results beforehand, and make an assessment of the actual risk that a vulnerability could be exploited, the result will be a much higher quality output.

It might be a lot to ask of an analyst, particularly an entry level analyst, to make such judgement calls on their own. This is where having a diverse security team comes in extremely handy. The ability to sound questions off other team members who may have a different understanding of the environment, in a formal or informal manner, is an incredibly powerful thing to have. If you have a red team, you can guarantee that they'll be able to provide some answers about the exploitability of a given finding; after all, that's a topic very much in their realm. There's no reason blue and red can't help each other out every once in a while!

If you're in a smaller security team, you might not be able to bounce ideas around internally. In this case, a good option might be to work with the lead developer, or the supervisor for an operations team to go through and discuss findings before tickets are opened. It will require time to be expended up front, but will save a lot more time later. Rather than having to close a bunch of tickets as 'won't fix' or 'not applicable', because they represent non-exploitable vulnerabilities, the findings could be flagged and suppressed in the scanning engine.

Prioritise clearly
A scan against a single host can yield hundreds of findings, which are classified as anything from 'informational' to 'critical' severity. If you take that raw list of findings and dump them on the table of an engineer who'll be responsible for patching, they're probably going to feel a little overwhelmed. This is where providing a clear, prioritised list comes into play. Of course, we're going to want the most critical vulnerabilities, for example those that could lead to remote code execution or data compromise, to be addressed first. Are the tickets we open set up to convey the relative importance of each, or do they all look the same? Most ticketing systems allow you to set a priority, and if that is the case with the one we're using, we should be sure to set those flags accordingly.

We should set expectations for the turnaround time for remediating a given vulnerability, and we should factor in knowledge of the environment to that expectation. This is usually baked into a vulnerability management policy, and might align with a compliance standard such as the PCI-DSS mentioned earlier. In many organisations, compliance standards are considered a little too lax, so a faster turnaround might be called for. For instance, we might have a 10-day rule on most critical issues, but if a particular critical issue is being actively exploited in the wild, impacts a web-facing server and can be triggered remotely, perhaps those 10 days should become 10 hours. Always start with the most exploitable and severe issues, and work down the list from there.

Incidentally, if we do decide to 'pull the alarm cord' to get a particular vulnerability patched at a highly accelerated rate, we should be 100 per cent sure that we absolutely need to do so, each time we do it. It can't be a standard reaction that we use for every nasty sounding issue. If it is, we'll start to lose the support of those that we're constantly pulling away from other work to make the fix. Of course, if we're dealing with another vulnerability like Heartbleed (Synopsys Inc., 2014) or Shellshock (Symantec Security Response, 2014) then we should absolutely go ahead and get things taken care of.

In September 2017, credit reporting giant Equifax disclosed a security incident that was to be one of the most significant data breaches in history. Highly sensitive personal information relating to more than 140 million people was exposed. Equifax faced considerable criticism for the time it took them to detect, respond to and disclose the breach, given that it impacted so many people.

The company later revealed that the vector for the intrusion that ultimately led to the security breach was a vulnerability (CVE-2017-5638) in Apache Struts, an open source framework for creating Java web applications (NIST, 2018). This vulnerability was rated as critical, as it allowed attackers to execute commands on vulnerable hosts remotely. Instead of being promptly patched within 48 hours, as was Equifax's policy for critical vulnerabilities, the issue went without remediation for several months.

In March 2019 the United States Senate Committee on Homeland Security and Governmental Affairs released a report detailing the issues that led to the Equifax breach (Permanent Subcommittee on Investigations, 2019). Failures and disconnection throughout the vulnerability management process was listed as a leading cause. According to the report, 'Equifax's system for vulnerability scanning was a global process that was disconnected from the company's regional patch management process.'

This is a key point, since the goal of vulnerability management is to drive remediation, which is typically dependent on patching. Equifax provides an example of what happens when scans are run, but patches are not applied as a result of those scans.

Learn the environment
Understanding the context of a vulnerability finding in the overall risk profile of an organisation is key. A critical vulnerability on a production server is more important than a critical vulnerability on a server in the test environment, if the test environment contains only garbage data and is accessible to a much smaller, internal audience, for example. This is where learning host names and knowing the basic function of each host, or group of hosts, that are scanned is a tremendously valuable exercise.

Additionally, learning to recognise false positives in scan results and filtering them out of any tickets will also make sure that we continue to deliver the right information to operations teams. Vulnerability scanners aren't perfect; sometimes they can think a piece of software is installed on a host, when in reality it isn't. If a finding has been flagged as a false positive one month, and then the operations engineer has to flag it as a false positive every subsequent month, well, frankly that is a waste of time. Security operations must take the input the first time and feed it back to the source to prevent a reoccurrence.

Ensuring it's not just about one person

Vulnerability management cannot be a task associated with one person. It requires the buy-in and support of multiple people. I already mentioned the importance of executive support; sometimes that might need to be leaned on more heavily than others. If you're in a one-person security team, then this might be especially true, as technically speaking you're going to be the only one pushing the buttons on the scanner.

Sharing the work, particularly the job of analysing findings and filtering out which issues should be tracked and remediated, falls very much into the category of 'many hands make light work'. Doing this ensures that you cannot forever be passing around the hot potato of vulnerability management, because it will have been cut into multiple, presumably very mushy, chunks of lukewarm potato.

An approach I like to take is rotating the role of vulnerability management lead between analysts on a monthly or fortnightly basis. This person will be responsible for ensuring the scans run, and will follow up on outstanding remediation work. However, they won't do that every single day for the rest of their career. They'll do it for the next couple of weeks and then hand over to the next person. This is a great way to knowledge share about the environment, and, if it's a task split between blue team analysts, makes them better defenders, since they have an idea of where the weak spots are more likely to be. It also avoids a single member of the team being labelled the resident nag, or whiner.

The vulnerability scanner

The core technical tool in any vulnerability management programme, the vulnerability scanner is a highly important security operations asset. It typically consists of a graphical user interface (GUI), most commonly delivered through a web browser; a database backend, for tracking findings and remediation state; and an engine for actually running the scanning process.

Given that vulnerability scans may need to reach across multiple network segments, or between different physical locations, most commercial scanning tools, such as Rapid 7 InsightVM,[1] Qualys Vulnerability Management[2] and Tenable Nessus,[3] support the use of multiple scan engine nodes. These nodes all report their findings back to a central database, but they allow the actual interrogation and scan traffic to originate from a source that is physically closer, or on the same network segment as the target. This is an important consideration when designing a scanning architecture, because the last thing we want to do is saturate a wide area network (WAN) link with scan traffic, or get inaccurate results because scan traffic is interfered with by an NAC list applied by a firewall.

Running the first scan

Before a scan can be run, targets must first be defined in the scan engine, and the scan configuration (or profile) should be set up. Targets are typically defined by individual IP address, IP address ranges or DNS name. In some cases, especially when deployed in an IaaS or otherwise virtualised environment, the scan engine may integrate via an API. This allows targets to be dynamically loaded into the engine. In virtualised environments, where servers may be provisioned automatically to handle increased load, this helps the scan engine stay in lock-step with reality. Ultimately, a hybrid approach leveraging both dynamically updated target lists and predefined IP address ranges is the best way to ensure no targets are missed.

Scan engines also allow for global exclusions to be set during targeting. The items entered into this list will never be scanned, even if they are included in a range of targets. But why would you want to prevent things from being scanned? Surely the whole point is to scan everything and figure out what is lurking, and vulnerable? A valid point, but as anyone who has spent time picking hundreds of pieces of wasted A4 paper from a networked printer that has just been on the receiving end of a scan will tell you, some things simply don't like being scanned. Network printers are the classic example. A few weird packets on their network interfaces and they'll spew paper and ink until they haven't any left to spew.

Scan configurations or profiles set the rules of engagement for a scan. They list all the things the scanner is and isn't allowed to do. Common parameters that can be set in a scan profile include:

- **Discovery scan technique.** Before a scan engine attempts deep interrogation of a target, it must first determine that a target is online. How should it do so? Ping every IP address, or go further, and run a TCP port scan? What type of TCP port scan, which TCP flags should be set? Which ports? You can go into very fine levels of detail on just this one topic to best suit your needs.

- **Authenticated vs. unauthenticated scanning.** Scan engines will typically attempt to use weak or default passwords to authenticate to a target as part of their routine work. However, if you have a set of known credentials that can give the engine a general level of access to a target, they can be stored and leveraged during the scan. The result is the engine gets much more insight into the configuration of the host, and can run a greater variety of checks. Running an unauthenticated scan might give you a general overview of the services running on the target, but an authenticated scan will allow you to run checks against the specific software versions that are installed.

- **Safe checks only.** In some cases, attempts to validate the existence of a given vulnerability could cause a machine to become unstable, and possibly crash. This might then lead to downtime and other disruption. Depending on the environment being targeted, this could be a very undesirable outcome. We have to decide what is more important to us, determining a particular vulnerability really exists, or reducing the risk of causing disruption. Commonly, that answer varies depending upon the context of the target. If the system belongs to a test environment, we might be able to take that risk. If it's in production, perhaps let's play things a little safe.

- **Number of simultaneous targets.** This setting allows you to choose how many targets can be scanned at the same time. The more hosts you have to scan, the higher this number might need to go, to ensure scans complete in a reasonable time frame. It's a trade-off, though, since the scan engine might run out of CPU and RAM if this number is too high.

- **Scan schedule.** When should the scan run? We don't want vulnerability scans to run at times when there is an increased risk of them causing disruption. Most enterprises have a 'busy period', when for some business-specific reason, there is increased demand for the services they offer. Therefore, scans are typically scheduled outside those periods, or generally outside primary business hours.

Being a good network citizen

In order to do their job, vulnerability scanners open many connections with many hosts, generating a lot of network traffic along the way. They have the potential to overwhelm firewall session tables, saturate links, trip IDS/IPS alarms, fill up log files, cause hosts to behave unexpectedly and generally be a noisy and unwelcome presence on the network. This doesn't really seem to fit with the whole service-focused security operations culture I mentioned earlier.

To make up for this uncouth behaviour, and get in front of any potential problems, there are a few proactive steps we can take to ensure that the vulnerability scanning experience goes as smoothly as possible for everyone. First of all, we should architect our scanning platform to reduce the amount of network devices that scan traffic needs to pass through. Scan engine nodes should live in the same subnets as their targets. This reduces load on devices such as firewalls and routers.

Second, we should be clear with the owners of the systems we're about to target, about what exactly a scan will be doing to their hosts. We should invite them to come forward with any concerns *prior* to the commencement of any scan. We can offer the opportunity to request a host be excluded from a scan, if there are significant concerns. Unfortunately, inviting exclusions can lead to a default response of 'yes, exclude all my things because of ... reasons!', so the exclusion request mechanism should include collection of an appropriate justification. Perhaps offer to run a test scan against the target that is of concern to see how it behaves in a controlled environment, to allay any fears.

Third, overcommunicate the scan schedule, and make it extremely clear what is in scope during a particular scan window. The only thing worse than something going wrong during a scan, is someone not being aware that a scan is occurring, and not considering it as a root cause. This can lead to bigger incidents than are really necessary. Ensure that contact information is up to date for the person running the particular scan, and build on-call procedures to support shutting off scans in an emergency. If an unrelated incident is already under way when a scan is due to start, be sure to postpone it, otherwise a confusing and stressful situation will become a lot more confusing and stressful.

That last paragraph was brought to you courtesy of my own screw up a few years ago. Under pressure to deliver a vulnerability scan for a new collection of hosts that hadn't been tested yet, I decided to kick off a scan overnight. Since it was a small subset of hosts, and I'd selected safe-only checks, I didn't expect it would cause too much of an issue. I let other members of my team know what I was doing via email, and scheduled the scan.

Unfortunately, a late architectural change to the target environment had placed a firewall that I wasn't aware of between what I thought was the closest scan engine and the targets. That firewall went down. Pagers were going off all over, except for one place: the security operations team. Since this was a scan that fell outside our normal windows, no one suspected the firewall problem would be caused by a scan, and since I'd limited the scope of my communication to our team, the operations centre didn't know the scan was occurring. Whoops.

The network team kept rebooting their firewall, but as the scan continued, the thing kept going down over and over again. When I was eventually summoned to the on-call bridge, all the pieces of the puzzle became clear and the neighbours several streets over could likely see the red aura originating from my highly embarrassed face. The scan was stopped, things were fixed and I arrived at the office the next day with many, many doughnuts for all of the people whose evenings had been disrupted. I also paid for lunch. Everyone had at least two beers.

The hunter becomes the hunted

Vulnerability scanning tools are some of the most sensitive systems on your network. If you think about it, they're pretty much the perfect toolkit for anyone malicious looking to cause damage and disruption. They contain a detailed map of the environment, a list of all the potential vulnerabilities that could provide an entry vector, the traffic that originates from them might be allowed through firewalls, and they'll probably even have a repository of credentials on them. Therefore, we should ensure that we give them the level of protection they deserve. Scan engines themselves need to be patched on a regular basis, and should be hardened as much as possible, given they're such valuable targets. This includes patching the underlying operating system and the vulnerability scanning application software itself, as frequently it will run with root level permission.

Reporting

The real value of the vulnerability scanning tool comes from the reporting it is capable of delivering, because ultimately that's where the information used to drive remediation work comes from. Vulnerability scans generate a lot of data about the discovered and targeted hosts, the services that are running on them, and of course the vulnerabilities detected within those services; as such, there is a need to slice and dice the data in a variety of different ways for the differing audiences of the report. Executives and security leadership, for instance, will want a high-level overview of an organisation's vulnerability posture, so they can ask questions about why specific areas of the business might have a greater exposure than others.

Depending on how remediation responsibilities are dished out, vulnerability reports might need to be delivered at the host level, or by application type. For instance, a hosting operations or infrastructure team might be responsible for patching a server's base operating system, but a service team might be responsible for patching applications and software running on that server.

Governance, regulatory and compliance tools

If vulnerability management is an integral part of any compliance standards your organisation is bound to adhere to, then in many cases there will be a desire to export a vulnerability management report into a governance, regulatory and compliance (GRC) tool. GRC tools allow internal auditors and compliance professionals the ability to track compliance-related activities and evidence, so that when audit time rolls around, the evidence is quickly available to hand. Many GRC tools support import of data directly from vulnerability management tools, because the vulnerability management tools offer specific 'data-only' report formats, such as CSV, JSON or XML. If compliance is a goal of the business, and a GRC tool is in use as part of the compliance programme, be sure to look for this two-way compatibility.

Encryption

Vulnerability management reports are sensitive documents, for many of the same reasons mentioned in regard to the scanner infrastructure. They contain sensitive lists of host names, IP addresses and vulnerabilities ready and waiting to be exploited on those IP addresses. If a vulnerability management report is to be extracted from a scan engine, it should be properly protected with file-level encryption to ensure those details remain confidential, even if the report file ends up in the wrong hands.

It's not uncommon for a vulnerability scan report to be used in due diligence by prospective customers and partners. During a prospect's vendor due diligence process, they might request a copy of the last internal vulnerability scan. This can put us in a tricky spot, since we'll want to be transparent, and show the health of our environment and prove that we're being diligent and scanning on a regular basis, but we'll want to make sure we're not exposing too much. To ensure this balance is maintained, vulnerability scanning tools frequently permit the construction of customised reporting formats, in which certain fields can be redacted. For example, we can very easily make a case for redacting IP address, hostname, low level vulnerability details and raw scan output. The report will still provide very clear insight into the health of the environment, but it will at least lack the details that would allow an outsider to piece together where the weak spots might be.

Integration with ticketing systems

As mentioned a couple of times already, vulnerability scanning platforms that integrate with ticketing and issue tracking systems fit better into existing processes. Typically, they achieve this by offering APIs that allow teams to develop custom integrations for access and sharing report data.

When evaluating a vulnerability scanning tool, study how these integrations could work, and be sure to scope in any custom development work that would need to occur.

Vulnerability scoring

Just like the broader cybersecurity marketplace, there are plenty of competing products vying for our attention in the vulnerability scanning space. A common way these products look to differentiate themselves is by introducing proprietary measures aimed at assisting security operations teams in understanding the true risk of a vulnerability being exploited, and therefore prioritising remediation accordingly. They do this by building on top of an industry standard and open vulnerability scoring method, known as the Common Vulnerability Scoring System (CVSS; FIRST, 2019).

The CVSS allows security researchers to assign a numerical score to a vulnerability based on its characteristics. Those scores can range from 0 to 10, with a score of 10 being the most critical classification of vulnerability. When scoring a vulnerability using CVSS 3.0 (current at the time of writing), the researcher selects from a series of weighted metrics that best describe the characteristics of the vulnerability. These weighted metrics drive a final score that represents the overall severity of the vulnerability, a measure known as the CVSS 3.0 Base Score. These metrics are as follows.

Access vector
The further away an attacker can be from the target that is subject to the vulnerability, the more severe the vulnerability is. For example, if, as an attacker, I can exploit a vulnerability from across the internet, that is much more severe than if I have to have physical access to the target. The following metrics are used to describe the access vector:

- network – attacker can exploit across the internet;
- adjacent – attacker must be on the same network subnet to exploit;
- local – attacker must have a valid session on the target to exploit;
- physical – attacker must be able to physically touch the target to exploit.

Attack complexity
This metric is used to describe how many factors outside the attacker's control would need to go their way for the vulnerability to be exploited. For example, would a system need to be configured in a specific way for the vulnerability to exist? If so, then the attack complexity would be scored as 'high'. If not, and the vulnerability could generally exist on a wide range of targets, and exploitation would be an easily repeatable process, attack complexity would be said to be 'low'.

Privileges required
This metric refers to the level of privilege an attacker would need to have on the target system to successfully exploit the vulnerability. The higher the privilege level required, the less severe the vulnerability. If no privileges are required on the target system, this will result in the highest score. None, low (a user with standard permissions) and high (a user with root, or administrative permissions) are the named values for this metric.

User interaction
Sometimes a vulnerability can be exploited at the will of an attacker, other times an authorised user of a system must be coerced or otherwise tricked into participating in the attack, perhaps by clicking on a malicious URL, for example. The CVSS score is reduced if user interaction is required.

Scope
This metric relates to the impact once a vulnerability has been exploited. Essentially, it asks the question 'does the vulnerability allow the attacker to impact a system component other than the vulnerable component?' For instance, if a vulnerability in a

virtualisation service that can be triggered by targeting a guest virtual machine allows an attacker to compromise the contents of the hypervisor running that virtual machine, the scope is said to be 'changed'. Otherwise, the scope is considered to be 'unchanged'. Changed scope will result in a higher CVSS score.

The final three metrics should be very familiar to us, and they relate directly to the impact on these three information security concepts. Each of these final three metrics can be scored as none, low and high. An answer of 'high' in any of the metrics will increase the final CVSS score.

Confidentiality
A high confidentiality impact is said to occur when the attacker can pick and choose what restricted information they can access. A low impact occurs when an attacker has no control over what bits of information they can access following the exploitation of the vulnerability.

Integrity
A high integrity impact occurs when an attacker can directly, and maliciously, modify data controlled by the vulnerable component at will, and with intent; for instance, to alter application configuration settings. A low impact means that modification can occur, but the attacker has no control over the specifics of the modification.

Availability
A high impact to availability occurs when the attacker has the ability to completely deny access to the vulnerable component, either during a specific exploitation window, or long after the exploitation has been completed. An example of a low availability impact would be reduced or degraded performance of the vulnerable component.

Once all these metrics have been determined by the researcher, the final CVSS base score is determined, and the vulnerability severity is calculated (see Table 8.1).

Table 8.1 CVSS 3.0

CVSS 3.0 base score	Vulnerability severity
0.1–3.9	Low
4.0–6.9	Medium
7.0–8.9	High
9.0–10	Critical

Beyond the base
Of course, vulnerabilities are dynamic beasts and context can play a huge role in how critical a vulnerability really is. What might be medium severity today might become critical tomorrow when someone writes a worm that exploits the vulnerability and spreads malware autonomously. What might be critical and web-facing in my environment, might only impact one barely used server, tucked away in a segmented network in yours.

It is this context that vulnerability scanners use to modify the base scores and attempt to give a more realistic severity rating, specific to your organisation. How exactly they do it is down to the individual software vendor.

It's worth noting that CVSS itself allows researchers to supply altered scores based on these factors too. Two further scores, alongside the base score, can be calculated:

The CVSS temporal score takes into account factors based on time. These can include the maturity of any exploit code, or the availability of an official patch for the vulnerability.

The CVSS environmental score takes into account factors based on the specific enterprise environment the vulnerability can be found in. This score allows security teams to modify impacts to confidentiality, integrity and availability based on their specific set of conditions.

EVOLUTION OF VULNERABILITY MANAGEMENT

The very nature of vulnerability management means it's always going to be a somewhat reactive process. We run the scans to discover the vulnerabilities after they've been made public. We encourage teams to apply patches to remediate vulnerabilities within a time frame that we consider appropriate for the level of risk associated with the vulnerability. The patch is applied, the ticket is closed. And repeat. It's a never-ending cycle of work that will never be complete. Perhaps that's another reason for the vulnerability management blues, described at the beginning of this chapter.

So how could we make this better? How could we switch things up, and become more proactive? How could we ensure that all vulnerabilities, regardless of severity, are patched as soon as possible, and how can we automate this?

A lot of companies are working on the answers to those questions, and they're getting a little help from technologies such as ephemeral application containers and CI/CD, as well as the increased reliance on PaaS and IaaS hosting models.

A container is a stripped-down virtual machine that runs an application, or a component of an application. In a microservices architecture, where various components of a hosted application are split into smaller pieces to enable greater resiliency and scaling, containers are becoming hugely popular ways to deliver a microservice.

Unlike traditional, long-running, or always-on server components of an application, containers are designed to have short lives, perhaps popping up during times of increased load, before being removed in a 'scale-down' procedure. Containers are based on container images, which are constructed and deployed during CI/CD processes. This is how companies that use CI/CD can release multiple times a day, if they really want to. They push a new copy of a master image into their environment, and phase out the old one. All this building and rebuilding provides a very good opportunity for security operations to kill off a vulnerability in a component installed on a container in very short order.

Each time a new container image is built, the latest version of a given system component can be installed, which will typically ensure that all applicable patches for that component are already included. Our mode of operation has switched from deploy and patch, to deploy patched.

Even earlier, leveraging databases of known vulnerabilities provided by vulnerability scanning tools during the development and build phase, it's possible to look up a list of components a developer is attempting to include in the build of their service. If any of those components appear in the database as being vulnerable without an available patch, notifications can be made to security operations, or depending on the severity of the vulnerability, the build could be blocked. Once again, the shift away from deploying, discovering and fixing later gives security the upper hand, and reduces risk.

Of course, containers and CI/CD are not going to be suitable for every situation, and chances are if we stopped a build on every vulnerability detection without tuning the process, that feature would soon be turned off, but these tools do seem to offer empowering options that will enable security operations to get a better handle on vulnerability management.

SUMMARY

In this chapter we've reviewed the highly important vulnerability management function of the security operations blue team. We talked about the importance of building a vulnerability management programme, rather than just throwing a scanning tool out there, pressing play and hoping for the best. Fitting into existing processes and offering those responsible for remediation a prioritised list of work are two key things we should be doing to ensure the success of our programme.

We talked about preventing the 'vulnerability management blues' in analysts, by rotating the roles and responsibilities of vulnerability management among team members.

We discussed vulnerability scanners, the key technical tool used to run a vulnerability management programme, including ensuring that vulnerability scanners are configured and tuned appropriately, so they don't cause damage or disruption as they go about probing the network. We noted the importance of securing the vulnerability management infrastructure as, if it were compromised, it would provide a great deal of highly sensitive and valuable material to an attacker.

We reviewed the common ways in which vulnerabilities are reported and scored, and the importance of this function in the vulnerability scanner. We reviewed the CVSS.

Finally, we reviewed the evolution of vulnerability management, and peeked into how new technologies and architecture approaches are providing us with new opportunities to reduce the need for retroactive patching.

The next chapter focuses on one of the key things a security operations team will need to be successful, and it's something that no vendor can sell you; trust. We'll talk about building trust across, and outside, the enterprise, including with users and hosting teams, as well as with external customers, partners and the wider security community.

REFERENCES

FIRST (Forum of Incident Response and Security Teams) (2019) Common Vulnerability Scoring System version 3.1: Specification document. Available at: https://www.first.org/cvss/specification-document

NIST (National Institute of Standards and Technology) (2018) National Vulnerability Database: CVE-2017-5638 detail. Available at: https://nvd.nist.gov/vuln/detail/CVE-2017-5638

Permanent Subcommittee on Investigations (2019) *How Equifax Neglected Cybersecurity and Suffered a Devastating Data Breach*. United States Senate Committee on Homeland Security and Governmental Affairs. Available at: https://www.carper.senate.gov/public/_cache/files/5/0/508a6447-853f-4f41-85e8-1927641557f3/D5CFA4A0FC19997FF41FB3A5CE9EB6F7.equifax-report-3.6.19.pdf

Symantec Security Response (2014) ShellShock: All you need to know about the Bash Bug vulnerability. Blog, 25 September. Available at: https://www.symantec.com/connect/blogs/shellshock-all-you-need-know-about-bash-bug-vulnerability

Synopsys Inc. (2014) The Heartbleed Bug. Available at: http://heartbleed.com/

9 BUILDING RELATIONSHIPS AND TRUST

The most technically adept security analysts, the most modern monitoring and logging tools fully deployed across the enterprise, blue and red team functions fully staffed, and a wide variety of processes documented in tremendous detail. Sounds like a security operations dream scenario, right? I'd say almost, there's just one more thing we need in place to ensure success: trust.

Consider that all of the accomplishments just listed are bricks, piled on top of one another to build a wall. Bricks are heavy things, of course, and generally, under normal circumstances, the wall would stay standing just fine. If, however, one of those bricks were to be knocked over, there's a chance it could knock into another, which in turn could lead to the collapse of the second brick and, maybe, the entire wall. To strengthen our wall, and stop it from collapsing so readily, we could use cement to join all those bricks together. Cement, in this cheesy but pretty accurate analogy, would be trust.

Trust is such a fundamental need at so many levels for a security team that I wanted to dedicate an entire chapter explaining the reasons why, and suggesting ways in which it can be built. So here we are!

Throughout the book I've touched on why trust is important. Early on, for example, I talked about the importance of hiring trustworthy security professionals, who you can be sure will protect the sensitive information they will be exposed to. Trust within the security team is one thing you absolutely must have in place in order to function effectively, but trust also needs to extend to the internal and external customers of our services.

The vast majority of my experiences running security operations teams have been positive. I've generally worked with very smart people from very diverse backgrounds, and together we've achieved a lot over the years. However, as anyone who has ever led a team of people will attest, things are rarely smooth sailing all of the time. Sometimes you're faced with making hard decisions, and I recall very vividly having to make a hard decision in regards to a member of a security operations team I was running at the time.

On the one hand, this employee was incredibly technically skilled. They were one of, if not the most, talented application security professionals I'd ever seen in action. An excellent red teamer, they could blow through applications with ease, and were finding bugs left, right and centre. They also had the ability to apply those technical skills defensively, although, to this day, I consider them a reluctant blue teamer.

On the other hand, the challenge was that for all the technical skill this person had, they lacked a significant amount of trust from other members of the security operations team. As a teammate, they were somewhat unreliable, didn't often show up in team meetings, and in some cases, flat out refused to partake in daily tasks because they were too busy doing other, 'more important' things.

After several attempts to make it clear that everyone in the team plays an equal role as far as daily work is concerned, and setting expectations around things like attendance in team meetings, there was no improvement, and I found myself face-to-face with a very hard decision. Do I continue to put up with the tension this person creates within the team because they're untrusted, in return for the high quality technical skills that are undoubtedly making our environment more secure?

The need for trust within the team won out over technical skill, and myself, HR and the employee had a sit down where I delivered the bad news. It was rough; even though I'd convinced myself it was the right move, I still felt awful. The sting lasted for a few days, but I did start to notice an improvement in team dynamics pretty quickly after the decision.

The lesson I learned from this was the value of trust. Prior to this occurrence, I would have likely considered technical skill to be the most important consideration when staffing for a security operations team. Technical skills can be replaced relatively easily, but trust cannot.

In this chapter, we'll talk about building trusting relationships with various departments with whom we do business, internal and external users of the applications we're working to protect, and with the wider information security community. We'll take a look at why these relationships lead to more secure departments. Finally, we'll discuss methods for demonstrating the effectiveness of security controls with data, so that we're not always relying on opinions to make an argument.

TRUST WITHIN THE ENTERPRISE

As an effective security operations team, we'll need to build trust at all levels of the enterprise we're working hard to protect. Doing so will not only make our jobs markedly easier, but actually possible. Trust needs to flow from the top down and the bottom up, meaning we need support from both executive sponsors, who'll provide things like budget and help shape the security culture, and the 'boots on the ground', who in most cases will be our eyes and ears.

Executives

At the senior levels of an organisation, trust is very much a two-way affair. Executives will want to trust that we're making the most of the investment they've made in the security programme, and that we're actually putting things in place to ensure a safer organisation. We'll want to trust that they recognise the work we're doing, understand the obstacles we face, and won't scapegoat the security team at the first sign of trouble.

One of the great challenges in security operations is that typically, when things are going well, we're out of sight and out of mind. Through our daily work, we'll prevent security incidents from ever seeing the light of day, perhaps because we intercepted a targeted phishing email, our vulnerability scan caught a newly discovered bug on an externally exposed port, or we prevented an employee from uploading customer data to their personal Google Drive account. It only takes that one time for something to go wrong, for us to be the centre of attention for all the wrong reasons. It's important that we tell stories of successes regularly, so that the first conversation that we have at the senior level isn't a negative one.

Briefing executives

The first step to establishing this dialogue is getting a regular meeting between security operations leadership and the wider executive leadership team on the calendar. Of course, every organisation is very different in terms of structure. Some will have a chief information security officer (CISO) who reports to the CEO; others will have a CISO that reports to the head of legal, or perhaps the security organisation won't have a CISO at all, and will instead report to the chief technology officer (CTO). This structure, whichever one it is, and the political factors that will inevitably come with it, will likely play a role in determining such logistical items as the attendee list, the agenda and the frequency of the meetings. With that in mind, let's talk in general terms about the best approach to take in regards to running a meeting with a senior executive or a group of senior executives.

In terms of frequency, holding a meeting every quarter seems to strike the right balance. It's not so frequent that the executive feels as though they're hearing the same information over and over again, yet the meetings are still close enough together that it's possible to provide updates on issues raised at the previous meeting. You can also send small periodic updates between meetings if you have content worth sharing. Another important point is that meetings with executives take time to prepare for; something worth remembering when setting the frequency. To make the most of the face time you do have, you'll want to make sure that all the material you will reference during the meeting is fully prepared ahead of time, and sent off a couple of days in advance, so that your audience can pre-read. For the time-crunched executive, this can be a huge benefit, and I'm generalising of course, but most appreciate the opportunity to get a sneak preview of what they're about to hear. Aside from sparing them any nasty surprises in a room full of people, it allows them to think up questions regarding areas they'd like to drill into in more depth while they have your attention.

As for the content, well, it typically takes a bit of experimentation and intelligence gathering to get the exact mixture just right. As a newbie presenting to a senior executive for the first time, there is no harm in asking people with more experience of presenting to that person the style that they enjoy. Some love PowerPoint slides full of intricate details, others do not. Some refuse any PowerPoint at all. I always like to open with a short story about an event or incident that has occurred since the last meeting: what went well in terms of the detection, what could've gone better and, perhaps most importantly, the net benefit of this piece of work to the customer and ultimately the business. As the security team grows, if people are willing and able, and it's an appropriate environment to do so, inviting analysts and engineers to demonstrate what they've been working on, or how they responded to a particular incident can work well in this setting. Information security can be a thankless job at times, and giving people the opportunity to tell a senior executive first-hand about the work they do is a tremendously engaging and rewarding thing to do.

After story time is over, it's time to get down to business. What are the top five high level things that pose a risk to our business, what are the challenges preventing us from fully addressing them, and what's the solution? Answer this question with bullet points, presenting just the facts as you do so. This serves a dual purpose. First, it allows us to honestly disclose challenges we face in securing the business in a structured format that, if done correctly, will not feel like or be perceived, as whining. It's therapeutic in a way: taking the emotion and frustration out of a blocked attempt to reduce risk in a given area, and logging it in the same manner as an auditor would following an audit. Second, if the proposed solution requires additional funding, or perhaps a nod of the executive head signifying support to get a thing taken care of, then this is a great forum to get that.

Finally, if you have data to support the work your team is doing, and how it is performing, it should be included in the meeting. Make sure, however, that the data you provide is relevant, allows for a consistent measure of performance against goals from one reporting period to the next, and is accurate. To these points, on the relevance of data, a trap far too many security teams fall into is attempting to use data to generate fear, and scare their executives into action. Remember, this is all about building trust, and using fear isn't a very effective way to do this. An example is using the number of application layer attacks a WAF blocks in a given period, for example, 'we prevented 6.5 million incidents this quarter'. We all know that isn't remotely true. Yes, we have WAFs triggering on multiple (many millions, in this case) HTTP requests, but we also know false positives happen, and a hit on a WAF rule doesn't constitute something that automatically would become an incident. Leave the big scary numbers where they belong, on the screens of SIEM tools displayed in the SOC.

Honesty is important. Data can be manipulated, and used to tell a story that best fits the narrative of the person telling that story. A lot of folks in technical leadership positions would probably admit (or maybe they wouldn't, actually) to preying on an executive's lack of understanding, or detailed knowledge of a particular topic and using data incorrectly to drive an outcome. It's a dangerous game, because while an executive might lack a particular piece of knowledge on one day, very little is standing between them doing the research and coming back with their own conclusions, if they so wish. If they do this, and it turns out the person supplying the data and controlling the narrative around that data might not have been telling the absolute truth, guess what? Goodbye trust!

Metrics or key performance indicators
The data points we use to measure performance of the security team are frequently called metrics or key performance indicators (KPIs). Metrics should tell us the things that are going well and highlight areas for improvement. Examples of metrics used to measure the performance of security operations teams include:

Percentages of events detected during the period that were reviewed and were not reviewed

Using percentages rather than numbers helps keep the slide free of those big scary numbers mentioned earlier; it also enables us to set a static target that we can measure against period-to-period. The ratio of reviewed vs. unreviewed events will have ups and downs, and we'll derive insight from that. Did a change in the environment generate more alerts for the team to handle? What are the possible solutions? Do we need more analysts, or higher quality event generation?

Number of potential incidents investigated during the period

This metric allows us to talk through the event to incident life cycle. It allows us to demonstrate clearly the filtering role that the security operations team performs on a daily basis, which is ultimately a key function of the team, in terms of the value it delivers.

Average time to resolve a confirmed incident

Since resolution of incidents is a cross-functional effort, this metric allows us to measure the amount of support we receive from teams outside security operations. As the incident response procedures become more mature, and trust is built between security operations and outside teams, incident resolution times should be reduced. If not, we can raise some of the reasons why.

Costs associated with a confirmed incident (outside security operations costs)

Tracking estimated costs associated with security incidents in a metric is a powerful thing indeed. After every incident is done, a tally of the people and hours involved in the response, combined with some salary data from HR, can be used as the basis for a compelling estimate of actual cost to the company. Money talks, and showing the correlation between the technical security incident and the real financial impact, will be useful insight for an executive.

Percentage of hosts with high or critical severity vulnerabilities open past agreed remediation targets

This metric provides a great talking point, because if the percentage increases dramatically, it provides a very clear indicator that something has changed, and provides us with the opportunity to address that. For example, perhaps a team started to prioritise working a new group of servers, and left some legacy systems unpatched.

Any business-specific security metrics

Earlier we looked at the importance of building detections that fit the business. Assuming we have some of these things in place, we'll likely want the opportunity to report on them. Here we can include metrics driven by these custom detection routines. For example, 'number of user accounts locked out due to abnormal behaviour'.

Remember though, that in an instant, the best thought out presentations can be cast aside into the abyss without warning. The executive ultimately controls the meeting, and can drive it in a completely different direction if they so choose. Be sure to read up on the latest 'headline breach', and be prepared to answer the question, 'would we be able to prevent this from happening to us?' I've found that to be a road I've been taken down many times.

When all is said and done, the goal of the meeting should be to build rapport between the top levels of the organisation and the security team. You'll want to make sure they get a sense of what is good, and what needs improvement. They should feel comfortable with the level of service you're providing and you should feel comfortable that they're firmly onside if you need them.

Internal customers

A common trap that technical teams, with the possible exception of IT support, can find themselves falling into is forgetting that there are insiders within their enterprise who are actually their customers. That's no one's fault of course; it makes perfect sense that any discussion of 'customers' conjures up thoughts of those outside our enterprise who pay us for our goods and services. However, for those of us in security operations, it is important to be firmly in the mindset that in addition to those external customers, the end users in our organisation who leverage the endpoints and systems we secure, and the technical teams who we work with to deliver that security, are also our customers.

Customers, no matter who they are, are there to be served. At the very start of this book I talked about the need to run a service-focused security operations organisation, and a major factor in allowing yourself to be served by an organisation is trust. Just as would be the case in an external customer relationship, if the internal customer doesn't trust the supplier, they'll go to the competition. In security operations, the 'competition' includes things like shadow IT, unapproved processes that violate policy and place the organisation at risk, and being too afraid to speak up and self-report potential incidents.

End users

Trust between end users and security operations teams takes time and effort to build, is an invaluable security tool, and can be lost in an instant. The building process begins with accessibility and awareness. We want people to know who we are and how to get in touch with us. We want them to know that they should reach out to us early on if they need to, and there are no negative consequences to doing so. Security operations should not be this mysterious force surrounded by folklore about the ways they operate and what happens if you get on the wrong side of them. Instead, we should be transparent about our approaches and the goals of our work, and invite further questions.

Different types of user will prefer different types of communication channel to reach out to the security operations team, so the onus is on us to provide as many of those channels as possible. Examples include:

- **Email.** A single email address for end users to reach out to the team with questions, concerns and anything in between. Procedures should be in place to ensure the team knows who is responsible for replying to a given email, and commonly the on-call analyst will take this responsibility. Receiving and reading the email is a good first step; having a well-coordinated response is the second.

- **Phone.** An oldie but a goodie. Sometimes there is no substitute for a phone call. Perhaps in the heat of the moment, when a user is panicked that they might have been compromised, or technical problems prevent them from reaching the team in any other way, a dedicated security operations phone number is the way to go.

- **Instant message (IM) and collaboration tools.** The majority of enterprises leverage some form of instant messaging platform to supplement email and, more intrusively, distract employees from the task at hand. So, if we're getting interrupted, it might as well be for a good reason. Having an official group or channel for end users to reach out to us allows the interruptions to flow in consistently, so they can be better managed and responded to as part of our daily operations.

- **Office hours/in person meetings.** Sometimes face-to-face meetings are the only way to seek clarity or make decisions. In a large enterprise we might not have the time to take meetings with everyone that desires one, but we might be able to support an 'office hours' type approach, where we set up a window for folks to drop in and ask questions in person or via video conference.

These channels provide great options for folks to come to us, but the second part of the trust generation method comes from the work we can do to make them aware of these channels and, more generally, the work we do in security operations. A little outreach can go a very long way. Security awareness methods include:

- **New hire orientation.** Having a member of the security team make a brief appearance in a new hire orientation sends a powerful signal. It conveys that the company is serious about security. It associates a face with the security function.

- **Posters, signage and graphics.** Having real estate on the walls of offices is a privilege that we should take full advantage of. High quality messaging can be delivered through printed materials, and this includes messaging specific to the function of and contact paths, for security operations.

- **Intranet sites.** Most enterprises have an intranet or collaboration portal that is used to deliver company messaging to employees. Security should have a spot on this site, and if it doesn't, that's a problem, so we should build our own. Intranet sites provide great opportunities to host training materials, including articles, videos and blog posts. Be aware, this type of content takes time and effort to maintain, so it's important to factor this into the team's workload if it's deployed.

There will likely be a broader security awareness programme in place, led by either the security or the compliance team. If that is the case, our job will be to align with that programme, and supplement the work that has already been done. If not, we might have to do a little more general information security awareness work. The goals of our awareness campaigns might include:

- **Educating users about when to contact security operations.** What are the indicators that might warrant a note to security operations? Should the user forward every funny-looking email? What about an error message, is that security or IT support? Prepare answers for questions like these to suit your environment and cover them in your awareness materials. Personally, I prefer overcommunication. I would rather redirect 10 typical end-user IT problems a day to IT, than miss one actual security incident.

- **Letting people know how to contact security operations.** Which of the communication channels listed above should be used first? What happens if something occurs outside business hours and the user needs a quick response?

Providing the avenues of communication and setting expectations for the appropriate route to take in a given situation, are key functions of awareness, and help reduce friction between the end user and the security analyst who ends up working with them. Even the most customer service-focused analyst might get a little perturbed if they're woken up by the on-call pager because someone received a funny-looking sales email.

- **Providing guidance on the correct way to do things.** We can't hold users accountable for doing the wrong thing, without having written guidance on how to do the right thing. Providing a solution is one of the most important things we can do to become a trusted entity.

- **Providing timely information about specific threats.** If there is an active campaign against the enterprise, or there is some event that has triggered heightened exposure of the company, it changes the risk profile. Depending on the circumstances, it can behove us to make a broader group of users aware of the increased risk. The users will appreciate the transparency too.

Technical teams

We rely heavily on other technical teams within the organisation to get things done. Security is never going to be a task we can do alone. Therefore, a special kind of trusting relationship has to be in place between security operations and those in technical roles at the enterprise.

Because of our reliance on them, it might not feel like they're our customers, but they are. They're getting a service from us, even though they might not have been the ones to sign up for it. We're helping protect the investment the company has made in them by keeping the products they've built away from any damaging headlines. We're saving them from late nights on the incident management phone bridge following a security incident. By working proactively with them, we're preventing a whole slew of reactive, stress-filled work later.

One of the single greatest causes of friction between technical teams and security teams is the sheer scale of our operation. In the security operations team we can be spread thinly across a wide variety of disciplines. I hope this book has demonstrated just how broad our scope can be. From the endpoint, across the network, to the applications and databases, and further still, we have a lot to secure. What that means is, we don't have anywhere near the specific level of expertise as a developer who works exclusively on one application, or the IT support professional who lives enterprise software problems day-in, day-out. We come into the conversation with the best intentions, but always a few steps behind in terms of the full body of knowledge needed to fully understand the situation. This causes problems because we don't actually like to admit this, and those we're working with have to spend time bringing us up to speed. For this reason, it can feel to them as if we're a bit of a burden, to say the least.

To counter this, address it head on. As a security professional, admit you don't have all the answers, but want to work with the developer, engineer or administrator to help address a security problem for the benefit of the company. Position that person as the subject matter expert, because they are. Explain the benefits of what you're attempting to implement, both in the short and long term. Ask what work you can take on to reduce the burden and for other ways you can help, including handling any approvals needed for the work to take place. Once the work is complete, take the time to say thank you, and recognise the contribution of the person (something that doesn't happen very often). They'll appreciate the upfront honesty and recognition, and if things go well the first time, then the second time, and every subsequent time, will likely run just as smoothly.

Human resources

Security teams and HR teams have a lot in common. Generally, people want to avoid both, thanks to a similar level of prejudice about what exactly each team does. However, when there is a particularly nasty or stressful situation requiring special support, HR and security are among the first ports of call, depending on the specifics. In the case study earlier in this chapter, I know I was super grateful to have the help and support of a tremendous HR professional. This mutual perception problem can be a great icebreaker.

Given that our work involves policy enforcement, there will be times when we need to lean on HR to help drive the consequences of policy violation. Sometimes that can include termination of an employee. Building rapport, expectations and specific procedures around these types of situation can make for a highly productive relationship.

One of the biggest security advantages to having a good relationship with HR comes when an involuntary termination situation arises. For reasons completely outside the scope of security, people might be shown the door. When that happens, if access to company information systems and data is not immediately cut, this presents a tremendous risk. Having a process in place for this situation is a must, but if the risk is elevated for whatever reason, an informal heads-up through a previously established relationship can further reduce the time needed to remove access from a freshly terminated former employee.

Take time to get to know the people in your HR team. Let them know the importance of alignment between security and HR, and make sure you have some processes in place for common situations that may occur. Finally, be sure to sell your capabilities to them. Security operations teams are frequently staffed by people with excellent investigative skills, and depending on the scope of the team, might include digital forensics capability too. A surprising number of HR teams don't know they have this capability so close to home within the organisation. The mutual benefits from this relationship will soon lead to a greater level of trust.

Marketing/PR

The role of the marketing team, and in particular the public relations (PR) function, is to have complete control over both internal and external messaging relating to the company. One of the key goals is to keep things consistent. Through the professionals that work in these teams, we get access to a pool of resources that can assist with routine, and not-so-routine messaging.

On the routine side of things, we can get digital artists and their tools to help produce catchy materials that deliver some of the awareness messaging mentioned earlier in the chapter. Delivering this message in alignment with company branding and style makes it feel as if the message is really a core part of the company culture. Few things are as frustrating to the security professional as seeing a key security message lost in a sea of terrible clipart, and written in the Comic Sans MS font.

On the less routine types of communication, having PR involved in crafting public and internally facing messaging around security incidents is a must. Even an internal communication might end up outside the organisation at some point, so working to ensure that if this happens the PR team is ready to respond to the fallout is a critical consideration. PR teams can take the facts of a security incident and craft the messaging in such a way as to limit panic.

We also need help from our PR teams. Typically, they're on the front line in the sometimes dark and murky world of social media. Everyone running a brand social media account needs to be aware of, and be able to recognise, certain types of non-malicious and malicious communication. This includes outright threats, against both physical and virtual assets, that are worthy of further investigation by the security operations team. It can also include genuine attempts by security researchers, or anyone else, to report security vulnerabilities in our products or services, in a responsible fashion. Such reports must be recognised, evaluated by security operations and responded to appropriately to ensure that both sides of the exchange are happy with the outcome.

Marketing and HR materials
The opposite of accidentally exposed would be 'purposefully exposed', and materials produced by the aforementioned marketing and PR teams would be prime examples of this. Of course, the whole point of a marketing department is to advertise a company's products and services, so no big surprises here. Earlier, we talked about the importance of having a good relationship with marketing for the purposes of detecting attempts at responsible vulnerability disclosure. In other words, the marketing team should perform an inbound check to filter and direct any messages that may be of importance to the security team. In a two-way relationship with marketing, security operations can offer significant value by performing a quick outbound check against any press releases, new advertising campaigns and other promotional material.

Now, you're probably thinking, 'we're not marketers, what value could we bring by reviewing marketing material?' First, at the very least, it is good for the blue team to be aware of a new marketing campaign. Marketing campaigns drive traffic to websites, cause new users to sign up for services and generally result in increased exposure for the company. A press release announcing a significant partnership or investment might attract the attention of that partner's enemies, or a financially motivated actor who now has interest in potentially getting access to some of that investment cash.

Second, a quick sanity check of marketing materials from the security perspective never hurt anyone. Marketers like to make big, bold claims about the products they're advertising, and sometimes those claims can include things about security. This has become more apparent in recent years, as security has become a key consideration for many product buyers. The wrong person seeing the bold security claim can lead to big problems for the blue team. For instance, if any materials submitted for publication to the world include any of the following terms, security operations would do well to make sure they never see the light of day:

- **Unhackable**, because nothing is unhackable, and there is no better way to discover this than by claiming it.

- **Bank-level security**, because not all banks implement technical security measures correctly, after all.

- **Military-grade cryptography**, because more often than not, it isn't, and that's fine, because generally we're selling software and services, not sharing invasion plans.

It's not just the claims in the materials that can be of interest. Simply exposing too much information about the architecture behind a service offering can also require a rewrite. I recall one particular example in which a developer was asked to submit a diagram of how a particular service was architected. Without context, and assuming it was to be used internally, they submitted a detailed technical diagram with server names and IP addresses, along with the software components running on those services. Imagine their surprise when that same diagram appeared in a marketing handout to be given to customers, some weeks later.

I can think of no better example of the evolution of information security and its role in marketing than a 2017 advertising campaign by US fast food chain, Jack in the Box. Just prior to the 2017 Super Bowl game, a traditional time for brands in the US to pull out all the stops in terms of their advertising efforts for the year, Jack, the brand mascot, was informed that he'd been hacked! Of course, in this particular instance, the breach was 'made for TV', so to speak, and wasn't real.

As part of the campaign, the brand launched a website, 'JackiLeaks', a clear play on national secrets leakers WikiLeaks. The site spent the next few weeks releasing some of Jack's biggest secrets. Needless to say, the intent of JackiLeaks was to sell burgers, not overthrow or embarrass governments.

What is incredibly interesting about this choice of campaign is that it was the first time a major brand had decided to play on the impact of a data breach. They were taking subject matter that is actually pretty serious, and making light of it. It's a sign of just how commonplace breaches have become, that the brand would feel comfortable that their audience would be familiar enough with the subject matter to get a kick out of it.

I do wonder, though, how the Jack in the Box security team felt about this one, and if they were consulted during the development of the campaign. Personally, I wouldn't want to tempt fate.

In recent years HR has found itself getting fully on board the marketing train, as they seek new and innovative ways to attract prospective employees. A new breed of website aimed at promoting the culture of a company has become a widely used platform for doing just this. These sites often feature detailed photographs of a company's offices, and groups of employees milling about looking happy to be at work. Of course, to make these photographs as natural as possible, they sit in front of computer screens and whiteboards, just as they would in real life. The problem, of course, is that frequently these computer screens and whiteboards don't have staged content. It's 100 per cent real. I can personally attest to having caught and sought the removal of two such photographs that showed a step-by-step plan for migrating a sensitive database. This desire to be open and inviting is often at odds with our work in defensive security, where we want to shield as much of the innards of our environment as possible. A balance can be had, with relative ease. Clearing whiteboards and blurring screens takes only a few seconds, you just need someone who remembers to ask for it to be done.

TRUST OUTSIDE THE ENTERPRISE

Beyond the physical and logical boundaries of the enterprise, perhaps more than ever, the security operations team is finding itself having to build and manage trusting relationships. Reasons for this include increased awareness among external end users about security issues, to the point where many feel comfortable asking to speak to a member of the security team about what they're seeing. Additionally, increased dependence on outside vendors to deliver more aspects of the enterprise's product or service, such as in an IaaS relationship, means that we're more likely to find ourselves on the phone with a SP than directing a remote hands service at a collocated datacentre.

External users

For some organisations, the idea of having a security team communicate directly with external end users of a product or service might send a shiver down their spine. Historically, such exchanges have been managed by customer support channels; these channels can provide structure for the exchange, and allow it to be measured in a manner that allows the organisation to prove how effective those channels actually are. Unfortunately, as we've all probably experienced, sometimes the need to measure the effectiveness of the support process can seem to be more important than the actual quality of the support experience.

In a B2B relationship, the supplier will typically present a named account manager to the customer to manage all aspects of their support experience, and this would be expected to include acting as a go-between in any exchanges between the customer and the security team.

In a business-to-consumer (B2C) relationship, the need to track every exchange with a customer is a given, to ensure a consistent set of information as the customer is passed between different support analysts, and the structure of various support levels often provides a barrier preventing the customer from getting direct information from the security team.

These traditional support models and the constraints they impose can lead to frustration for customers, support teams and security teams alike. Therefore, more modern approaches of permitting, encouraging or providing direct access to and from security teams are gaining momentum. Personally, I'm a big fan of this, and I think it's a great way to give an analyst a level of job satisfaction that they might not otherwise have been able to experience. It's a great feeling to be able to deliver an insightful answer in a relatively deep level of detail to a worried consumer. A common example of this is when a user thinks their account might have been compromised. Assuming all the logs are in place, it should be a relatively short task for the analyst to give this assessment to the user, and provide guidance based on their findings.

Of course, there should be some rules in place. We can't ditch the tracking of interactions with customers just because they come to security. Therefore, perhaps aligning security operations with a customer support ticketing system is one example of a decent approach. Additionally, depending upon their confidence in the analyst, and I mean this in the nicest possible way, a manager might elect to review any response before it is finally sent to the customer. Security folks can sometimes be very direct in their assessment of a given situation, and since customer support training isn't typically on the agenda, it figures that sometimes a little help on language choice or tone is in order.

So, there are two stages to building trust with external users. The first is to start by building trust with the customer support function in your organisation. Win them over by fitting into their processes where possible and proving that you can be trusted to talk to users directly. After some successes, which may not come immediately (sometimes no matter what you tell people, even if it's the truth, they don't believe you), the tide will shift, and it'll be hard to remember a time when customer support teams placed themselves between the customer and the security team.

Partners

In a partner relationship there is likely to be sharing of data, and much of it will relate to the end users of the platform. In such relationships, it's important that both sides are very clear on each other's responsibilities relating to that data. Ultimately, the customer isn't going to care if their data was compromised from a partner organisation if they only ever shared it with the platform provider.

Where possible, or if required by law, consumers should be empowered to know when their data is being passed to a partner. This might not be strictly a security operations function; indeed, it typically falls in the realm of privacy engineering, but as technical security professionals, nothing will stop us from making the request to share such insight.

If a security operations team can't trust the partners on their platform, this doesn't bode well for end users. Making the effort to introduce ourselves to partner security contacts, before we write them into our incident response plans, is a great way to get to know them and discover how they run their security programme day-to-day. Of course, due diligence should have been completed prior to any data being shared, but as we all know, the way things look on paper can be quite different from reality.

Most partners will have a named contact inside your organisation. To avoid stepping out of bounds and making their job harder, be sure to include them in any conversations with the partner about security.

Vendors

Much like platform partnerships, if a vendor is responsible for a key element of delivering our service, we need to have mutual trust for the sake of our customers.

If we have custom software developed by an outside vendor, we need to know who to reach out to in the event of a security vulnerability being discovered. If our IaaS provider is experiencing a DDoS attack, we should make sure they know how to reach us and let us know.

A list of critical vendors and their technical contacts, should be kept up to date and in the incident response playbook. Some vendors will have more mature security programmes than we do, in which case we should look to leverage that programme as much as possible to fill any gaps we might have, for example, leveraging flow logging from an IaaS provider if we don't have an IDS in place. Others will have less mature programmes, and we'll need to spend cycles making sure we're doing all we can to compensate for that.

As before, proactive outreach and routine communication between the vendor and the security team can provide tremendous results for both sides.

The information security community

The modern enterprise needs a good relationship with the information security community, and you don't get that by making a statement including the line 'we take the security of your data very seriously', following a breach that could have been prevented, had a bug report been appropriately triaged and remediated.

We need to provide channels for security researchers, and others who stumble upon vulnerabilities, to reach out to us, and they should receive a decent response when they do. I touched on this topic a little earlier, when I spoke about PR receiving bug reports over social media. Quite honestly, social media should not be the avenue a researcher is forced to take because no others are available. Having a well-publicised email address, along with Pretty Good Privacy (PGP) email encryption key that can be used to submit vulnerability reports is a simple, but often overlooked item.

Putting that email address into service, and building procedures to promptly respond to bug reports when they arrive will not take much of an investment from either a financial or a time perspective.

Bug bounties
Taking the responsible disclosure route even further, and building a bug bounty programme that formally sets rules for the rewards given to those who responsibly disclose security vulnerabilities can be the ultimate sign of an enterprise ready to work with the security community. It can also be a minefield.

A bug bounty requires more thought than simply creating a portal to report a vulnerability and a prize list for doing so. Having executive approval for the payouts is key, and needs to be obtained as early as possible. Being realistic about the bounty you can afford to pay might also discourage those who want to hold out for more.

Consider the pros and cons for your specific situation, and make a decision that best fits your enterprise. Some companies have done really well through bug bounties; others would probably be better off spending the money on more precise penetration testing.

Open-source

For those of us who've worked in the technical side of information security, there is a very strong chance that we've leveraged open-source software along the way. So how sweet would it be to be able to contribute and give back to the open-source community any tools that we develop ourselves along the way. It's an approach that is growing, and is often well-received by the information security community – a great way to build trust in the company, its products and its security team.

Netflix famously hosts an open-source site,[1] where it has released a number of open-source tools relevant to security and other technical disciplines.

SUMMARY

Throughout this chapter, we've focused on the importance of trust to a security operations team. We've talked about internal trust within the team, trust within the enterprise and trust beyond the enterprise.

We've discussed building trust with executives through regularly scheduled meetings, and using metrics to demonstrate with data the good and not-so-good elements of our security operations programme.

We've talked about treating end users and technical teams in our enterprise as customers, and how that changes our approach to be more service-focused. We discussed ways to build awareness of the security operations team, and how to make ourselves more accessible.

We covered the importance of relationships with key internal teams, such as HR, marketing/PR and customer support. Finally, we discussed the growing importance of external relationships with outside customers, partners, vendors and the information security community.

In the next chapter, we're going to need that trust we've just discussed at length. The focus will be on the ways in which we can extend our defensive capabilities beyond the mostly internal technical controls we've focused on so far. The chapter talks about the role of security operations in employee safety and brand protection, and looks at ways in which we can grow our offerings beyond the walls of the enterprise and evolve into a modern security operations team.

10 BEYOND THE ENTERPRISE

Much of the defensive security operations work we've discussed so far in this book has been naturally very introspective. For the most part, we're comfortable controlling what goes on within the physical and virtual walls of our enterprise – we have influence and we have tools that give us plenty of insight in detecting and responding to potential security incidents. Given this, blue teams can sometimes be tempted to close their eyes and cover their ears against the world outside their immediate control. By doing this, we're potentially missing out on a great deal of insight and information that could increase our value, from both a security and a service perspective.

The internet is clearly a goldmine of information, and there have never been more opportunities to ingest, process and apply this information in new and creative ways. APIs allow us to build integrations that can automate these steps against a number of public and private data sources. Perhaps the best example of this comes from the realm of social media. Love it or loathe it, social media has fundamentally changed the ways in which people communicate and share information with one another. While the overwhelming majority of such interactions are positive, so I'm told, there is of course a non-trivial amount of negativity too. Threats, harassment, bullying, trolling and predatory grooming are some examples of the worst in human behaviour to which social media has given increased reach. So, as defenders, if someone is threatening our company, or even an employee via social media, should we just ignore it, because it's outside of our immediate purview and control? The answer of course is, no, we should go looking for the threat and respond accordingly, in a manner that aligns with the legal frameworks applicable to us.

An organisation's employees are both its biggest asset and biggest risk. Keeping them happy can play a big role in determining which way the pendulum swings on this one. Most successful companies will invest significant amounts of money on things like employee engagement and employee benefits. In recent years, benefits have grown to include things like free meals, gym memberships, dog-friendly offices, flexible working hours, support for remote working and private health insurance (which is an absolute must in countries like the United States). I like to think of a well-run security operations team as being an employee benefit in line with some of the offerings just mentioned, although of course, I don't think we'll come close to topping access to healthcare, or even being able to play with dogs in the office.

Asking the question 'what can we do to help keep our employees safe?' will likely yield answers that span both the physical and virtual realms, and that if implemented, would increase happiness and reduce risk.

Access to a security operations team that will assist with a security issue that might not fall strictly within the realms of an enterprise security problem, is very welcome for many employees who are making their way through the minefield of information security threats that lurk in their connected lives. If we're able to offer assistance and guidance when possible, we absolutely should, since it will help build trust and ultimately improve the security of our enterprise.

This chapter takes the blue team outside the relative comfort of the enterprise, and looks at monitoring external data sources for information that we can leverage to build better defences, increase employee safety, and increase the variety and level of services we offer to keep the enterprise secure.

OPEN-SOURCE INTELLIGENCE

Whenever you hear the term 'intelligence' bandied around, if you're anything like me, your mind probably jumps to information obtained by clandestine means. The asset on the inside feeding their handler secrets obtained by leveraging a position of trust within a target group or organisation. While that is a perfectly legitimate way to collect intelligence, the truth is that there is plenty of intelligence already out there in the open, ready to be collected and analysed, no spies required. In fact, all you really need is a web browser and a search engine.

The name for such information is open-source intelligence (OSINT), and it would be remiss if blue teamers weren't exploiting it to enhance defences. Let's take a look at some examples of OSINT in action.

Google hacking

The Google search engine spends its days hoovering up and indexing content on the internet. It knows where things are, lots of things, and that is why it has become the front door to the internet for so many people. The majority of the things it finds are designed to be found, and indeed a whole industry exists to make things more likely to be found.

Inevitably, though, it can also stumble across things that really shouldn't have been found, but through some misconfiguration or error, have been exposed to the open internet. Things like confidential documents, database backups or configuration files, to name but a few examples. Add into the mix the fact that Google is capable of being driven to find content in much more specific ways than the simple free text searches the majority of people use, and you've got quite a powerful OSINT tool on your hands.

The term 'search operators' is used to describe the various parameters that can be used within a Google search to discover very specific result sets. For example, if you wish to concentrate your search on a specific site, say example.com, you'd use the operator 'site:example.com' in the search box. Results would be limited to materials found on example.com. Replace example.com with your enterprise's domains, and you'll have a targeted search that may uncover some information you didn't know was out there. To add to the specificity, another operator can allow you to limit your search results to a particular file type, the 'filetype' operator. Say you were looking for PDF files on your own domains, a combination of 'filetype:pdf site:example.com', would get you there.

Other examples of Google search operators are shown in Table 10.1. Remember, these operators can be combined in a single search, which leads to highly specific results.

Table 10.1 Examples of Google search operators

Operator	Function	Example
allintext: / intext:	The 'all in text' and 'in text' operators tell Google to look for a specific term in the main body of the text on a website. The singular 'intext:' can be used on individual words, whereas 'allintext:' can be used on multiple words.	'intext:security' finds pages containing the word 'security'. 'allintext:security breach' finds pages containing the words 'security breach'.
allintitle: / intitle:	As above, but limits the scope of the keyword search to values found in the HTML title tag.	'intitle:security' finds pages containing the word 'security' in the title. 'allintitle:security breach' finds pages containing the words 'security breach' in the title.
allinurl: / inurl:	As above, but limits the scope of the keyword search to the full URL, rather than the body of the webpage.	'inurl:security' would find pages with a URL such as 'https://www.example.com/security'. 'allinurl:security breach' would find pages with a URL such as 'https://www.example.com/security/breach'.
filetype:	One of the most powerful operators from a security perspective, this limits search results to a specific filetype.	'filetype:txt' will limit results to text files.
site:	Limits search results to the specified site.	'site:example.com' returns results only from example.com
cache:	Returns search results from the most recently cached version of a site. Handy for looking for content that may have been exposed and subsequently removed.	'cache:example.com' will return results from the most recently cached version of example.com, providing there is a cached version in Google's index.

These techniques have been used by attackers and red teams alike for years, usually as an initial information-gathering step in a targeted attack or penetration test. These types of event are typically time bound: a penetration test has a start and end date for instance. There is value to be had on the defensive side by maintaining a regular routine of scouring for any changes to the search engine footprint of an organisation, just as you'd run port scans during the vulnerability management process to look for changes to the network profile of a host or firewall. Repeatedly running targeted searches on Google can help discover some new exposure. Hopefully, your team will be the ones to find it, before anyone else does. Well, anyone other than Google, of course.

Entire books have been dedicated to Google hacking (e.g. Long et al., 2016), containing hundreds of pages of examples of ways in which the search engine has been leveraged to find sensitive information and vulnerable hosts, but to whet your appetite, I've listed a few examples of Google search terms, so-called Google Dorks, in Table 10.2.

Table 10.2 Examples of Google Dorks

Search term (Dork)	Result
intitle:'iDRAC-login'	Locates login pages for Dell Remote Access Controllers
intitle:'Login - Xfinity' AND 'Gateway > Login'	Identifies exposed login pages for Xfinity (Comcast) routers used for residential connections
filetype:pub 'ssh-rsa'	Identifies secure shell (SSH) public keys
filetype:env intext:AWS_SECRET	Locates files containing Amazon Web Services (AWS) secret keys in environment variables
intitle:'Index of /private/'	Looks for indexed versions of pages that contain /private/ in the path, which as you can imagine, would likely be sensitive in nature

Additionally, the Google Hacking Database[1] serves as an online reference, containing many example search strings.

Shodan

While Google spends its days looking for content served up over HTTP, another search engine that concentrates on finding internet-connected computers is hard at work looking at every exposed port and service. Shodan[2] is a search engine for computers, which works by connecting to public IP addresses on various ports and recording the response (Figure 10.1). Shodan is a great OSINT tool for finding hosts that maybe, just maybe, shouldn't be publicly accessible. The Shodan site is chock full of stories of some of the more interesting internet-connected hosts it's discovered over the years, a wind turbine being my personal favourite.

As the IoT has become more prolific in recent years, Shodan has become a more powerful tool, with a penchant for finding horrifically insecure devices accidentally exposed by folks who may not have grasped what they were doing. This includes on both personal and business networks.

Compromised credential dumps

One of the worst user habits we frequently observe is password reuse across multiple sites. On a very much related note, one of the worst SP habits we frequently observe is not supporting, let alone requiring, MFA.

Figure 10.1 Shodan

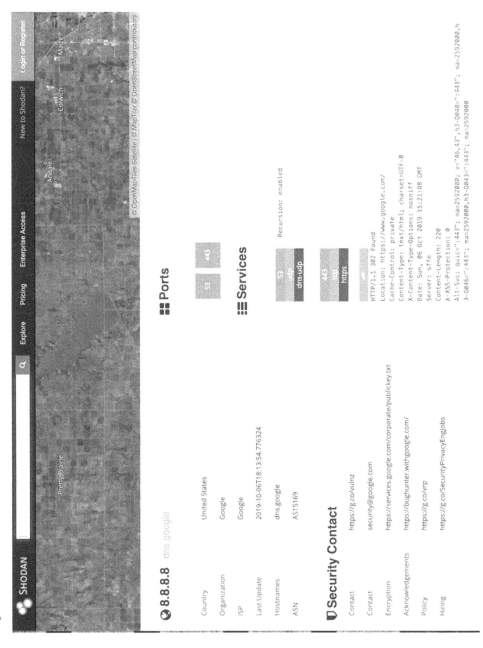

When a password becomes compromised, either through a breach of a credential database or during a phishing attack, it'll frequently find its way onto the internet in clear text, along with the username or email address associated with it. If the same credential set is used on a website in addition to the one it's been compromised from, there is very clearly a risk to the user that these credentials could be used to gain access to that second site, third site, fourth site and so on.

An attack that involves leveraging stolen credential sets at scale to attempt to gain access to a web application is known as a credential stuffing attack. We can help protect our users from such attacks, not just by offering MFA, but by actively scouring for compromised credentials online, and warning them that their credentials have been compromised. Taking this further, we can completely prevent them from reusing a previously compromised password. A blue team can prevent someone else's breach from becoming their problem.

Implementation of such features has become more commonplace, but they aren't without their challenges. A user might not understand the messaging, and might believe their password has been compromised from your application. So, if you're planning on implementing such a feature, expect and prepare for angry users to ask questions, but for the most part, they'll actually be pretty happy when you explain to them how they're being protected by your application.

We can of course apply the same logic to employee accounts, and prevent them from leveraging previously compromised passwords on internal systems. This will clearly result in a security advantage for the company. Indeed, this can be a great way to pilot such integrations, before rolling them out to external users.

So how do you discover sets of credentials that have been previously compromised? A number of threat intelligence feed providers include compromised credential discovery in their offerings, and some dedicated services have also popped up, perhaps most famously, Have I Been Pwned?[3] which offers both a UI and API for searching its large database of compromised user accounts and passwords.

Google alerts

There is definitely a stigma around the act of Googling yourself, but as security operations professionals, we have good reason to do so. Google alerts allow teams to automate this process, so I guess you could even claim that it's not really self-Googling if a software application is doing it on your behalf. The purpose of doing so is to get a heads up when your company, or perhaps key figures associated with your company, are included in new content that Google has discovered.

Alerts are configured based on keywords, and can be set to focus on a specific source within Google's treasure trove of information, such as news articles, blog posts or general web content. Alternatively, you can just ask Google to look everywhere to see what it can find. The alerts can run daily, or in real time, and can even be focused on a specific region, so if you're exclusively UK-based, for example, you can filter out noise from across the pond.

Upon discovering what is deemed to be relevant content, the Google alert will send an email at the configured frequency, containing links to the discovered content. Through a little bit of coding, it's possible to extend a Google alert to generate an event directly in a SIEM tool. A very powerful, free, OSINT capability.

SOCIAL MEDIA MONITORING

During the introduction to this chapter, I noted social media as a potentially highly valuable source of threat information for defenders. Social media chatter can contain anything from the general background noise of mixed positive and negative feedback directed at a brand, to a user expressing concern that a potential security incident might have occurred, or perhaps a disgruntled former employee disclosing information about the company that might be damaging, and everything else in between.

The key to leveraging this information well is to automate the process of looking for it. Thanks to APIs offered by the major players in the social media realm, it's possible to build integrations directly into our SIEM solutions. There are also an array of open-source and commercial products, such as Hootsuite,[4] SentiOne[5] and ZeroFox[6] that can take care of these integrations for us.

Before we get stuck in to some examples of how we can leverage the major social media platforms, it's worth noting that when I refer to the collection of information posted on them I'm strictly speaking about publicly accessible information. It's not right, nor may it be legal in certain jurisdictions, to access private content on social media for the purposes of security operations. This is especially true when it comes to accessing content posted by employees. However, as a slight exception to this rule, if a report comes in of a threat made in private on social media, then by all means it should be addressed, and the appropriate authorities involved.

Twitter

The majority of content posted to Twitter is open to the masses to view and digest. A lot of information can be conveyed in 280-character tweets, and it provides a platform for brands to advertise to and support their users, celebrities to interact with their fans, people to read the news and presidents to run their countries. The Twitter API allows us to search through the millions of daily tweets for keyword combinations that might be of interest to us. Examples of the types of keywords that can deliver actionable intelligence include:

- **Company names and company Twitter account handles.** Although most companies with a social media presence have full-time staff that monitor activity on them, they might not be able to read every message in a timely fashion, so the more eyes on the thread, the better. While we won't jump in to every customer service conversation that pops up, we can get a head start on anything that might require security awareness or intervention.

- **Executive names and their Twitter handles.** Twitter allows customers a direct line to the CEO of a company, so why bother starting with anyone lower down the food chain if you have a grievance? Unfortunately, using the veil of anonymity that the internet provides, some people might rapidly escalate their tone from complaining to harassing.

- **Location-based keywords.** Looking for information such as street names associated with the physical location of a company's offices can add value from a physical security perspective. Geo-tagged tweets (i.e. tweets tagged with a GPS location) can also be filtered so that any tweet that was sent from a specific location pops up in the search results.

- **Any combination of the above, plus security-related keywords.** Searching for 'company name + breach' or 'company name + hacked', for example, can lead to some interesting discoveries. These days, many users are defaulting to considering any outage or problem on a web application to be a security incident, even if the root cause isn't security related. These searches can help identify these whispers and be used to direct a PR-counteroffensive to ensure they don't become screams.

Facebook

Unlike Twitter, the majority of content posted to Facebook is access-restricted based on a user's privacy settings. As we all know, in some cases users will unintentionally post content to Facebook in a more open manner than perhaps they were expecting. Privacy settings and control have been a hot topic for Facebook over the years.

Facebook's Graph API is the principal tool for querying the social network's vast array of data, and provided the permissions assigned to a given object make it accessible to the requester (say a public post on a brand page, for example), searching can be automated via a Graph API HTTP request.

Following the fallout from the Cambridge Analytica scandal discussed earlier in this book, Facebook has dialled down the capabilities of the Graph API to access content without user consent. Certain content, such as public posts, can only be retrieved without associated user identifiers.

Instagram

The Facebook-owned, image-centric Instagram may draw comments from users that are of concern to us in security operations. Given the association with Facebook, Instagram has also undergone a fairly wide-ranging restricting and limiting of its API's capabilities following the increase in awareness around user privacy. As a result, some of the broader search capabilities that were once in place have been dialled back.

However, the Instagram Graph API allows automated collection of comment data on brand-posted content, and can be a powerful way to look for potential issues that need security attention. Additionally, it's also still possible to search for brand name or company 'mentions', alongside specific hashtags that may be of interest.

Finally, it's a good idea to check those images that brands are posting for some of the classic 'oversharing' risks mentioned earlier, including whiteboards, computer screen content and paperwork.

LinkedIn

The 'professional' social network, LinkedIn, provides a platform for everyone to behave in a slightly more grown up fashion, and share content related to their careers, alongside various motivational messages and other ground-breaking business concepts. Of course, just like any platform, there is always scope for misuse, and given the platform allows direct messaging to its users, in a very similar manner to regular email, the possibility of email-like threats, including phishing and abusive communication is omnipresent.

The majority of content in a LinkedIn profile is designed to be public and discoverable by people seeking information on the person posting it. Just as with other social networks, users can overshare and divulge information that may not really be for public consumption, or may not align with the values and beliefs of the individual's employer. Unfortunately, given the very clear association between the person's employer and their independently posted content, sometimes the line between employer's position and employee's position is not as clear as it would be on other social networks. This can lead to problems.

Companies and brands also serve up public pages on LinkedIn, and post content that can be commented on. As with some of the other platforms just discussed, those comments can invite unwelcome language and content.

The LinkedIn platform is also leveraged by job seekers to apply for open positions. Sometimes job postings can be a valuable source of insight for an attacker seeking to gain more information about the technologies in use at a given company. A balance must be had between explaining the technologies and skills you're looking for, and not giving away sensitive information for free. One way to achieve this is to ensure you provide a gating and review procedure for any new job descriptions.

Of all the social networks we've just discussed, LinkedIn has the most restrictive API access, which can make automated searching tricky. Still, it can be worth building a monitoring procedure, given the size of the LinkedIn user base and the potential for problems to amplify.

Glassdoor

While not exactly a social networking site, given the fact that most of its content is posted by anonymous users, Glassdoor is worthy of a mention here. Glassdoor provides a platform for employees to provide reviews of their companies. As you can probably imagine, this results in a mixed bag of content, some positive, some negative, but all of it very public. Security operations and HR teams should be aware of this and monitor the Glassdoor site for any comments that may cross the line from fair and appropriate feedback, to threatening or otherwise abusive comments.

EMPLOYEE SAFETY

Keeping fellow employees safe from online security threats while at work is of course what we spend a considerable chunk of our time doing. Those threats do not vanish when the employee leaves the office, and they also do not limit themselves to the virtual realm. The nature of a given threat means it could also extend to an employee's family members.

Of course, the truth is that we simply cannot monitor and be a shield for every employee and their family; this simply isn't practical. There are, however, plenty of things we can do to make the security knowledge that we possess more accessible, and encourage our employees to share it with their family members more freely. The great news is that most of those things can be done at little to no cost.

Making security personal

Let's take a look at how we can push enterprise security operations knowledge out of the enterprise, and into the homes of our employees.

Provide quick summaries of information security news stories

We're now firmly in a time when the mainstream media is comfortable carrying an information security story in the main section of their website or publication, rather than burying it in the technical or science section. It doesn't hurt that there seems to be a limitless supply of stories either. These stories will inevitably trigger questions from our user base, so it's a really good idea to get out in front of those questions. Don't answer the same question on the same vulnerability 10 times when you can provide a single answer to every person in your organisation.

Whether it's a smartphone vulnerability, a breach of a popular website impacting millions of people, or a new wave of phishing, there are frequently things users can do to lessen the impact. Apply the latest software updates quickly, change your password on other sites if you're guilty of reuse and be on the lookout for the following characteristics that may indicate you are at risk from this particular issue; these are reasonable responses that all users can take. Give them summarised versions of those news stories, so they don't have to figure it all out themselves, and provide it in a format that encourages them to share your advice.

Emails work well, but make sure users know the content is okay to be forwarded externally. I find using two different formats, one for serious, 'internal only' type communications, and a different one for public information, works well. Subject line tagging and protective marking can also help make this distinction clearer. Internal blog posts can work but won't be shareable via a link, so make sure that an option to save a shareable PDF is present.

We're not Reuters, so we can't quite cover every story, but it'll become apparent which stories are worthy of this treatment, usually based on the number of people that might ask about it.

Offer workshops on information security topics

A really great way to connect with your users is to offer short workshops, perhaps during a lunch hour, on various information security topics. Providing advice on how to lock down a social media profile, deploy a DNS-based web content filtering system, ensure that a wireless network is secure, and deploy parental controls on a given platform, are all examples of topics for such talks.

Running this type of event allows users to get to know you and your team, which can lead to a more trusting relationship, and they promote good security hygiene at home, which translates into the enterprise environment.

Executive cyber security services

The executives in your company will likely be among the highest profile employees, and will have access to some of the most sensitive material. They're extremely valuable targets to a malicious actor, and they'll go after them in whatever way they can.

In a larger security operations team, it is sometimes possible to spend more time focused on a high-profile executive, perhaps gaining permission to run some penetration testing on the executive's personal IT equipment across the internet, or maybe even travelling to their home to review wireless network and personal device security settings. Doing this will clearly result in benefits to both the executive and the organisation, perhaps the only downside is that resource constraints mean it's not something we can offer more broadly.

In the summer of 2009, the identity of Britain's next top spymaster was revealed through a publicly accessible Facebook post. The incoming chief of MI6, known as 'C', and the only publicly acknowledged MI6 employee, Sir John Sawyers, was exposed thanks to a post by family members on his wife's Facebook profile page, which lacked any access controls.

An innocent, 'congrats Uncle C', started a tidal wave of embarrassing media coverage, with UK newspapers gobbling up and reprinting photographs of C in his swimming trunks. Perhaps more seriously from a security perspective, the Facebook page was also used to reveal the location of the apartment Sir John and his family were staying in.

While not all high-profile individuals will be in positions as sensitive as the head of the UK's foreign intelligence agency, this example still shows just how serious the security posture of family members can be in the highly connected world of social media.

Duty of care

When we arrive at work, it's reasonable to assume that our employer will have done everything they can to ensure they're providing us with as safe a work environment as possible. Not only does this extend to physical safety measures, such as ensuring that our work environment is free of hazards that could lead to injury, but it also extends to mental health. Harassment at work would be an example of something that could have an adverse impact on your mental wellbeing. Harassment can of course occur electronically, through instant messages and emails. Anyone who ever went through high school in the internet era can probably attest to that.

In security operations, we can help our employer ensure they're meeting their duty of care in a couple of different ways. Many of the technical security tools discussed in this book, particularly DLP and content filtering tools, can also be used to take on harassment. DLP, for instance, can be tuned to look for threatening, offensive or racist language.

If a company is providing virtual access to their employees, either through phone lines, emails or chat windows, keeping these environments as safe as possible falls under the duty of care. For example, it should be possible for a customer service representative to quickly end an instant messenger conversation, if the conversation goes off the rails and becomes abusive or threatening. In any environment where it's possible to send files directly to an employee, especially images, checks on content, things like skin detection, or perhaps even cryptographic hash comparisons against known pornographic image types can be used to filter out unwanted content. If implementing such preventive controls is not possible, another option might be to have a remove and report button, where security operations can get an incident report directly from the employee and take the appropriate level of action.

These days, knowing where someone works along with their name is pretty much all the information you need to track them down online. For more vulnerable groups, especially younger women, this can present a risk. Support from an employer for things like aliases, and all the technical infrastructure to support an alias or alternative name in services like email, in applications and on business cards, can make a world of difference. Unfortunately, in a lot of cases such things are not considered; this is typically because the people designing the systems haven't had to experience this particular type of harassment themselves. Diversity when it comes to application design is a wonderful thing, as it can help open eyes to these types of concern.

Situational awareness

Pushing information to employees to assist them with improving their situational awareness while at work can be a tremendously valuable role fulfilled by security operations. For instance, monitoring travel news sites for train cancellations and passing that information to a central point within the organisation might not seem like a safety or security responsibility, but if we consider that it could lead to an employee deciding to take a different commute option, rather than getting stranded at a train station later in the evening, you can start to see why it might be valuable.

Staying on top of changing weather conditions is another example of keeping an eye on the world around us. I'd like to think I'm pretty aware and capable of making my own decisions about safety, but in July of 2007, like many others, I was caught out by some terrible flooding in the West Midlands, UK, and spent a night sleeping in my car on the side of the road. At no point was I given an instruction to leave the office early because roads were becoming rivers. I really wish I had been; it was an extremely uncomfortable night spent listening to the RAF helicopter pluck people off the rooftops of flooded homes nearby.

Enterprise travel systems

It's relatively easy to keep tabs on employees when they're in the same building, day after day. However, a lot of people travel for work, on planes, trains and in their own vehicles. Keeping on top of those travellers can be a full-time job depending on the size of your company and the number of employees on the move. Many companies leverage enterprise travel booking and management systems, either allowing employees to book directly or through a travel agent. There are cost advantages to the company of doing this, of course: it allows them to set travel policies and ensure that folks aren't constantly flying first class and staying at five-star hotels.

Importantly, these types of travel management system provide valuable reporting with data that allows you to see employees' flight and hotel details. Just like any data, it's only valuable if it's used. Systems like Concur[7] have powerful APIs that allow full itineraries to be exported and used elsewhere, perhaps even in your SIEM. If something were to happen to an aircraft, or perhaps if there was a terrorist attack in a given location, this data could quickly be used to locate potentially impacted employees.

As you may have guessed from the photograph on the front cover of this book, and some of my analogies, such as the MEL, I'm a little bit of an aviation nerd. I was able to put my nerdiness to good use within the last couple of years, as I put together what I consider to be a pretty neat integration of two data sources into our SIEM.

First, we pull in travel itineraries from our enterprise travel management software. This helps us keep an eye on the flights our employees are booked onto. That, in and of itself, has proven to be useful information on a couple of occasions.

Second, to add additional value, leveraging the service Flightradar24,[8] which uses crowdsourced ADS-B transponder data to track the location of aircraft in real time (Figure 10.2), we can be on the lookout for aircraft that have potential problems. Aircraft will frequently transmit a special transponder code if they're in distress. A transponder code is a four-digit number that allows air traffic controllers to identify the aircraft they're seeing on their radar screens.

- The code 7500 is used to indicate a hijacking, '75, taken alive'.
- The code 7600 is used to indicate radio failure, '76, in a fix'.
- The code 7700 is used to indicate a general emergency, '77, going to heaven'.

Flightradar24 tracks transponder codes, so they are loaded into our data when we detect we have an aircraft with an employee on business travel on it. Should we get a correlation between any such flight and one of these emergency codes, a SIEM event is generated.

It gives security operations awareness that the employee might need support, perhaps if a flight is diverted, and is a very powerful example of how open-source information and company data can be combined in new and innovative ways to ensure that an employer is meeting their duty of care.

To combine the physical and technical realms, this idea could be expanded to suppress or more accurately curate 'unusual sign in location' alerts generated by a SIEM.

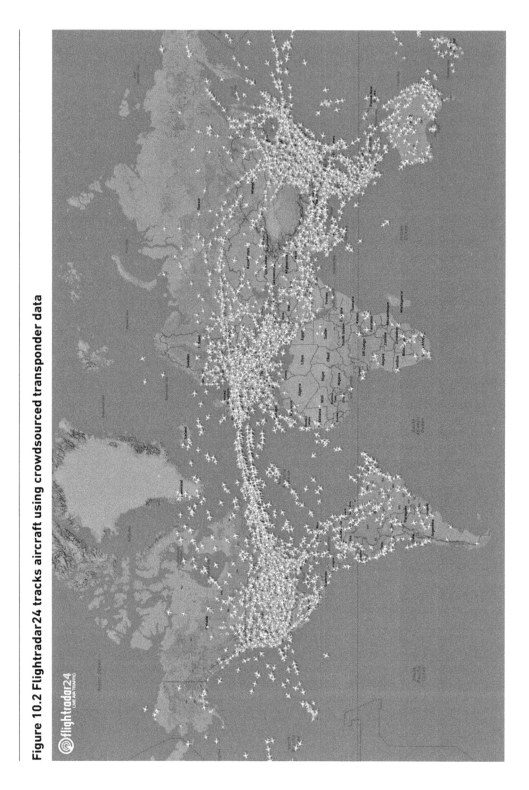

Figure 10.2 Flightradar24 tracks aircraft using crowdsourced transponder data

SUMMARY

During this chapter we reviewed ways in which defensive security operations professionals can take a look outside the enterprise for information which can assist them in their objectives. We started by looking at OSINT techniques, including the use of highly targeted Google searches to find sensitive material that has been indexed by Google. We looked at Shodan, a search engine for finding internet-connected machines. Then, we discussed using Google Alerts to inform us of new material detected by Google.

We talked about leveraging dumps of compromised credentials to protect users who may reuse the same password over and over from credential stuffing attacks.

Next, we talked about social media monitoring, and looked at examples of how we could leverage some of the most popular social networks to gain intelligence into threats to our company and employees.

We looked at ways to improve employee safety, both physically and online. We talked about offering informal training sessions that pertain to securing personally owned devices. We discussed offering useful summaries of information security stories, and the actions that users should take as a result of those stories.

Finally, we talked about duty of care, and the need to build in technical controls to protect our employees from abuse and harassment via online channels. We mentioned a couple of ways in which we can improve situational awareness, and finished the chapter by discussing integrations with enterprise travel management tools, for the purposes of helping to keep business travel safe.

The next chapter shifts things around a bit, as we go full red team, and talk about key offensive functions including penetration testing and threat hunting.

REFERENCE

Long, J., Gardner, B. and Brown, J. (2016) *Google Hacking for Penetration Testers*. Syngress, Waltham, MA.

PART II
RED TEAMS

11 RED TEAMING AND THREAT HUNTING

At the beginning of this book, I ran through the typical life cycle of a security operations team. So far, as we've progressed through the chapters, we've tracked along nicely with that life cycle. From early inception in response to a specific business need, to the birth and eventual maturity of defensive, or blue team, capabilities. Now, it's time to put our work to the test, as we switch gears, turn red, and change our focus to offensive security operations.

The purpose of a red team is to simulate the approach of an adversary, testing our defences and validating the hard work we've put in, but also to ensure that we, as a security operations team, are constantly in a state of ongoing improvement. That's something we always need to remember. Everyone is working towards the same goal. Everyone is on the same team, regardless of whether they are 'blue' or 'red'. It's imperative that both sides have a great working relationship, share information in a two-way fashion, and never become truly adversarial. Having fun with one another is one thing, and highly encouraged, but there must always be mutual respect along the way.

To achieve their objectives, the red team will undertake a series of activities, including penetration testing, both in the digital and physical realms, proactive threat hunting and bespoke tool development. We'll discuss each of these activities throughout the remaining pages of this book. Within this chapter specifically, we'll look at building out the red team, in terms of the people we hire and the culture they operate in, setting the rules of engagement, digital penetration testing and threat hunting.

Before we begin, one final note. The approval of red team hires, especially the first hire, has traditionally been one of the trickiest to get pushed through the process. Some might be nervous about what could be uncovered when an offensively minded security professional gets free rein to spend all day exploring an enterprise's applications and networks. Some may protest that by having an insider perspective, the red teamer will be forever tainted by what they've seen. Fortunately, this attitude is becoming less common, and folks are waking up to the not so bold idea that an employee finding a problem is markedly better than someone outside the enterprise doing so. Either way, if you're sitting here reading this after getting approval to go find your first full-time red teamer, you must have done a good job building enough trust and demonstrating enough value to this point, so by all means take a minute to congratulate yourself!

WHAT IS RED TEAMING?

When a malicious actor decides to target an organisation, there are no rules. They aren't going to pause to consider a scope of work. They aren't going to limit their activities to occur only during business hours. The path of least resistance will be taken, even if that path goes directly through an employee's personal online accounts and presence, to get at their employer.

The purpose of red teaming is to simulate this lawlessness as closely as possible. Of course, the difference is that the red team has explicit approval to conduct activities that, if not approved, would clearly be illegal.

Activities performed by red teams can be focused on exploiting vulnerabilities in technical or physical security systems, as well as taking advantage of human behaviours, perhaps through techniques like phishing or social engineering (both topics we'll discuss later in the book).

When it comes to the testing of technical and physical security from a red team perspective, penetration testing is the prime activity *du jour*, and one covered extensively in this chapter. Red teams typically run a combination of ongoing testing and campaign-based tests, in which they are given a specific target objective, typically lasting multiple weeks or months.

Given the wide variety of techniques at a red team's disposal, they lend themselves to a diverse array of skills and backgrounds when staffing.

BUILDING YOUR RED TEAM

Just as the founding member of an enterprise security function can have a profound effect on the perception of the team for years, so too can the founding member of an enterprise red team. Perception has a direct impact on effectiveness, and that is especially true when it comes to red team work. A person could be the most technically gifted penetration tester the planet has ever seen, but if they cannot communicate their findings effectively, their technical skills will go to waste. Therefore, a balance between technical, communicative and interpersonal skills must be sought. As the hiring manager, the specifics of that balance fall to your discretion. For example, you might lean more to the technical side, with the understanding that you will have to be more hands-on with the communication aspects. These decisions when building teams are what management and leadership are all about.

Red teamer skills

When sitting down with a candidate for a red team position, there are typically three main areas of focus a hiring manager will evaluate:

- **Technical skills.** Broadly speaking, red team work can be categorised as a specialism. Within the umbrella of red team work, things can become even more specialised still. Penetration testing skills, for example, can be concentrated on applications, infrastructure or hardware.

- **Creativity.** Technical skills alone, although highly important, won't be enough to cut it as a highly effective red teamer. You've got to get creative from time to time, whether that's during exploit development or figuring out how to get past a physical security control.

- **Personal.** As previously stated, the value derived from a red teamer's technical skills and creativity will never be maximised unless they have reasonable communication abilities and interpersonal skills. No one likes a new person showing up at their work, pointing out all their mistakes, and handing them a series of new problems to deal with. They need to be tactful, and while security operations leaders can help to some degree, we won't be there all the time.

We'd been interviewing extensively for a red team position that was proving incredibly difficult to fill. One day we lined up five interviews back to back to try to finally select a candidate. I happened to have a device called a PwnPlug,[1] which is a little covert penetration testing drop box which took the physical form of a power adaptor, sitting on my desk at the time. As I headed to the conference room where the interviews were going to be taking place, I took it, and plugged it in the outlet behind me, so that it would be visible to our interviewees.

I didn't really have a grand plan, I just thought it would be interesting to see how many, if any, of the candidates would notice it. Given that they were interviewing for a role in which observational skills are important, and one in which they might ultimately be using tools like the PwnPlug, I figured this little test couldn't hurt.

Candidate one didn't notice. Candidate two said nothing. Candidate three walked into the room, pointed directly at the PwnPlug, and said, 'you do realise there is a PwnPlug there, right?' After we'd wrapped up the interview, the candidate asked if there was any time for them to have a demo of the plug. I had a few minutes, so obliged. Ultimately, candidate three got the position, although not just because they'd spotted the object hidden in plain sight, there were other reasons too. I liked this improvised test so much, I used it a couple more times for subsequent roles, with similar results.

A common approach to interviewing red team candidates applying for penetration testing roles is to present them with a 'capture the flag' type challenge, in which they are asked to compromise a purposefully vulnerable web application or system. This is a good way to assess both technical skills and creativity, but as the interviewer, it's important to focus on the candidate's approach to solving the problem, rather than whether or not they actually hit the solution in the time allowed. It's also important to make it absolutely clear to the candidate at the beginning that if they don't capture the flags it doesn't automatically mean they've failed the interview. Why? Because an interview isn't a normal representation of a typical day at work. An interview is a high-pressure, time-reduced scenario, where a person is so far out of their comfort zone, they can sometimes be unable to answer basic questions in a manner in which they usually would.

Focus on the ways in which the candidate assesses potential vectors to get into the application, how familiar they are with the tools that could aid them in meeting the objective, and then how well they can communicate what they're trying to do, and what they might do next if they had more time.

As for assessing personal skills, typically, you can do that during natural conversation, and by gauging their responses to specific questions. How they react to the idea of partaking in a 'capture the flag' can also be very telling. I once had a candidate for a penetration test lead position flat out refuse to even look at a vulnerable web application I'd prepared. Their reasoning was because 'I've never seen a challenge like this that mirrors the real world enough to make it worth my time'. Needless to say, they didn't make the cut. Even if the idea of doing a technical test makes the candidate nervous, the majority of people that are suited for this type of role will jump at the opportunity to have a go, and let their technical skills do some of the talking.

Rules of engagement

On the one hand a malicious actor positioned outside the enterprise starting to size up a potential target have free rein to go after what resources they want, in whatever fashion they desire. They're not bound by such corporate restraints as the business and political pressures that surround us all in our daily work. On the other hand, the red team, which is supposed to mirror a malicious attacker's approach as closely as possible, will have some limitations placed on them. Our job as leaders in security operations is to remove as many of those limitations as practicable, but it's still a reasonable expectation of the business that we play by some rules, and our activities are bound by appropriate guidelines.

In the world of penetration testing and red teaming, the rules of engagement serve as those guidelines. Frequently used when working with external contract penetration testers, they're equally important when working with internal teams. Provisions that may find their way into the rules of engagement include not performing application or infrastructure penetration testing during change or release windows, or perhaps aligning with a HR approved approach to running phishing simulations.

While having published rules of engagement may seem like a hindrance to our team, they can actually help us out. Rules of engagement establish expectations, and they reduce, or even eliminate, the opportunity for someone to come back at us after the fact and claim they were treated unfairly, or were tricked, and that the results of a given test shouldn't stand.

There might also be some legal considerations that come into play when crafting the rules of engagement. When considering physical penetration testing for example, those working directly for our company might have been given authorisation to attempt a break in to the primary datacentre. However, if that datacentre is co-located and hosted by a third party, without the third-party's authorisation to perform the testing, the potential for breaking the law is very real. Procedures for informing and seeking approval from all appropriate parties to begin a test should be included in the rules of engagement, and kept up to date.

Where to start

While a newly established red team can be directed to simply 'have at it', and explore the enterprise, testing things as they find them; more often than not, we'll want to provide some direction and prioritisation based on risk. After all, we'll need a way to measure effectiveness of the team and, with sporadic findings from all over the place, it can be hard to bundle them together in such a way as to make this possible. However, if we have regularly delivered penetration test reports for specific targets, the output and operation of the team is less likely to be called into question.

Risk plays a leading role in almost all decisions we make in information security, and prioritising the work of the red team is no exception. If the majority of a company's revenue is generated through one particular web application, that application is likely going to be a higher priority for the security team overall, and at the top of the target list for the red team's penetration testing efforts.

Early, and often

The earlier in the software development life cycle (SDLC) a security vulnerability is identified, the cheaper it is to fix. If vulnerable code is discovered and remediated before it ever gets anywhere near production, the company will save valuable time, money and, of course, will not have placed itself or its users at risk in the process. To increase the chances of early detection, the red team should be invited into the development process, and tasked with performing penetration tests in test or staging environments.

Tight alignment between the development team and the red team means that as new features are finished, they can be tested. Likewise, any major changes to an existing application or feature can be subjected to the same level of testing. As the process matures, and both the development team and the red team become comfortable with each other, slowly but surely, a two-way pipeline of testing and remediation work will form. Frequent testing will lead to more secure software and a more secure company.

In addition to the ongoing penetration testing efforts that occur during the SDLC, time should be set aside for the red team to conduct scheduled stand-alone tests that result in the publication of a formal report, perhaps on a quarterly, biannual or annual basis. These 'from scratch' tests should assess the state of the application at a given moment in time, and should be conducted to a standard that is appropriate for dissemination to customers, or in support of regulatory and compliance requirements.

Since the red team works for the same organisation, they can also provide guidance to the blue team on any discovered vulnerabilities and how best to detect and respond to any potential exposure that may occur as a result of that vulnerability.

Red team tools

The majority of penetration testers are more than comfortable using open-source tools to perform their testing, so rarely do people consider the need to purchase commercial products to support them in their endeavours. The Kali Linux[2] distribution, for example, comes pre-loaded with a variety of open-source tools. This pre-loading is one of the main reasons Kali is so frequently recommended, a great deal of time can be saved by not having to individually install and configure each of the tools manually. It is worth noting, however, that there are more than a few commercial penetration testing tools out there that can aid with various penetration testing tasks and, as with all good security tools, if there is budget available and a need to be met, they should be at the very least evaluated. Examples of such tools include the web application testing tool Burp Suite,[3] OSINT mapper Maltego[4] and the commercial version of the penetration testing framework Metasploit.[5]

With their suite of tools in place, it's somewhat ironic that the red team is one of the most likely teams to require an exception to violate all of the security policies the security organisation enforces on others. The discovery of some of the tools that will be present on a typical red teamer's laptop would likely start to ring alarm bells if they showed up anywhere else. Now, these exceptions may all make perfect sense, but in the early days of the red team, they can sometimes lead to friction. In organisations where IT is responsible for enforcing policy and control over the endpoint, for instance, getting them to agree to allow the red team to work off domain or off image can involve more discussions than you'd probably like to have. It's possible to see both sides of the argument; we typically claim no exceptions, and that everyone should be treated equally, but then go a little *Animal Farm* (Orwell, 1945) and suggest that the rules don't apply to our own people. Therefore, be prepared to make some compromises.

One option might be to issue red teamers with two laptops. A corporate standard one, for doing routine things, like checking email and accessing enterprise applications, and then a testing one which enables them to do what they need to do to ensure they can test effectively. Most testers will want a Linux-based laptop, and will legitimately need root access to ensure everything runs as it should without interference from permissions restrictions. Alternatively, permitting virtual machines to be installed on corporate laptops can be another approach, but this can still lead to issues with interference from the host security controls.

Whatever the final decision on the approach, have the conversation and make sure all parties are in agreement, and, ideally, have this decision made before the first red teamer walks into the building. Frequently, a red teamer's first experiences involve being caught up in these discussions and debates, and that's not really a good way to start a new position, when all you really want to do is get stuck in right away.

PENETRATION TESTING

The goal of the penetration test is to simulate the actions of a malicious actor in order to identify vulnerabilities in applications and services. I've talked a lot about penetration testing, and now it's time to dive a little deeper into this scientific process. The descriptive term I just used, 'scientific process', is very important to call out, as unfortunately it's something that is forgotten with a somewhat alarming frequency. Regardless of who is performing a penetration test, whether they are working for an internal red team or an external consultancy, the test should always follow a defined methodology, and result in the delivery of a report that contains enough detail that a third party could repeat the test and arrive at the same conclusion. Sadly, in the heavily commoditised world of modern penetration testing services, reports can sometimes read more like marketing materials than scientific documents. Incidentally, this can be one of the justifications for having an internal red team; if you directly manage the team, you have full control over both the methodology used and the reporting standards.

Penetration testing methodologies

There are several published penetration testing methodologies, crafted by various industry bodies, government entities and private enterprise. The aim of each of them is to define a standard approach to testing, and just as importantly, reporting. The idea being that if we're all working to a baseline standard, it'll be easier for consumers of penetration testing reports to understand and derive a certain amount of value from the output of the test. Standard methodologies are also frequently used to define the level of testing required to meet a regulatory or compliance need. Let's look at some examples of penetration testing methodologies.

Open-Source Security Testing Methodology Manual (OSTMM)

Created and maintained by the non-profit Institute for Security and Open Methodologies (ISECOM), with the first version released in the early 2000s, the Open-Source Security Testing Methodology Manual (OSTMM)[6] provides a methodology for testing the effectiveness of operational security. In addition to the methodology itself, ISECOM offers training for penetration testers who are conducting testing according to its guidelines, and can also validate that reports delivered following the OSTMM aligned test meet all of ISECOM's requirements.

The OSTMM describes how a tester should properly scope and plan a test prior to commencing any testing, and describes the five 'channels' over a which a tester might find themselves interacting with a target. Those channels are physical, human, wireless, data networks and telecommunications. As a result, the OSTMM provides good coverage for testing any range of target types, from web applications, to infrastructure and even entire enterprises.

The reporting format described in OSTMM is known as the Security Test Audit Report (STAR), and leverages a number of mathematical formulae to provide a numerical score to measure the security level of a target.

Penetration Testing Execution Standard (PTES)

In 2009, a group of penetration testing consultants from across the industry were beginning to get fed up with the dramatically variable standard of penetration testing practices in use around the world, and as a direct result came together to craft a standard. Called the Penetration Testing Execution Standard (PTES),[7] this testing methodology walks a tester through seven defined phases of running a penetration test:

- **Pre-engagement**, which includes scoping and setting rules of engagement.

- **Intelligence gathering**, which includes collecting OSINT on a target.

- **Threat modelling**, which includes the identification and risk classification of assets, and potential threats to those assets.

- **Vulnerability analysis**, which includes discovery of potential weaknesses in targets that could be leveraged by an attacker.

- **Exploitation**, which includes taking advantage of the vulnerabilities identified in the previous phase and exploiting them to gain access to a target.

- **Post-exploitation**, which includes leveraging and maintaining the tester's new found foothold in the target organisation to expose other assets in scope for testing.

- **Reporting**, which defines the content and structure of a penetration test report.

In addition to the main body of the standard, the group behind PTES has also produced a series of technical guidelines, which includes examples of the tools that can be leveraged during each phase of the PTES penetration testing process.

Technical guide to information security testing and assessment (NIST 800-115)

It wouldn't be a good standards discussion without input from the folks at NIST, and when it comes to penetration testing, their document 800-115 (Scarfone et al., 2008) provides a high-level overview of the various steps they recommend a penetration tester follow while performing a test.

The NIST methodology is broken into three phases:

- **Planning**, which talks through topics such as scoping, ensuring that requirements are met and setting rules of engagement.

- **Execution**, which includes the discovery of vulnerabilities through specific activities selected based on the nature of the target being assessed, and the type of testing being performed.

- **Post-execution**, which includes report creation and delivery.

The technical guide 800-115 is called out specifically as an industry standard penetration testing methodology in the PCI-DSS, and as such, has found its way onto the desks of many security professionals working to protect payment card environments.

As the quote attributed to computer scientist Andrew S. Tanenbaum goes, 'the nice thing about standards is that there are so many of them to choose from'. Whichever methodology is ultimately chosen as the basis for a given programme of testing, it should be fully understood and applied correctly by the testers across the red team. Decisions to deviate from the standard should not be taken lightly, as we'll want to ensure a consistent product for all our internal and external customers.

Prior to the test

Before the first keystroke in support of a penetration test is ever registered, there is important pre-work to be done. Pre-work is one of those terms that no one ever gets excited about. It's work before work, and given that most people working in penetration testing like the excitement of exploitation, any additional steps we have to take that keep us from doing what we truly love can be frustrating. The truth is that we have to do this important work to ensure that we can keep doing what we're doing, because mistakes during penetration tests can lead to major problems, which can reduce the trust placed in us, and dramatically reduce the likelihood that we'll be allowed to test again.

We've already discussed the rules of engagement, an important pre-work item, and something that can usually be set once for an internal red team (unlike an external team, where precise rules may need to be set on a per-client basis). Still, if you're working with a new team, or on a new target, it is worth ensuring that everyone is up to speed on your published rules before testing commences.

Scoping is another major area of focus for the pre-work phase of a penetration test. It is incredibly important to ensure that scope is locked down and extremely clear to all involved in the test. In the era of platforms and partnerships, IaaS and SaaS, and personally owned devices in the enterprise, setting rules for what the test can and cannot touch is a more important step than ever before.

For example, if a test is on an application hosted on shared infrastructure, are we allowed to attempt to compromise that infrastructure (like a real attacker would), or are we scoped only to target the application?

We should always take the time to ask the question 'what do I do if something goes wrong during this test?' Any time you subject an application or service to a condition that it wasn't expecting to find itself in, such as putting it on the receiving end of malformed requests generated during a penetration test, you run the risk of causing it to become unstable, or possibly even unresponsive. If it's an application in production, no prizes for guessing that this could be a very disruptive, costly thing for a business to deal with. Therefore, preparing for this scenario, and taking steps to reduce the impact should it materialise, are a key part of pre-test planning. Knowing who should be notified if things go wrong, having up-to-date contact information for them, and being aware of specific time windows that are more favourable for running the test, are all examples of things we can do in support of this effort.

In some cases, particularly in larger organisations, penetration tests might be run like projects, with a project-manager type figure ensuring that the scope is set, the requirements and goals of the test are defined and the appropriate resources are assigned. I really like this setup, because it means penetration testers can avoid becoming involved in every aspect of the pre-work process, and can stay focused on the actual work of testing. Unfortunately, for many testers, resource constraints mean that they are just as involved in the pre-work as they are in the testing.

The test

When it's time to begin testing in earnest, simply throwing a URL or IP address into a tool, pressing 'play', sitting back and waiting for vulnerabilities to pop up automatically doesn't quite cut it. Instead, a multi-phase process, which involves varying levels of interaction between the tester and the target, should be followed. Some of these phases were alluded to earlier in the discussion on penetration testing methodologies, and indeed, the specific names of, and tasks to be undertaken as a part of, those phases will vary slightly between methodologies. However, they all roughly follow the same pattern, which I will now summarise.

Information gathering phase
The first phase of a test is centred on learning as much information about your target as possible, without actually interacting with it. Commonly, this involves reviewing open-source information that will provide insight into the infrastructure hosting an application, such as domain and IP registration records (often queried using WHOIS services) records. Depending on the nature of the target, it can also include learning about the structure of an organisation and key employees, or mapping out relationships between the target and its customers or partners.

Of course, an internal red team will likely have access to a great deal of both public and private information, which, practically speaking, could negate the need for actually executing much of the work performed as part of the intelligence gathering phase. That said, staying true to the mantra of simulating the actions of a malicious attacker operating from a position outside the organisation, we should still run through this phase where possible – you never know what you'll discover, after all. It's possible that some open-source information might expose more about your target than intended, perhaps through an incorrectly secured directory on a webserver that is subsequently indexed by a search engine.

Scanning and discovery phase

As the test evolves into its second phase, more active techniques are used to gain insight into the target environment. This includes running scans against IP addresses to discover open ports, and information on the services listening on those ports.

Tools like the de-facto standard port scanner nmap[8] can, of course, go beyond simply detecting if a TCP port is open or closed. By analysing the way in which a target responds to different types of probe on different ports, it is capable of fingerprinting specific applications and operating systems in use, and the associated version numbers. This can then lead the tester on a path of research into possible vulnerabilities that might apply to the target, based on this newly discovered information.

Where a web application is our target, we'd likely use this phase to look for potential entry vectors within the application, such as form input fields or file upload functions.

As the attacker, or tester, moves to a more active posture they will likely generate events that will flow down into log files, trip IDS/IPS and generally provide an opportunity to test our preventive and detective security controls. This, of course, includes the blue team. As we begin any penetration testing engagement with an enterprise red team, there are decisions to be made regarding the level of notice or awareness that the blue team should have about what is occurring. In some cases, the rules simply state that all tests are performed in a 'double-blind' manner, meaning the blue team does not get a heads up about what the red teamers are testing at that given point in time. In others, the red team will notify the blue team, or perhaps senior members of the blue team, so that they can intervene if a response to a test has the possibility of creating an incident or leading to another problem.

Exploitation phase

Next, we move on to actually attempting exploitation of potential vulnerabilities identified within the previous phase. How this happens depends entirely on the nature of those vulnerabilities. In the case of a web application, we might attempt to use a user-driven input to cause a XSS vulnerability, by inserting some JavaScript and seeing if it is executed in the context of the page rather than being sanitised before it is displayed back to the user. In the case of a vulnerable Secure File Transfer Protocol (SFTP) service, we might line up some specifically crafted and carefully vetted exploit code discovered online, and point it towards our target.

This phase of the test is the most critical phase in terms of things that could go wrong, so a tester should be mindful of the potential negative impacts they might have on their target, and keep the phone nearby at all times when engaged in exploitation.

Once exploitation has been achieved, and the tester has a foothold on the target, care should be taken to record exactly the levels of exposure that could have resulted should the compromise have occurred at the hands of someone truly malicious. This includes as a direct result of the first compromise, and as a result of any lateral movement that may occur from that first target. In some methodologies, exploitation and post-exploitation are distinct phases.

Clean-up phase

One of the golden rules of penetration testing is that we never leave a system more vulnerable than it was when we first found it. So, for example, if we've uploaded a web shell to a web application to facilitate access to the underlying web server host, we'd remove that shell on the way out. We don't want it to be there for someone else to leverage. If we weren't able to remove it, we'd ensure that someone else who can knows about it, so that they can remove it on our behalf.

In most penetration testing methodologies, the final phase of the test cycle is dedicated to tidy up work, to ensure that we restore the environment to its pre-test state.

Reporting

Upon completion of the test, it's time to produce the report, which, as the only tangible output of the penetration testing process, is a critical document. Recall that the penetration testing process is supposed to be scientific and therefore the report is a scientific document. An independent third-party tester should be able to pick up the report and accurately repeat the test based on what they read. That means they'll need details such as the tools used, the version numbers of those tools, and tool configuration settings leveraged during the test. They'll also need the raw output from those tools to be able to run a fair comparison of what they're seeing versus what the original tester saw.

That level of detail can quickly add up to hundreds of pages of data, and not everyone who reads the report will be doing so with the idea of validating its findings. Most will simply want to digest the findings so they can set about fixing what needs to be fixed. That is why it is important to have a well-defined report structure that allows different elements of the report to be accessible to different audiences. Many penetration testing methodologies will prescribe the structure and layout of a report and, of course, if you're following that methodology, you should base your report on those guidelines. That said, as with the actual penetration testing process, most standards roughly agree on the following report elements.

An executive summary

The opening section of the report is just as it sounds, a summary of what was tested, why, and what was found, written for a principally non-technical executive audience. The summary should be as concise as possible, spell out clearly the risk to the business if the discovered vulnerabilities are not addressed and end with fact-based conclusions. It all sounds so simple, right? However, executive summaries are tricky to get right, and they are a prime example of where good communication skills come in.

Most penetration testers love to go into great detail about what they found, how they found it and what this means for the future of civilisation as we know it. Truth is, the executive summary should answer only a couple of questions: Is the target of the test secure, or not? If not, what should we do to make it so?

Summary of vulnerabilities

Occasionally, you will get an executive summary reader who'll want to know more. And then of course, you'll have the next layer in your report's audience, the technical folks who'll actually be charged with addressing the findings in the report. That's why placing a summary of the discovered vulnerabilities immediately after the executive summary is a logical progression.

This is a great section to place graphs and charts that help tell the story of the test. Grouping vulnerability findings by severity and displaying them in a pie chart, for instance, can give an immediate overview of the scale of the work that is about to land following a report.

You might also group vulnerabilities by target system, or by category (e.g. weak or default credentials, XSS), depending on how the team(s) receiving the report are organised.

Test team information

The report should contain the names of all testers involved in the testing and report process. This isn't simply so they can be tracked down and yelled at, although I cannot guarantee this will not happen. Instead, it makes it easier for folks to seek clarification on any issues in the report. Of course, if you are in an internal red team, your contact information is likely going to be the email address that you use at work. Still, it's a good idea to get into the habit of putting this information in a report, if only to keep track of who tested what, and when. As tests are repeated year-on-year, it's a good idea to rotate out testers if possible. A fresh set of eyes on the same application can yield different results.

Overview of the methodology used

Recall that this is a scientific document, and while a company may use a standard methodology that is documented separately, if this report ends up being used externally without that document to complement it, it would be pretty hard to reproduce the test without the missing detail.

For this reason, a copy of the methodology used should be included. Most methodologies are of course many pages long, so in the interests of saving trees and bytes, a summarised version can be included.

Scope of work

During the pre-test work, when scoping was agreed, it should have been documented in a scope of work document. As a quick reference, it's always a good idea to include this original document in the report.

Lists of tools used

A penetration test report represents the state of a target at a given moment in time. The tools we use as penetration testers, just like any other types of software, evolve. New features are added, and new configuration options are made available to us. This is why it's important to record the tools we used to perform a given test, and just as important to record the version numbers associated with these tools, in the report.

Vulnerability details

The meat of the report will be a breakdown of each discovered vulnerability that we originally referenced in the vulnerability summary, including associated severity, how the vulnerability was discovered, the results of any exploitation and a suggested remediation.

Screenshots and tool output should be included to better aid the report readers who will likely be a combination of those seeking to understand and remediate the vulnerabilities, and security, legal and risk professionals who'll be looking to ensure that the presence of a vulnerability doesn't trigger contractual or regulatory reporting requirements.

For each vulnerability finding, the detail section should start with a summary of the issue, followed by the names/IP addresses of any impacted assets, before opening up into the full detail. It's within these sections that the details can quickly start to become overwhelming, so having decent formatting, and using things like page breaks to clearly define when one vulnerability description ends and another begins, really pays dividends.

Appendices

In order to keep the vulnerability descriptions to a reasonable length, the tester might choose to omit or truncate certain tool output or technical information in the earlier sections of the report. It is still important to record this information, so appendices can be used for this purpose.

Just as with vulnerability scan output, which I covered earlier, penetration test reports are extremely sensitive. Perhaps even more sensitive, since they do the job of translating raw tool output into an actionable guide for compromising a target. Therefore, reports should be protectively marked, and secured appropriately, behind adequate authentication and encryption.

Re-testing

All that hard work will have been for nothing if the findings aren't taken on board and remediated. A re-test can be leveraged to ensure that any remediation work has been completed correctly. More often than not, re-tests can be more targeted and focused than the original penetration test, and as such often take less time to complete.

Decisions about a re-test strategy or policy should be made before the original test is conducted. For instance, should the identification of any vulnerability result in a full-blown repeat of the first test, or are smaller, focused re-tests the way to go?

THREAT HUNTING

While penetration testing is a great way for the red team to identify possible entry vectors that an attacker may leverage, threat hunting focuses on identifying those attackers that have already penetrated the organisation, and are lurking under the radar, out of sight of the blue team and their existing tools. I've noted several times in this book how signature-based detections, such as AV software and IDS/IPS, rely on existing knowledge of the threat in order to build the signatures, which can put the defenders on the back foot.

Given that blue teamers are often too busy keeping an eye on known threats, having a dedicated red team spending time hunting for new ones can be really valuable. In recent years, the term 'threat hunting' has been coined to refer to this activity. While traditionally a manual activity, the security industry has responded by creating various specialist tools that help with the process of joining the dots together to identify activity that could be attributed to an attacker. These identifiers, known collectively as tactics, techniques and procedures (TTPs), to borrow an old military term, provide a line of enquiry for the threat hunter to establish whether a compromise has truly occurred.

Evolution of threat hunting

Finding a potentially malicious file on a machine, creating a hash of that file and checking it against a database of known malicious files to confirm or deny its status is a form of manual threat hunting. Observing a network connection between a host and a potential command and control server is another. Clearly, given the rate files move around the enterprise, and the number of network connections that are opened and closed every single second, these processes do not scale very well, and therefore we might need a little automation assistance from specialist tools.

Before an enterprise red team can begin to start to move past basic manual threat hunting methods, there are a lot of foundational things that need to be in place. First and foremost, threat hunters need data, lots of it. We need as much data as we can gather, and we need to keep gathering it. Fortunately, if we have a SIEM tool already aggregating log data from multiple sources, we already have a great deal of data to work with. The key is to look at the logs that don't trigger events in the SIEM, which may seem counter-intuitive, but it's where we're most likely to identify new, previously undetected threat actors.

Application of threat intelligence
As a first iteration on manual threat hunting, we can take threat intelligence information from various sources and do comparisons with what we're seeing in our logs. Bear in mind, new indicators of compromise are discovered daily and added to threat feeds. Even if you're doing comparisons to threat feeds in real time as part of the SIEM's normal workload, it's possible that a threat feed match event today wouldn't have been a match yesterday. Taking the time to replay historical logs and look for new alerts can sometimes lead to new insights. To make things run even more effectively, this process should be automated where possible.

Building threat hunting procedures
Just as a security operations blue team will have daily procedures for checking defensive systems, the same principle can be applied to threat hunting. Let's say we have a particularly critical system, and we can safely hypothesise it would be the most valuable target for a motivated attacker seeking to gain access to our enterprise; how might they go about it? Would they try to phish people that they know are likely to have access to that system? Would they leverage social engineering against support staff to force a password reset? Once we've modelled the potential threats, we can start to think of ways that we could track them down.

In the case of phishing, we could look at email logs for all successfully delivered messages to users of that system; do we see any abnormalities in the sending mail server IP addresses? Do we see an email from an address provided by a free email provider that we've never seen before?

As for the social engineering risk, could we subscribe to a feed from the helpdesk ticketing system, and trigger a log entry whenever the term 'password reset' is found in the ticket?

Then, how could we automate the process of scouring these two particular log sources on a regular basis and generating output that we can review to determine whether a suspected threat discovered in them is real.

Leveraging machine learning

The final evolution in the threat hunting life cycle (at the time of writing) is using machine learning to automate the process of identifying previously unidentified threats from large datasets. Machine learning is a branch of artificial intelligence focused on algorithms which allow computers to 'learn' from the data they are presented with. This allows them to identify patterns and anomalies in data, and make decisions based on those discoveries; including the decision that the data is indicating the presence of a threat.

Unsurprisingly, the idea of algorithms rapidly exploring security logging datasets and plucking seemingly invisible threats out of that mountain of data has triggered a wave of machine learning-focused information security start-ups, and has caused many long-established players to evaluate their own approach to machine learning. While there is tremendous value to be had here, a word of caution. Not all machine learning algorithms are created equally, and some may not truly be machine learning algorithms at all. Be sure to evaluate any products before agreeing to buy them, and push hard with questions on exactly how machine learning is implemented in the product.

MITRE ATT&CK

No mention of threat hunting would be complete without a nod to the MITRE ATT&CK framework.[9] The framework, developed in the early 2010s by the non-profit MITRE corporation, is an open-sourced repository of attacker TTPs, based on those discovered following real-world attacks against enterprise systems. As a result, it is a tremendously powerful resource for threat hunters.

The framework is arranged in a tabular format, which is more or less a spreadsheet. Each column represents a phase in the attack, and if you think back to the phases of a penetration test discussed a little earlier, they are roughly aligned. For each of those phases, multiple TTPs are listed, and it's possible for the threat hunter to click through each one to explore real life examples of how those TTPs were leveraged in a previous attack.

For example, in the initial access phase of an attack, a TTP listed in the framework is 'Spear phishing link', and then several examples of advanced persistent threat (APT) campaigns that leveraged spear phishing links are reviewable on the MITRE ATT&CK website.

The ATT&CK framework has become a highly valuable resource for red and blue teamers alike.

SUMMARY

In this chapter, I introduced the offensively focused red team, who have the job of simulating an adversary on multiple fronts, including both digital and physical penetration testing, threat hunting and bespoke tool development.

We talked about the initial build out of the red team, the challenges and resistance you might face, and the traits that lead to good red team hires. Technical skills are undoubtedly important, but equal consideration should also be given to creativity and communication skills.

We discussed the importance of establishing rules of engagement, to protect both testers and targets alike.

We looked in-depth at digital penetration testing, a scientific process that should be conducted in accordance with a published methodology. We listed the phases of a penetration test.

We covered the importance of reporting, as the only tangible output from the penetration testing process, and how the content and structure of the report directly impacts its value.

Finally, we introduced the concept of threat hunting, and explained how it evolves as an organisation's threat hunting programme gains maturity.

The next chapter continues to look at red team functions, with a focus on the art of building bespoke tools.

REFERENCES

Orwell, G. (1945) *Animal Farm*. Secker and Warburg, London.

Scarfone, K., Souppaya, M., Cody, A. and Orebaugh, A. (2008) *Technical Guide to Information Security Testing and Assessment: Recommendations of the National Institute of Standards and Technology*. NIST, Gaithersburg, MD. Available at: https://nvlpubs.nist.gov/nistpubs/Legacy/SP/nistspecialpublication800-115.pdf

12 BUILDING BESPOKE TOOLS

The majority of folks who work in information security will tell you they're never short of things to keep them busy. There are always improvements and enhancements to be made, changes to respond to, incidents to investigate and, of course, a never-ending tidal wave of newly discovered software vulnerabilities and malware. To overcome this, a commonly cited mantra is 'work smarter, not harder', and one of the ways we can work smarter is by building bespoke tools to automate or expedite a specific repeatable process or function that is core to our work.

Although any information security function can benefit from the use of custom tools, in the world of the red team, the need for automation and bespoke tooling is particularly prevalent. This is because it allows us to concentrate on precisely what we should be concentrating on, finding security vulnerabilities. If the first morning of every test is spent setting up the test environment in the same way we've set it up every other time we've tested a particular target, well, that doesn't seem like the best use of our time.

In organisations that make their money by developing and selling software, it's highly likely that there is already a wide variety of automated test tooling in place. Just as with security testing, other types of software tests benefit hugely from automation to reduce the burden on the test teams. It's critical in organisations that leverage continuous deployment and continuous integration that tests are automated to keep up with the release cadence. Given this, there may well be opportunities for the red team to include some security testing in these existing suites, or simply leverage the tools to create their own.

This chapter covers the development of bespoke tools to support red team activities. We'll talk about test automation, exploitation development, tools for social engineering and, finally, tools that allow us to bring all our findings together in a well-structured report.

TEST AUTOMATION

If your organisation employs software quality assurance (QA) engineers, their job is to subject the software the organisation is building to a barrage of tests, at various points in the SDLC. Their objective is to identify defects that could have an impact on the quality of the finished product. Their role is similar to that of a penetration tester. While in QA the traditional focus is on bugs that affect things like overall function, user experience or performance of the application, one can very easily argue that security is indeed a component of quality.

With this in mind, red teamers can do worse than spend time with their friends in QA. Not just because they're a good source of knowledge about the buggiest components in the software we're looking to compromise, but because they have already lived through, and automated, some of the same repetitive tasks we're going to need as part of our own testing programme.

Test automation tools

There are many products out there, both commercial and open-source, that support the scripting and performance of different types of software test. Examples of such tools include Selenium,[1] Katalon[2] and Cypress.[3]

These tools allow testers to build tests and run them automatically from various browsers, record the test as it happens, and debug the results. Given that, essentially, they are providing an automation service to any web application functionality, there is no reason why they cannot be used to perform repetitive administrative tasks, in addition to formal tests.

Creating test users or accounts
When testing a web application, one of the most common initial tasks for the tester is to set up the application environment in which they'll be working. This typically includes steps such as registering a user account in the application, which may include validation of email address and other identifying data.

While the same test accounts can be used over and over, and simply reset, in the majority of cases, to make the test as realistic as possible, a new, clean environment will need to be established each time. Automating the sign-up process can really help here, as keeping track of which email addresses are associated with which test accounts can become quite tiresome.

There are many other variables, such as product offerings and permissions levels, associated with user accounts that might need to be included and established as part of any user registration process. These various test cases can also be automated through these tools.

Relationships between accounts
In some applications, to leverage the full suite of features that the application affords, a single user account might not cut it. For example, in an application where a workflow is initiated by one user and handed off to another (say, a manager) for approval, the tester will need to create accounts on both sides of the process to ensure that the test provides full coverage.

Automating other functionality
Some vulnerabilities will not manifest until a certain function of an application is triggered, or a task is completed by a user. This is where our friends in QA can likely help us out once again. They will most likely have prepared end-to-end test cases for the

majority of features and functions in the application. If we can leverage them to enhance our security tests and save time, then there is no reason for us not to.

Application programming interface testing

Not all interaction with web applications occurs via a web browser. In the integration era, where partners exchange data between their various software platforms, APIs are commonly used. An API allows two pieces of software to exchange data in a structured format, via the internet across organisational boundaries or internally between two components in the same application.

APIs should be tested to the same extent that front-end web UIs are tested, if not more so. The reason why? Many developers make the mistake of assuming that all data coming through an API is somehow more trustworthy than data coming from a user via a UI. In cases where the APIs are internally accessible only, this is more understandable; however, in cases where partners are exchanging data, the principle of 'trust, but verify' should always apply.

If data is going to be rendered and processed in an application you are responsible for, you are responsible for ensuring the sanity of the data the application is rendering. Ultimately, it'll be your application that is at risk of compromise if you don't. API testing tools include the aforementioned Katalon, as well as SoapUI[4] and Postman.[5]

Aside from incoming data sanity, when testing APIs for security, some of the common issues penetration testers should look for include:

- Ensuring authentication and authorisation is correctly applied, and API clients cannot obtain access to data beyond their approved scope.
- Checking that rate limits are correctly applied, as APIs can be abused to rapidly extract data from a platform, or cause a denial-of-service condition.
- Ensuring that all API activity occurs over a secure channel (HTTPS), and any attempts to downgrade the level of security fail.

EXPLOITATION TOOLS

In addition to the tools that support the logistical aspects of penetration testing, it is of course possible to develop custom exploitation tools, and this is a topic near to the hearts of red teamers, penetration testers and security researchers alike. Custom exploits are routinely developed, disclosed, sold, shared and traded between parties. Exploits are written to provide proof of concept (PoC) for a discovered vulnerability, or to automate the process of exploiting a vulnerability, so the vulnerability can be reliably triggered during subsequent attempts. A highly valuable resource, you can find plenty of examples of exploit code in Offensive Security's Exploit Database.[6]

The motivation and actions taken by the enterprise red team in regards to custom exploit development will differ from those of a more maliciously minded individual, of course. In our case, the likely outcomes of identifying a vulnerability and building a custom exploit to leverage it may include:

- Immediately submitting the finding to an in-house development team to fix the vulnerability the exploit leverages. Incidentally, including a PoC exploit in your vulnerability submission really does assist the development team in applying applicable remediations.

- Responsibly disclosing the vulnerability to a third-party vendor, or open-source project so that a fix can be provided. Many vendors offer approved channels for such disclosures, so they should be leveraged where possible.

- In some cases, the exploit might be leveraged as part of a longer-term engagement focused on testing the organisation's defences, including the blue team. In this event, the exploit and vulnerability it leverages might not be immediately disclosed. Ultimately though, this is a judgement call. The red team should always act in the best interest of the organisation and its customers, so if there is a risk in not disclosing promptly, this should be weighed up against the outcome of a test that was allowed to go on for longer.

Exploit development techniques

Red teamers use a number of techniques when identifying vulnerabilities and developing exploit code, and each of these techniques is worthy of its own book, or books. Given that, I can't go into the level of detail that each one truly deserves in this book, instead I can cover them at a high level:

- **Fuzzing.** A common technique used in exploit development, fuzzing involves injecting a string of random data into an input for a piece of software, and monitoring how it reacts to that data. Doing this can allow the tester to identify cases where the application hasn't been configured to properly handle the unexpected input, which can be indicative of a potential vulnerability.

- **Reverse engineering.** A technique used to understand how compiled software behaves on a machine when it is executed, to identify potential areas of vulnerability. The reverse engineering process typically involves using specialised tools to disassemble and debug running code. Examples of commonly used tools that fall into this category include IDA Pro (Hex-Rays, 2019) and OllyDbg.[7] Reverse engineering is also frequently used in a defensive manner by malware analysts and researchers, to understand how a particular strain of malicious software is functioning.

- **Network traffic and protocol analysis.** In the case of targets that may have exposed network services, understanding and manipulating the structure of the packets associated with the service can provide an opportunity to identify potential vulnerabilities. To assist in this process, red teamers can leverage protocol analysis tools such as Wireshark.[8]

- **Web application traffic proxying.** When working with a target that is a web application, a commonly used vulnerability identification mechanism is to use a proxy tool, such as Burp Suite (referenced in Chapter 11) or OWASP Zed

Attack Proxy,[9] to intercept and manipulate HTTP requests from the client to the application. Doing this can lead to an understanding of how the application is set up, and identify any opportunities for web application-specific vulnerabilities, such as those found in the OWASP Top Ten (OWASP, 2019).

Exploitation frameworks

The process of constructing custom exploits can be expedited through the use of pre-existing exploit frameworks. These tools allow the exploit author to reuse common components, such as payloads that are executed on the target host following the successful exploitation of a vulnerability. Additionally, community contributed exploits can be loaded into the frameworks with ease, to assist in the overall penetration testing process. The Metasploit framework[10] and the Browser Exploitation Framework (BeEF)[11] are two examples of commonly used exploitation frameworks.

As I've mentioned previously, AWS is, at the time of writing, the most widely used IaaS provider globally. The penetration testers at US-based Rhino Security Labs, including Spencer Gietzen, became acutely aware of this when they found a number of their clients were requesting penetration tests of environments hosted exclusively on AWS.

While every customer's individual AWS environment will be different, there are a standard set of security technologies, including a wide-reaching IAM policy engine, monitoring tools such as Cloudtrail and GuardDuty, and orchestration tools like AWS Systems Manager. A vulnerability, or abuse technique, in any of these common tools in one customer's environment will also be present in another customer's environment, provided the AWS security team hasn't already made a change to remove the vector.

Rather than start from scratch in every penetration test, Rhino built an AWS exploitation framework, known as Pacu,[12] which allowed them to rapidly leverage their proven techniques for testing AWS environments. Even better, they open-sourced the framework, so that other penetration testers and red teams can leverage it in their own testing.

As with any popular product that can be exploited, AWS is in a constant tug of war with those seeking to subvert the security features they've built. A vulnerability today, could very well be addressed tomorrow. To counter this, the Pacu framework is modular, and allows for new tricks and techniques to be easily loaded into the tool as code modules. It's also possible for contributors to write their own code and contribute it to the framework.

Pacu is a pretty cool example of an exploitation tool built to save time leveraging common vulnerabilities, so that an engagement can be more focused on identifying customer-specific issues that could potentially be more damaging to that customer.

SOCIAL ENGINEERING TOOLS

As an attacker, among the most viable paths to gaining entry to an enterprise are the human beings working in that enterprise. Red teamers should be testing this entry vector with some frequency. Social engineering is the act of using psychological pressure to convince a person to behave in a certain way, frequently with the goal of obtaining sensitive information and, in some cases, to facilitate a further intrusion into an environment.

Social engineering methods include phishing, spear-phishing, SMS-based phishing, in-person and telephone-based phishing. Glancing at that list, there are clearly some methods that can lend themselves to automation better than others. Phishing campaigns and SMS-based phishing can be automated with relative ease and directed at different groups within the enterprise. Telephone-based social engineering can also be automated, but this would rely on the target falling victim to one of those awful robo-calls, which, although they must work in some cases, are just more annoying than anything else.

Phishing tools

Phishing emails are part of the background hum of life on the internet, and, therefore, phishing tests conducted by red teamers should follow the same pattern. Having a specific day called out on the calendar as 'phishing simulation day', and sending the same fake-malicious email to a hundred people will likely result in the IT helpdesk receiving a spike in users reporting the email. The recipients of the emails will confer, and once one of them becomes aware that the email is a test, it could blow the entire test for the remaining victims. Until a recipient who was out of the office at the time comes back a week later, and falls for the campaign on a delayed schedule.

Instead of big-bang tests, a slow trickle of phishing simulation emails as part of a sustained campaign will likely result in more realistic results. Unfortunately for the wider security programme, but fortunately for the red team, these results will likely yield more examples of disclosure that can then be leveraged to achieve further penetration. At a technical level, the slow and steady approach also avoids setting off email filtering tools and technologies, the effectiveness of which should be evaluated as part of the test.

There are many commercial SPs who offer the tools needed to craft, schedule and track the responses to phishing simulations. They can even take your users through a short training programme if they fall for the phish. Given this, you might be wondering why this topic would come up in this chapter about building custom tooling. Well, while there are reasons to buy in a service to do this for you, there are also several other reasons that make it a good candidate for building a custom tool.

- **Cost.** I'm speaking fairly generally here, but one of the main justifications in 'build vs. buy' is the money saved by developing your own tool. Phishing simulation tools use common libraries, perform common functions and don't have to be overly complex to be effective; as such, they are good candidates for in-house construction. There are still costs, of course; it would be naïve to assume otherwise. Engineering time and the compute power to run the tool will all need to be paid for indirectly, but on balance, the cost savings are easier to realise.

- **Sensitivity.** During a phishing simulation we will likely collect a significant amount of sensitive data, including identifiers such as email addresses of our targets and credentials, including passwords. This type of data is something that we typically don't ever want to see leave the safety of our environment under any circumstance, even in a controlled test. If we store the looted credentials in our own tool, they don't ever have to leave the environment.

- **Customisation.** If you build your own tool, the only limit to the way emails are formatted and their content is your imagination. If you rely on a commercial product, you can find yourself limited by the vendor's imagination. This is a limitation that real attackers do not have, so why impose it on yourself?

If you do elect to build your own phishing simulation tool, it'll need to support a handful of functions to be effective:

- Send emails as part of campaigns: these emails typically contain links to phishing websites.

- Create and run phishing pages, which can be very simple HTML forms that capture what is entered in them. They might even have a simple website cloning feature, to leverage existing sites as a template.

- Track who emails have been sent to, and at what time.

- Track responses, and the level of response. For example, was a malicious link clicked and were credentials entered?

- Produce simple reports about phishing success rates. You'll need these to help justify getting more training in place if the results are particularly bad for the organisation.

REPORTING TOOLS

Writing reports, especially penetration test reports, is something of an art form that is often neglected, or an afterthought to the main body of testing. This is somewhat understandable. If you were to survey the majority of technically minded penetration testers and red teamers, you'll likely find that reporting rarely falls into the top five most enjoyable parts of the job. To overcome this particular challenge, and simplify the report creation process, reporting tools can be used to reduce the burden on the tester as much as possible, and make for a better customer experience for the recipient of the report.

In the previous chapter, we covered the content of a penetration testing report in some depth; here our focus is on another important aspect, the formatting and layout. The book you're currently reading has been laid out and typeset by a trained professional, and I'm extremely grateful for this because it really isn't something I'd be very good at. I'd much rather concentrate on the words I'm writing and the content they're conveying. In much the same way, penetration testers shouldn't be spending time concentrating on layout aspects of the report, such as which typeface is used and what exact shade it should be. Instead, they should be able to spend cycles accurately documenting their findings at the level of detail required in a scientific test.

Building a brand

The biggest brands in the world use a common set of colours, logos and taglines to make their products instantly recognisable and attributable to them. Of course, they have armies of marketing and branding professionals at their disposal, and significant budgets too. So, while we, as an internal security operations team, might not have the resources to compete at a global scale, we shouldn't worry, because that's not what we're trying to do. We should, however, consider building an internal brand and incorporating it on our reporting output.

A well-formatted penetration test report can be a highly effective branding tool. Having a document that reads and is presented like a digestible scientific paper does wonders for the credibility of the team that created it. Folks will appreciate the consistency too, and in cases where outsiders, like customers, auditors and partners, receive copies of internally produced penetration test reports, they'll subconsciously begin to associate the report with the test team. This can only be a good thing, provided the content is just as good as the presentation.

If you can, leverage an internal resource in marketing or PR, who might help you create a report layout or template. It seems like a minor thing, but it can really make all the difference.

While we were working for a penetration testing consultancy a decade ago, a colleague of mine, who I'm still pretty sure is one of the smartest people on the planet (for a variety of reasons), saw an opportunity for a bespoke reporting tool.

After every engagement we had a pretty short (if any) window to produce a report for the client. The majority of the time we weren't short of things to write. Our customers were mostly government clients who had very specific standards and requirements to meet, and so any deviations from those standards would constitute a finding.

We were acutely aware of the need to always deliver our standard reports in a consistent format. We were a young company, with four employees, and were literally based out of the back of a barn in Worcestershire, UK. The consistency we desired would help us establish our brand, let alone provide a decent customer experience. To this end, we had a Microsoft Word template that we used for reports. However, it wasn't perfect. It still required more than its fair share of manual manipulation, and even after that it wasn't completely consistent. We needed a better tool for automation of report creation.

During a break between engagements, my aforementioned smart colleague sat down and crafted a report writing tool in Python that leveraged the LaTeX typesetting system to format the final document. Instead of worrying about the format, information was added to report sections through a simple UI. When all the information was added, the tester would hit a 'generate report' button, and the tool would use a built-in template to output a PDF document. The content was stored in an XML file and could be edited and adjusted as needed. This tool probably had a more dramatic impact on the company from a daily operations perspective than anything else in its history. I'm positive it indirectly led to more findings in penetration tests, because we felt less pressured to make time for report writing.

I wanted to call this out because a report generation tool doesn't sound very 'sexy' or interesting, especially when you consider the other types of tool we might build for offensive security work. Well, sometimes functional is sexy. The tool has stood the test of time too; even though this particular company was acquired some 3 years ago, the reporting tool is still in active use, a decade later.

SUMMARY

In this chapter I introduced the concept of building bespoke testing tools to assist the red team in delivering value. We talked about working with existing QA test tools to automate tasks such as environment preparation, and we covered the importance of testing APIs as part of our testing programme.

Next, we looked at the development of custom exploits, introducing some common development techniques, and covering how exploitation frameworks can be leveraged to expedite this process.

We covered using custom tools to automate non-technical attacks, such as social engineering through phishing. Finally, we discussed building tools to assist in the production of well-structured and consistently formatted reports.

The next chapter focuses on an aspect of security that is so fundamentally important to the entire security operations programme, yet is frequently left to linger without a formal owner in place – physical security.

REFERENCES

Hex-Rays (2019) About IDA. Available at: https://www.hex-rays.com/products/ida/

OWASP (2019) OWASP Top Ten Project. Available at: https://www.owasp.org/index.php/Category:OWASP_Top_Ten_Project

13 PHYSICAL SECURITY

The majority of the techniques and tools we've covered throughout the preceding chapters of this book will mean very little if appropriate physical security measures are not designed, put into practice and tested on a regular basis. Physical security is a fundamental component of any enterprise security programme, and it's increasingly important that at the very least it's aligned with, if not fully owned by, the information security department and its security operations team.

The challenge with physical security is that in many small to mid-sized companies, it's a secondary thought. It's an area that frequently doesn't have a clearly defined 'owner', or is partially owned by many different people, and as such it doesn't get the full attention that it deserves. Frequently, the facilities department will have overall responsibility for physical security, typically as an extension of being in charge of things like badging operations, but won't have dedicated physical security specialists. As a result, it'll fall into the category of something that is a secondary concern, quietly maintained, but not really advanced. Until, just as with information security, a physical security incident occurs, and it's suddenly centre of attention once again.

Immediately following a physical security incident, in cases where a dedicated enterprise security team exists, but has not been given a clear remit to own the responsibility for physical security, there might very well be a finger pointing exercise between the facilities and the security organisations. A case of 'we thought you were doing this', and 'oh, we thought you were in charge', from the other side. Finger pointing doesn't do anyone any good of course, so it's better to tackle the issue of ownership head on prior to any incident occurring. Regardless of who owns physical security, it's an enterprise-wide concern, and everyone has a role to play in helping to ensure it's implemented correctly. We just have to make sure they know where they should go if they have questions.

In this chapter we'll look at various physical security controls, how they're implemented, and the role security operations can play in their deployment and subsequent operationalisation. We'll talk about environmental security, which is a sub-area of physical security that seeks to prevent damage and disruption caused by environmental risks such as fire, flood, extreme weather and earthquakes. Next, we'll take a look at the ways in which traditional physical security systems are taking advantage of technology to improve their worth, and how this convergence benefits us in security operations. Finally, we'll talk through the process of physical security testing, a common red team responsibility.

PHYSICAL SECURITY CONTROLS

Just as with their counterparts in the digital realm, the security controls that we can deploy in support of a physical security programme can be classified as preventive, detective or administrative. The purpose of preventive controls, unsurprisingly, is to prevent a breach of physical security from occurring in the first place. Detective controls will not prevent a breach that has already occurred, but will allow us to figure out that something untoward may have happened, or is still happening. Finally, administrative controls are designed to alter behaviours, to lessen the risk of a particular physical security problem occurring. Let's take a look at some common examples of physical security controls in each of those categories.

Preventive controls

The best security incident is the security incident that didn't occur, because we prevented it. This is especially true in the case of physical security, where incidents will likely have a more direct impact on life safety. We're all familiar with the controls I'm about to discuss, as we apply many of them in our own homes, but of course, at a much smaller scale than in an enterprise setting. In the enterprise, the larger the scope of the physical security operation, the more complex these controls become to deploy and manage effectively. In a geographically dispersed company, there may be a requirement to allow employees to travel between office locations with a single badge, for example.

The nature of the facility being protected will also have a direct impact on the way in which these controls are applied. In a datacentre, where only a select group of approved individuals should have access to the secure floor where servers and equipment are racked, there will be more physical controls than in a typical office environment, where visitors are expected.

In some cases, information security, and other types of regulatory and compliance standard that an organisation is subject to, will have requirements for preventive physical security controls that should be enforced to ensure compliance with that standard. For example, the ISO 27001 (ISO, 2019) standard, although primarily an information security standard, lists requirements for ensuring physical and environmental security in areas that contain sensitive or critical information, and information processing facilities.

Access controls and locks

Just as with files and folders, the principle of least privilege should apply to physical spaces within an enterprise, and access-controlled doors are typically how this principle is enforced. Server rooms and networking closets, for example, should be off limits to those folks who have no business need to access them. In some environments, this principle extends to specific spaces within the office environment itself, where perhaps access to different areas within the facility is granted on a 'need to know' basis. This is especially common in high security environments such as those run by defence contractors or intelligence and security agencies.

Smart card readers that are connected to a central server, or perhaps into a cloud environment, are commonly used to enforce physical access controls. An employee is assigned a smart card (or badge), and then granted access to a selection of doors through the access control platform based on that smart card's identification data.

When the smart card reader reads the identification number, it sends it to its central platform to confirm that it should permit access to the door it is associated with. If the answer is, yes, the lock is mechanically opened, if not, the lock remains locked. In some cases, an alarm might go off, or perhaps the failed access attempt is simply recorded in an audit log.

The biggest flaw with smart cards is that the check is being made against the card and not the person carrying the card. Smart cards can be lost, stolen or simply passed around between people, and all of a sudden, another person has obtained a level of access that they might not have been entitled to. Therefore, smart cards alone are typically an acceptable control in low to moderate security environments, but as we get into high security environments, MFA should be used. In a datacentre, for example, the smart card, along with a biometric control (more on these next), could be used to validate that the subject holding the card is indeed the person it was issued to.

Depending on the technology the smart card system is based on, it might also be possible for a malicious actor to clone the data on the smart card itself. If an attacker has physical access to the card, and the right equipment, cloning can be a fairly trivial task. In the case of contactless cards that leverage radio-frequency identification (RFID), it's possible to buy a cloning device online for less than £10, and in these cases the attacker needs only to get within the proximity of the device to make the clone (see Figure 13.1). Again, these risks can be mitigated by the addition of a second factor.

Figure 13.1 An RFID cloner and blank cards

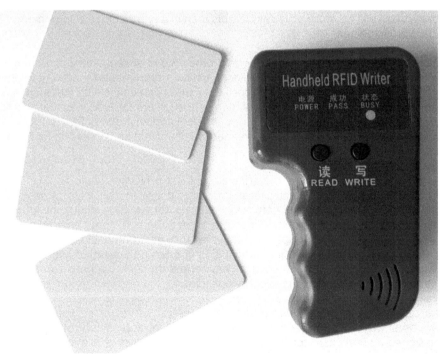

The majority of folks reading this book will have stayed in a hotel which leveraged a smart card as a room key. There's also a very strong possibility that the particular system in use in that hotel was manufactured by a company called Onity, as their locks are installed in around half of all hotels worldwide.

In 2012, security researcher Cody Brocious gave a talk at the world famous Black Hat security conference in Las Vegas, entitled 'My Arduino Can Beat Up Your Hotel Room Lock', which would become a major headache for Onity and its customers, as it revealed a serious flaw in their locks.

Cody had studied the locks in great detail, focusing on both the mechanical elements and the onboard software logic that the lock leveraged to determine if it should remain locked, or open itself to provide access. During his research, Cody discovered that when the locks were installed, a 32-bit value called a 'site code' was written to the lock's memory. This value was unique to the hotel, and was not viewable by any of the hotel staff. There were other values stored in the lock too, including special values for key cards that had advanced functions, such as programming, and the hotel master key.

Cody explained during his talk that at the base of the lock there is a small programming port, which can be used by a programming device to send the lock commands.

Under normal circumstances, the hotel's staff can use a programming device and the programming port to issue an open command to the lock. The device submits the 'open' command, which was determined to be the same for every lock, along with that 32-bit site code value mentioned earlier. Unfortunately for Onity, Cody had crafted a piece of kit that could read that site code from the lock memory in mere seconds, and then send an open command to the lock. The net effect was he'd created a device that could open an Onity lock almost instantaneously.

The device was built on the Arduino platform, and cost around £75 to build. Arduino is an open-source electronics platform based on easy-to-use hardware and software.

There was no way to completely fix the core issue of the weak site code storage, without replacing the circuitry in each lock, and with 10 million of them out there this would be a costly and time-consuming exercise.

Onity produced little plugs to cover the programming port, but many pointed out that if someone went to the trouble of creating a lock bypass device, they probably would be able to find a way to remove such a plug, using a screwdriver for example.

This case study is a classic example of how software elements of physical access controls must also be designed to ensure high levels of security.

Another mechanism commonly used to enhance the security of a smart card is to require the user to input a PIN on a pad while entering the space. This PIN is a 'something you know', which along with the smart card (something you have) represents a reasonably low cost multifactor physical entry control. Such controls also typically support a duress PIN, which is a special number that will trigger a silent alarm if the user is being asked to provide access under duress.

Locks may also be used on specific drawers and cupboards to keep sensitive paper files and other materials protected from those who have no requirement to access them. There are various types of mechanical lock out there, including warded padlocks, combination locks, pin tumbler and disc tumbler locks. When selecting which type to use for a specific purpose, the use of a lock grading system, such as the Central European Norm (CEN) and American National Standards Institute's (ANSI) lock grading systems should be considered. These standards lay out the requirements a lock must meet in order to achieve a given grade. Under ANSI's standard, a grade one lock has demonstrated it has reached a 'high security standard', while under the CEN standard, the highest security locks are classified as grade six.

Biometrics

Biometric systems rely on a physical characteristic of the user to authenticate them, a 'something you are' in the world of authentication factors. Common examples of such controls include fingerprint scanners, facial recognition, handprint scanners and iris scanners.

In recent years, the reduced cost of biometric technology has seen some of these controls implemented in our personal devices, which can make for a very convenient and secure user experience. However, biometric systems can still be prone to error. Such errors are classified as false rejections, in the event they cause an authorised user to be rejected, or false acceptances, which is when an unauthorised user is permitted access. Manufacturers of biometric systems publish the rates of these errors, and they should be considered when selecting a biometric system for commercial use.

Fencing

No, not the sword-based combat sport in this particular example, although that could be quite the deterrent if someone was not expecting it, but the barrier built around a property to prevent unwanted subjects gaining access and to introduce a layer of privacy.

Fences of course come in varying sizes, and can be made from materials including wood, plastics or metal. The typical height for a fence is a little over 2 metres, or 7 feet. In high-security settings, such as airports, fences can of course be much higher, with a sprinkling of barbed wire at the top for good measure. The higher the fence, and the stronger the materials used to construct it, the more security it will afford.

The type of a fence required for a given scenario and the construction materials used will depend on all sorts of factors that are well outside the scope of this book, many of which will be driven by locally applicable legislation. I know, for example, if I were to construct a 9-foot steel fence around my home, I'd be driven out of the neighbourhood by a group of angry neighbours, as restrictive covenants prevent me from doing so.

Bollards

A quick wander past any local supermarket or government building in a capital city will likely yield the sighting of a bollard or two. These are short vertical posts designed to prevent vehicles from crashing into buildings, either deliberately or accidentally. Deliberate attempts to drive a vehicle into a building might be related to criminal activity, such as a 'ram raid' style robbery attempt against a supermarket, or a terrorist attack, such as an attempted car bombing of a government facility.

Bollard placement should be considered at the design phase of a construction project to ensure they blend in with the surrounding environment.

Lighting

Illuminating an area does not directly prevent a crime from occurring, but does provide less opportunity for criminals to move through an area undetected. The use of security lighting in spaces such as car parks is commonplace, and is designed to make an area feel safer during night hours and to reduce the likelihood that a criminal will feel empowered to break into a vehicle.

Security lighting is a key element of a concept known as 'crime prevention through environmental design' (CPTED), which is an architectural principle that originated in the 1960s. This principle aimed to reduce crime and create safer spaces by creating more open areas that permit natural surveillance.

Depending on the situation, security lighting can run on a continuous basis through the hours of darkness, or be tied to an infrared motion sensor. In the latter case, the lights only come on when motion is detected, which can be less intrusive and more cost effective than continuous illumination.

Detective controls

If we cannot prevent a physical security incident, the next best thing is having a reliable detective control to alert us to an event that may have occurred, or might still be in progress. In some cases, it simply might not be possible to deploy a preventive control.

Think about a supermarket environment. If every product was kept under lock and key, the shopping experience would be a much slower and more painful experience than it already is. The most valuable items, such as electronics and high-end alcohol, may be stored behind preventive controls (locks). However, the majority of the goods on the shop floor are ready to take from the shelves. The supermarkets run the risk that occasionally those goods might be shoplifted, but they use detective controls such as closed-circuit television (CCTV) cameras and security guards who patrol the space to address that risk as best they can.

CCTV

While the presence of surveillance cameras alone might be enough to deter a malicious actor and therefore prevent an incident, technically speaking they are a form of detective control. Whether they are used in real time to observe an incident in progress, or reviewed after the fact, they are an extremely powerful tool.

CCTV has come a long way over the years. From the days of tape-based, grainy, time lapse footage in the earliest systems, to the ultra-clear 4K hard disk and cloud-based video systems that are accessible to residential consumers in the present, the proven success of CCTV has made it a popular choice for a variety of uses.

Modern CCTV systems can be extended to include motion detection functions, read vehicle number plates and recognise human faces. The mere presence of a surveillance system, let alone the addition of these types of additional features, has triggered conversations around rights to privacy for innocent people who might be captured on such systems. Therefore, when planning a CCTV deployment, it is important to be aware of any legal and privacy issues that might crop up along the way. Working with employee groups, such as unions and works councils (where applicable), can help ensure that such issues are raised and mediated before any money is committed to the CCTV project.

CCTV itself should be considered a sensitive system. Controlling who has permission to view camera streams or search through video footage is tremendously important, as is establishing and enforcing polices for appropriate use. This is especially true of systems that store video digitally, and may use IP-connected cameras. Appropriate authentication and auditability on camera and digital video recorder interfaces is a must, and a great example of ways information security-minded security operations can cross over into the realm of physical security, by helping to ensure these controls are in place.

In September 2019, the owner and an employee of a British CCTV installation and monitoring company were jailed for 14 months and 5 months respectively, after being found guilty of computer misuse. Sherry Bray, the director of Camera Security Services Ltd, and her employee Christopher Ashford, were found guilty of having unnecessarily accessed footage of a post-mortem examination taking place at Bournemouth Mortuary. Screenshots of the footage later leaked out to the internet and were widely distributed through social media.

The case received heightened public attention, because the subject of the autopsy was professional footballer Emiliano Sala, who had been killed in a plane crash a few weeks earlier. Footage of a separate post-mortem involving another man had also been shared, an act that was also covered by the charges.

During the trial, a company culture of unauthorised viewing and sharing of footage obtained from CCTV cameras, with a lack of auditability was described by the prosecutor. Although the two suspects in question didn't post the screenshot to social media directly, their actions in sharing the footage, obtained through their privileged access to the CCTV system ultimately resulted in the leak.

Emiliano Sala's family provided a victim impact statement, in which they noted the additional stress and upset this incident had caused them following Emiliano's death.

Alarm systems and motion detection

If there is no reason for there to be movement in a particular space between certain hours of the day, setting a motion detector-based alarm system can be a great way to become alerted to something untoward happening. Most motion detection systems use passive infrared (PIR) sensors to detect the change in temperature caused by the body heat radiating from (presumably) a human being walking in front of the sensor. Most PIR sensors can detect movement up to 10 metres away.

Placement of motion sensors is important to avoid detecting movement that could cause false positive activations, perhaps outside the secure space. Anyone who has ever played the role of 'named contact' on a monitored business alarm system will have no doubt enjoyed receiving a call at three in the morning to go to the office because motion has been detected. Upon arrival, discovering that someone left an oscillating desk fan switched on and the temperature differential was finally large enough to trip the sensor and trigger an alarm might be a relief, but it'll also probably ruin your day.

What happens when an alarm is triggered is a consideration that must be made prior to installation of an alarm system. Many alarm systems can be monitored by third party alarm response centres that will typically reach out to a named contact first, and if they're unable to get a response, will notify law enforcement. These arrangements should be tracked and maintained. If an alarm goes off for the first time in 3 years, and the only named contact the alarm company has, has been retired for the last year, then that person isn't going to be best placed to respond.

Other types of sensor, besides motion detectors, can be installed in an alarm system. Magnetic contact sensors can be placed on doors and windows, to detect when they are opened, and trigger an alarm if the system is in an armed state. Glass break sensors contain microphones that listen for audio frequencies that match those which occur when glass is shattered. If they're detected, an alarm is tripped.

Propped door alarms

Usually tied into the badging system, propped door alarms can give a security team heads up that someone has left a door that is typically access controlled propped open. This works by sensing the door has not been returned to the closed state in a timely fashion after an access granted event. People prop doors open for a variety of reasons, including moving large things around, or popping outside for a break when they've forgotten their badge. Unfortunately though, it presents one of the biggest risks to physical access controls, and is a behaviour that should be corrected if detected.

Audit logs

Many of the physical security controls just discussed are capable of producing audit logs. Just as with information security controls, like firewalls and IDS, those log files are only useful if they are retained and searchable in a speedy fashion. Unfortunately, many of the default conditions for badging systems and alarm systems are to retain logs only for a short period, and as such it can be necessary to work on ways of getting them out of their native platforms.

Depending on the manufacturer or vendor of the system in question, the device might support the syslog protocol to offload logs to a syslog server, or may offer an API that allows events to be pushed or pulled into a log aggregation platform.

The audit logs produced by these controls are themselves a detective control, as they can allow you to piece together a person's movements throughout a building, for example.

As with all audit logs, they are a form of self-reporting, vulnerable to manipulation and errors. System clocks on the devices that generate them should be set using network time protocol (NTP), and Coordinated Universal Time (UTC) should be used to avoid having to account for shifts in local time caused by daylight savings.

Administrative controls

In much the same way that an information security policy won't actively prevent a malicious actor from attempting to compromise an organisation, having an administrative physical control will not directly prevent someone from breaking a window to grab things from a desk. What it will do is influence behaviours to hopefully reduce the risk of that occurring. For example, having a 'clear desk policy' is an administrative physical security control that aims to encourage people to put things away when they leave in the evening. This could make all the difference between a casual smash-and-grabber deciding to smash that window and take a laptop that has been left on a desk, or seeing an empty desk and moving on.

Physical security policies
In addition to the clear desk policy just described, it's possible to craft various policies and procedures for enhancing physical security. Examples of things that might appear in such policies include:

- Keeping badges visible at all times, to aid in identification of unauthorised persons.
- Ensuring all visitors have checked in with a central point (usually the front desk) when they arrive on site.
- Escorting visitors and guests while they are in the organisation's facility.
- Ensuring that doors to secure areas close properly, and reporting any that don't to the appropriate contact at the organisation as soon as possible.
- Locking away laptop computers if they are to be left in the office.
- Reporting suspicious behaviour to an appropriate contact as soon as possible.
- Shredding sensitive documents, or placing them in a specially marked receptacle for shredding.
- Using screen privacy protectors when travelling.
- Refraining from discussing business-sensitive information when outside the organisation (for instance while travelling, or having breakfast in a hotel).
- Locking computers the second they are left unattended, which for some reason seems to be the most difficult behaviour to instil in people in all of information security.

A number of these items might seem to fall into the realm of common sense, but, just as with information security policies, if they aren't documented and presented to an employee to be digested and understood, they aren't enforceable.

Visitor logs

When an outsider comes to visit an office or other type of facility, they should have a legitimate reason for doing so, and their identity should be validated before they gain access. This is why having procedures around handling visitors appropriately, and ensuring they are followed at all times, is so important. Yes, really, at all times. Even if the visitor is the CEO's spouse, or the VP's golden retriever. Okay, maybe the dog gets a pass.

Having the right person on a front desk can make all the difference to the experience of handling incoming visitors. If the person is engaging and welcoming, it's possible to take a visitor through the procedures without them knowing that they are being screened, and their identity is being checked.

A typical flow for a visitor interaction is as follows:

- Welcome the visitor, ask them to sign in on a log (physical or digital), check ID. Ensure that the name on the log matches the name of the ID.

- Ask them who they are here to see, make contact with that person so they can start to make their way to the visitor area to escort their guest.

- Print a visitor badge and request that the visitor take a seat until their escort arrives. Under no circumstances should the visitor be allowed to enter a secure space unescorted.

- Ensure that the visitor is collected by their escort.

- Upon departure, have the visitor sign out and return their visitor badge.

The output of this process is a visitor escorted into the facility, presumably happy with the experience, and a visitor log. That log can be used as a detective control if an incident occurs and needs to be investigated after the fact. It's also a safety tool, as it can be used to identify which visitors are in the building in the event of an evacuation.

Social engineering is the art of human manipulation, to trick someone into performing a specific action for you. In the event that a visitor isn't really who they say they are, one of the best social engineering techniques to gain access to a space is to ask where the toilets are. In the event that they're inside the secure space and an escort hasn't yet arrived, this can be a great way to get early, unescorted access. It makes perfect sense, everyone needs to use them at some point, it's hard to challenge.

The best solution is to have restrooms outside the secure space, but in many cases this simply isn't possible. Therefore, by all means the person should be allowed in, but with an appropriate escort. The great news for that escort is that they get to hang around outside the restroom area and wait for their escortee to finish what they're doing. If you have this role, I recommend having a phone to play with to distract you as you wait for the person to return, and perhaps even pretend you didn't notice them as they come back, in a sort of 'oh, done already, didn't notice you there, let's go!' fashion. Yes, it's truly a bit awkward for some reason, but not as awkward as explaining why you let someone unescorted into the office who turned out to be conducting corporate espionage.

Two-person rule

In some spaces the level of sensitivity is such that having a person working alone is considered too much of a risk. Think very highly secure datacentre environments, weapons facilities or aircraft flight decks. In the last example, many airlines introduced two-person rules in their flight decks following the 2015 tragedy of Germanwings Flight 9525, in which a suicidal pilot deliberately crashed an airliner in the French Alps.

Training

Finally, including some of the items just discussed in new hire training, to make physical security procedures a part of everyone's vocabulary is highly recommended. The training doesn't have to be long, but it should convey the essential positions on physical security adopted by an enterprise.

Specific safety training, including things like fire drills, may be required by law and should be performed in accordance with that law.

It's a sad reality that one of the more common types of physical security training that employers, particularly in the United States, are providing is active shooter drills. Given the prevalence of firearms in the US, they never seem to be that far away. The controls, or lack thereof, that prevent these weapons from ending up in the hands of the 'wrong' type of people have been the source of much debate in a country that prides itself on its constitutional right to bear arms.

ENVIRONMENTAL SECURITY

Not every threat to physical security comes our way as a result of the direct actions of our human counterparts. In some cases, the planet we're all riding around on likes to throw us a few curveballs, through natural disasters and extremes in weather. In some cases, it can be easier to predict the likelihood of such a disaster occurring and take steps to mitigate the risk. For instance, placing key data processing facilities away from geological fault lines to reduce the opportunity for earthquake-related disruption.

Damage caused by fire and flood are two other examples of risk that fall into this category. I've worked in an office that was flooded extensively due to a burst water pipe following a particularly cold winter. Dealing with the aftermath is disrupting and it's important to have a recovery plan in place.

Business continuity planning and disaster recovery

Typically, the enterprise function designed to plan how a business will respond to a natural disaster, other environmental security event, or significant technical equipment failure is known as business continuity planning and disaster recovery (BCP/DR). BCP/DR can be a part of an enterprise security department or its own independent function, typically reporting up through the chief financial officer (CFO). The role played by security operations in a BCP/DR programme varies depending on how the organisation is structured. At the very least, security operations should be aware of various environmental security controls that may prevent the need to trigger a BCP/DR event. These controls can include backup generators that negate the need to close down an office in the event of a power outage, or redundant network links that kick in, in the event of an outage, which need to be monitored with the same amount of rigour as the primary ones. We may even be asked to build them into an overall facility security strategy.

Fire

The best response to the risk of fire is to ensure it doesn't happen, using fire prevention techniques to eliminate the opportunity for it to begin in the first place, or prevent it from spreading and taking hold of a facility. The use of fire-resistant construction materials will have probably the biggest impact here, as well as good practices, such as not leaving cardboard and other combustible material in areas where it is likely to become exposed to heat.

If you've ever been in a datacentre environment, you'll likely have seen signs stating that cardboard boxes should not be left on the datacentre floor. This is for good reason, of course. The boxes that servers, switches and other hardware are shipped in make a great fuel source for a fire.

If prevention fails, we have two other layers of fire control to work with. Fire detection relies on the use of heat and smoke sensors to trigger an alarm informing us of a potential fire. At this point, of course, the biggest concern is getting everyone out of a building and calling the fire brigade to respond. We all know how important fire detection systems are, and how important it is to keep them well maintained. In many jurisdictions, it's a legal requirement to have appropriate fire detection controls in place.

Fire suppression is more likely to be found in commercial settings, than residential, owing to cost, but it affords us a more active defence against a fire that is beginning to take hold. There are three 'ingredients' that lead to a fire: oxygen, heat and fuel. By removing one of these three ingredients with a fire suppression system, we can put out the fire.

Water sprinklers are an example of such a system. Most of us have likely seen sprinkler systems in commercial buildings and been warned not to hang clothes from them in hotels (quite why anyone would want to hang clothes from a ceiling mounted sprinkler is something I've never been able to fathom, it doesn't seem at all convenient). Water aids in fire suppression in a couple of ways. First, by displacing oxygen that is feeding the fire and, second, in the case of fires started by solid combustibles, by turning to steam and cooling the surface of the fuel source.

Of course, water itself can be an environmental security risk. The damage caused by water sprinklers can be just as devastating as fire, the trade-off being that they may well prevent the fire from spreading. While water is great at suppression of fires started by solid combustibles, such as wood and paper material, it's not a suitable suppression method for electrical fires. Given our roles in information technology, it's more likely that an electrical fire will be the type we come across.

Gas-based fire suppression systems are frequently used in datacentre environments. These work by inserting an inert gas, such as argon, into a space to displace the oxygen and supress the fire. The advantage to these systems is that they result in no water damage, which when you're dealing with sensitive electronics, such as computing equipment, is clearly a major concern.

Handheld fire extinguishers are another example of a fire suppression system that can be used to target smaller fires. Different types of extinguisher exist for different types of fire, and are labelled accordingly.

Temperature control

Having lots of servers in a space can generate lots of heat. Therefore, having suitable temperature controls, such as those afforded by a heating, ventilation and air conditioning (HVAC) system, is an important part of building design, especially in the case of a datacentre or server room environment.

Overheating of computing devices can cause them to shut down to prevent permanent damage from component expansion, which is a form of denial of service.

A common consideration for a security operations, or BCP/DR team, is how to respond in the event of an HVAC failure, which can occur more frequently than you'd expect. Typical responses include gracefully shutting down servers that may not be critical to operations to reduce the amount of heat output in a room in the short term, or bringing in temporary portable air conditioners to reduce the temperature.

Water

We're taught from a young age that water and electricity don't mix. So no big surprise then, that when we're considering the environmental security of a facility, we'd do well to keep water pipes away from computing equipment. Water pipes can burst, and push gallons of the stuff out at an alarming rate. When that happens, we don't want it to happen anywhere near our servers and other hardware. Should it happen, it is a good idea to ensure that those who are likely to be on scene first know how to shut water and electricity off safely, perhaps by clearly labelling shut-off values, to prevent the situation from becoming any worse.

Dust

If you've ever opened up the tower of a desktop computer, or server that has been running for 6 months or longer, you've probably found some dust in there. In cases where it's been even longer than that, you may struggle to see the computer's components through the dust layer.

As cooling fans suck in air, they suck in dust too. In most environments, you cannot completely eliminate dust, with the exception being facilities that handle microchips and other sensitive electronics, which have special vacuum and filtration systems to remove particles from the air.

The presence of dust can have an adverse effect on equipment cooling, and as such can cause things to overheat. Therefore, there are worse ideas than scheduling downtime for systems to facilitate the removal of dust from hardware.

Power supply

Although you may think the electricity that comes into our homes and businesses from the power grid is delivered in a relatively consistent and stable fashion, the truth is, it's subject to regular fluctuations that can cause damage to sensitive equipment. Surges, spikes and sags in the incoming voltage are all very real things that happen on a daily basis. It's for this reason that electricity coming from the grid is known as 'dirty' power.

A surge is a prolonged overvoltage situation, in which the power company's equipment delivers more voltage than intended (110 V in the US, 230 V in Europe). Surge protectors can help prevent damage to equipment in the event of such an occurrence. A spike is a short overvoltage situation. A sag on the other hand, is a short low-voltage situation. If a sag becomes prolonged, you have what is known as a 'brownout' in which the grid is not able to deliver enough voltage to power equipment fully. If the voltage stops completely, perhaps due to damage to overhead lines during a wind storm, you have a power cut.

To address the problems associated with dirty power, uninterruptable power supplies (UPS) are brought in to clean up the incoming supply. UPS systems sit in line between the utility power and the customer's equipment (servers and network switches, for example). Using a bank of batteries to ensure a consistent supply at all times, UPS systems deliver what is known as clean power. In the event of a power cut, the UPS detects the loss of incoming power, and picks up the load using electricity stored in its batteries. Of course, the greater the load, the more capacity the UPS needs to ensure it can run the equipment that is reliant on it.

Ensuring that security critical equipment, including physical security controls such as CCTV systems, have appropriate clean power and backup, should be part of the security operations remit.

CONVERGENT PHYSICAL SECURITY

Almost all of the physical security controls we've just discussed can be connected to a computer network for monitoring purposes. CCTV cameras, access controls and badging systems, UPSs, fire detection and suppression, and alarms, can all deliver status reports in real time. In security operations we can leverage this information to get a more accurate picture of what is occurring in our enterprise.

If we have the opportunity, grabbing the output produced by physical security controls and making it accessible through our SIEM and other tools, is a great example of making the most of what we already have in place, and breaking down barriers between siloed tools.

For example, a badge log could be brought into a SIEM solution. If a badge reader is in view of a CCTV camera, a link to the archived video footage at the time the badge swipe was recorded could be used to validate that the person swiping the badge was indeed the person the badge was issued to. Finally, this information could be referenced against a technical element, such as a computer login event. It's all very powerful stuff when put together like this.

PHYSICAL SECURITY TESTING

A core function of a red team, physical security testing involves attempting to breach physical security controls and gain access to a target. Just like digital penetration testing, it's a process that requires preparation, including the development of a plan that lists a set of objectives for the test. Also, perhaps most importantly, achieving all the requisite clearances to attempt to gain entry, and taking steps to ensure the health and safety of both the testers and those being tested.

Physical security testing can be a risky business. In a true test of physical security, the tester will be acting in a manner that is indistinguishable from that of an actual intruder, and could come into contact with someone who doesn't know a test is occurring. People are unpredictable in abnormal situations and the flight or fight mechanism has no built-in test mode. Therefore, if the 'fight' mode kicks in, the tester best have a plan in place to disengage and calm down the situation before things turn dangerous. Most commonly, testers carry what is known colloquially as the 'get out of jail free card', which is a piece of paper explaining they're authorised to be where they are, and provides contact information for the person who provided that authorisation. Additionally, having someone who knows about the test nearby to help provide that assurance, but not actively interfere with the test until it becomes necessary, is never a bad idea.

Creative physical security testing

Physical security testing doesn't have to involve breaking in to a location to be effective. For example, if there is a local café or pub near a target business, simply patronising those locations can reveal a lot. People like to talk about work outside of work, and

During my time as a penetration tester, I performed a handful of physical security assessments. Perhaps the closest I came to suffering actual physical harm was during a test in Glasgow, Scotland. This particular test was performed in support of a UK Government requirement to assess various non-profit organisations. In exchange for a clean assessment, the non-profit would be given access to a greater array of government data, some of which was sensitive in nature. The objective of the test was to gain access to the internal network of the non-profit and run a port scan. If I was prevented at any point from doing that, they'd have passed.

I scoped out the location the day before, and prepared my cover. I printed a fake ID badge and posed as a journalist from a local newspaper. I noted that access was pretty locked down to the building, and there was no way of gaining entry without being buzzed in and speaking to a receptionist.

When it was time to perform the test, I got buzzed in, claiming I had a meeting with the head of PR from the non-profit, whose name I'd looked up on LinkedIn the day before. I suggested to the receptionist that I knew where this person sat, and I could just find my own way there. Sure enough, I was allowed to make my own way unescorted to the top floor of the building, where I found an empty conference room. Having ducked into the room, I removed my laptop from my bag, plugged it into a wall socket and began to scan away. I had about 30 minutes alone before the receptionist and three or four others found me. They did not look pleased, and the receptionist angrily made her way toward me. I received a single shove, and was asked, 'excuse me, who are you?', but in slightly more direct language. It was at that point I revealed the nature of my role, and provided the get-out-of-jail free card, along with the name of my local contact.

'You're lucky she didn't break your neck', joked my contact during the subsequent debrief. Needless to say, signing in with that receptionist while I moved onto other stages of the engagement for the next couple of days was an interesting experience. I don't think she was a fan of mine.

unfortunately that can lead to information disclosure. As the 13th-century poet Rumi said, 'the quieter you become, the more you are able to hear'. Of course, be aware that the owner of a business might not really appreciate you using it as a listening post, but if you're paying for their goods and services, most won't be too bothered.

Company secrets, organisational politics, upcoming deals and general happenings in the work environment are typical topics of conversation. I've worked with a number of organisations who've preached the art of not discussing sensitive information outside the office as part of their security awareness programmes, and helped them validate the effectiveness of those programmes by simply spending the day sitting and listening.

Rogue device sweeps

Another aspect of physical security testing is looking for unauthorised, or rogue equipment. Common examples include rogue wireless access points, but in the days of small, cheap and reasonably powerful computers, the 'drop box' method of gaining access to internal networks is a very real risk. An attacker with physical access may install a small machine in a network that reverse connects to a host under the attacker's control. Simply dropping a USB drive loaded with malware on the ground near a target is another option. This can be a very effective way to break out of a network, when breaking in has become a little too difficult.

The general rule to be followed when looking for rogue devices: if it's not properly labelled, with a documented purpose, its presence should be questioned.

SUMMARY

In this chapter, we looked at physical security, a critical component of an enterprise security programme. We reviewed different categories of physical security control, including preventive controls such as locks and fencing, detective controls, including CCTV and alarm systems, and administrative controls, like policies and training.

We looked at environmental security, a sub-area of physical security that concentrates on threats posted by the environment, including extreme weather, fire and flood. We introduced the BCP/DR function.

We discussed how physical security controls are leveraging technology to enhance their capabilities, and how we can use this convergence to our advantage, for example, correlating physical security events in the SIEM.

Finally, we turned to physical security testing, a common red team function. We talked about ensuring such testing is conducted legally and safely.

REFERENCE

ISO (2019) ISO/IEC 27001 Information Security Management. Available at: https://www.iso.org/isoiec-27001-information-security.html

14 CONCLUSION

Over the course of the preceding 13 chapters, we've covered a great deal of material that will enable you to put your security operations programme into practice. If you're about to start this process, I hope that you're excited about the possibilities. You should be.

If you're part of an established information security programme, I hope the book has highlighted new areas of focus for you, or conjured up ideas of how your existing processes could be enhanced to meet the ever-evolving challenge of keeping a business operating as safely as possible.

SECURITY OPERATIONS IN A NEW AGE OF SECURITY AND PRIVACY

Having worked in information security for over a decade, I personally have never felt that the work we do has been appreciated the way that it is now. It really does feel like we've turned a corner in the last few years, with the adoption of the GDPR in 2018, and similar legislation in the United States by way of the California Consumer Privacy Act (CCPA). Consumers are being given what are essentially 'audit rights', in relation to their personal data and the businesses they chose to engage with. Society has no choice but to take notice.

This is happening because of the unrelenting stream of data breaches and security incidents that fill the headlines these days. Folks are, quite rightly, getting frustrated with being told how seriously companies take their security when they have just been breached, setting up credit monitoring, and replacing compromised credit cards. Knowing which businesses I can trust, perhaps by exercising my rights under GDPR to find out which are transparent about their data handling practices, is becoming just as important to me as a consumer at home as it is to me as a CISO at work. And I'm not the only one. Ultimately, we're all our own CISO, after all.

You can't have privacy without security

While the legislation that we just mentioned is better categorised as privacy legislation, as opposed to security legislation, you simply cannot have privacy without security. In the modern enterprise, you cannot have security without security operations. While tools, policies and procedures can get you some of the way there, without having a dedicated team to deploy, operate, tune and continually improve them, they aren't going to be fully effective. Hiring people who can spend time actively working on all the various tasks and disciplines described in this book is the only effective path. As we enter this new era of renewed trust and transparency requirements, this will likely become more apparent, as legislation becomes more stringent and detailed.

Companies that make exercising the privacy rights afforded to consumers as slick and seamless a process as any other interaction with the brand will have an advantage over those who delay, and deliver the bare minimum in order to be compliant.

When an organisation makes an effort to be truly transparent, it'll likely be because they have faith in their security operations programme. They'll trust that by revealing the amount of information they collect, how it's used and other previously 'secretive' practices, they won't be opening themselves up to additional risk. I truly believe that'll be a significant differentiator for any business in the 21st century.

GREAT POWER DEMANDS GREAT PEOPLE

Being an integral part of the business is of course a positive thing for a security operations team. There is no doubt about that. However, it can also lead to higher levels of stress among security operations employees, as more pressure is placed upon their shoulders. Browse any online information security community and you'll see countless posts on the topic of avoiding burnout and taking a break from the screen to clear your mind. These are important topics. This work is hard, and it's unforgiving at times. We all need to take care of ourselves, and each other.

People make the difference in information security. At the beginning of this book, I talked about the different types of people that you can hire into your team. We spend so much time at work, having good people you can trust to share that time with comes highly recommended. I listed a bunch of people in the acknowledgements to this book that I've had the pleasure of working with for many years, at many different companies! There's a reason we've all stuck together when we can: it's because we trust each other, know each other's strengths and weaknesses and like the work we do together, no matter the mission of the company. We know we make a difference to the people we're working to protect, and that is hugely satisfying when we do it together.

No matter which phase of your information security career you are at, always take the time to surround yourself with good people. If you have the privilege of putting together a team, then this should be your first priority.

THE FUTURE OF SECURITY OPERATIONS

In some organisations, particularly larger ones, just as soon as a centralised security team has been put together, it is decentralised and security professionals deployed into smaller business units. Perhaps embedding security engineers into development teams, or allowing subsidiaries to take more direct control over their own security rather than being held accountable by a parent company.

DevSecOps is a term that has sprung into the mainstream in recent years, and is a prime example of this decentralisation. In the DevSecOps model, DevOps teams have a dedicated security function to ensure the code and infrastructure they're building is built with security in mind, which you could be forgiven for thinking sounds like something that should always happen anyway.

So, does this decentralisation mean the end of the road for the security operations team? Not at all. Security operations functions will always be a necessary component of any information security programme. They all need to be performed and owned by some group in the organisation. Even if we distribute security operations functions into smaller teams, the same tools, processes and people will need to be involved. As long as the roles and responsibilities are well-defined between the smaller teams, so nothing gets missed, there is no reason this model cannot be successful. Think of it as being à la carte security, you just have to make sure that between everyone at the dinner, you order one of everything on the menu.

NEVER STOP BUILDING

Putting security operations into practice is an iterative process. Once you've built the foundational elements, based on the concepts discussed above, and start to deliver value, your programme will grow, and there are few limits to where it will end up.

That's the great thing about information security in general, and especially the hands-on world of security operations. The teams and programmes we put into place today will hopefully persist for years to come, and make for a more secure connected experience for all of us.

I'm sure we can all agree, there are few career paths more satisfying than this.

ENDNOTES

CHAPTER 3

1. A digit representing the sum of the correct digits in a piece of stored or transmitted digital data, against which later comparisons can be made to detect errors in the data.
2. https://suricata-ids.org/
3. https://www.snort.org/
4. https://www.elastic.co/products
5. https://www.graylog.org/products/open-source
6. https://www.symantec.com/products/data-loss-prevention
7. https://www.forcepoint.com/product/dlp-data-loss-prevention
8. https://www.extrahop.com/
9. https://www.versive.com/
10. https://www.netskope.com
11. https://www.skyhighnetworks.com/
12. https://aws.amazon.com/
13. https://cloud.google.com/
14. https://azure.microsoft.com/en-us/

CHAPTER 4

1. https://www.jamf.com/
2. https://www.samanage.com/
3. https://www.microsoft.com/en-us/cloud-platform/system-center-configuration-manager
4. https://www.jamf.com/products/jamf-pro/device-management/
5. https://manager.mosyle.com/for-it-macos
6. https://www.munki.org/munki/

CHAPTER 5

1. https://www.virustotal.com/#/home/search
2. https://totalhash.cymru.com/
3. https://www.cisecurity.org/cis-benchmarks/
4. https://www.alienvault.com/solutions/siem-log-management
5. https://www.splunk.com/
6. https://www.mysql.com/
7. https://www.postgresql.org/
8. https://www.microsoft.com/en-us/sql-server/default.aspx
9. https://www.oracle.com/database/

CHAPTER 6

1. https://github.com/
2. https://bitbucket.org/
3. https://fidoalliance.org/
4. https://www.onelogin.com/
5. https://www.okta.com/
6. https://auth0.com/

CHAPTER 8

1. https://www.rapid7.com/products/insightvm/
2. https://www.qualys.com/apps/vulnerability-management/
3. https://www.tenable.com/products/nessus/nessus-professional

CHAPTER 9

1. Netflix Open Source Software Center. https://netflix.github.io/

CHAPTER 10

1. Offensive Security's Exploit Database Archive. https://www.exploit-db.com/google-hacking-database
2. https://www.shodan.io/
3. https://haveibeenpwned.com/

4. https://hootsuite.com/

5. https://sentione.com/

6. https://www.zerofox.com/

7. https://www.concur.com/

8. https://www.flightradar24.com/

CHAPTER 11

1. Pwn Plug R3 Pulse Sensor. https://www.pwnieexpress.com/pulse-pwn-plug-r3

2. https://www.kali.org/

3. https://portswigger.net/burp

4. https://www.paterva.com/web7/buy/maltego-clients.php

5. https://www.rapid7.com/products/metasploit/

6. ISECOM Research. https://www.isecom.org/research.html#content5-9d

7. www.pentest-standard.org/index.php/Main_Page

8. https://nmap.org/

9. https://attack.mitre.org/

CHAPTER 12

1. https://www.seleniumhq.org/

2. https://www.katalon.com/

3. https://www.cypress.io/

4. https://www.soapui.org/

5. https://www.getpostman.com/

6. https://www.exploit-db.com/

7. www.ollydbg.de/

8. https://www.wireshark.org/

9. https://www.zaproxy.org/

10. https://www.metasploit.com/

11. https://beefproject.com/

12. https://rhinosecuritylabs.com/aws/pacu-open-source-aws-exploitation-framework/

INDEX

NICs (network interface controllers) 38, 84, 94

NIST (National Institute of Standards and Technology) 2–3, 103–4, 113, 114, 180

noise 3, 26, 29, 46, 48, 116, 118, 126, 160, 161

non-technical detection 120–1

north–south monitoring 50

NPM (network performance monitoring) tools 29, 30, 31, 53

NTP (network time protocol) 206

number of potential incidents investigated (performance metric) 144

off domain machines 61–2

'on the business' 6

'on-call' response 121–2

Onity 201

open-source tools 69, 129, 154, 177, 179, 181–2, 187, 201
building bespoke tools 190, 192
external data sources 156–61
monitoring networks and clouds 30, 47, 48

OSI (open systems interconnection) model 33–8, 40

OSTMM (Open-Source Security Testing Methodology Manual) 179

OU (Organisational Unit) 67

OWASP (Open Web Application Security Project) 37

PaaS (platform-as-a-service) 91, 137

packets 33, 36, 39, 41

Pacu framework 193

partners, building trust with 152

passion 18

passwords
logging 81
resetting 186–7
reuse of 102, 158, 160, 164
strength/complexity of 61, 62, 72, 80
weak 35, 41, 103, 131

payment terminals 59

PCI-DSS (Payment Card Industry Data Security Standard) 40, 126, 128, 180

penetration testing 8, 12, 13, 173, 178, 187

building a red team 174–7

building bespoke tools 191, 193, 195, 196–7

clean-up phase 183

establishing a security operations team 20, 21

exploitation phase 182–3

external data sources 153, 157, 165, 161

information gathering phase 181–2

methodologies 178–80, 184

physical security 174, 212

pre-test planning 180–1

reporting 183–5

re-testing 185

scanning and discovery phase 182

tools 184

percentages of events reviewed (performance metric) 144

permission levels 1, 87–8, 98, 100

personal skills 175

personas 19–20

PFS (perfect forward secrecy) 43, 51

PGP (Pretty Good Privacy) encryption 153

phishing 12, 80, 102, 142, 174, 176, 186–7
building bespoke tools 194–5
external data sources 160, 163, 164
incident response 113, 119, 120

phone (end user channel) 145

physical layer (open systems interconnection model) 34

physical security 14, 21, 58, 162, 198, 213–14
access controls and locks 199–202
administrative controls 206–8
CCTV 203–4, 211
convergent 211
detective controls 203–6
environmental security 83, 208–11
monitoring networks and clouds 34, 50
open systems interconnection model 34
penetration testing 174, 212

policies 206
preventative controls 199–203
protecting data 82–3
security controls 199–208
smart card readers 199–202
testing 212–13

PIR (passive infrared) sensors 205

playbook, incident response 115

PoC (proof of concept) 191–2

port scanning 36

ports 32–3, 36, 39

posters, signage and graphics 146

post-mortem (incident response process) 114–15

power supply 211

PowerPoint 142

PR (public relations) teams 148–51, 196

presentation layer (open systems interconnection model) 37

preventative controls (physical security) 199–203

'principal' roles 22

prioritising (vulnerability management) 128–9

priority framework 23–4

privacy 74, 76–7, 152, 153, 162, 204, 215–16

privileges required (vulnerability scoring metric) 135

Profile Managers 69–70, 71

propped door alarms 205

protecting data 10, 74–5, 95–6
availability 75, 78–9
backups 94–5
cloud storage 85–91
confidentiality 75, 76–7
database security 91–4
encryption 76, 82, 85, 88, 94–5
identity and access management 80, 87–8, 95–6
integrity 75, 77–8
logging 80–2, 88–9, 90, 92–3
securing servers 79–85

protocols 33, 35–6, 37, 38, 40, 43, 50, 88

provisioning/deprovisioning (IAM terminology) 98, 106–8

PTES (Penetration Testing Execution Standard) 179

purchasing decisions 45

www.ingramcontent.com/pod-product-compliance
Lightning Source LLC
Chambersburg PA
CBHW060541060326
40690CB00017B/3563